THE CENTENARY
OF THE
CAR

THE CENTENARY
OF THE
CAR
1885-1985

ANDREW WHYTE

Foreword by
JACKIE STEWART

OCTOPUS BOOKS

First published in 1984 by Octopus Books Limited, 59 Grosvenor Street, London W1

© 1984 Octopus Books Limited

ISBN 0 7064 2006 3

Printed in Spain by Cayfosa Barcelona

Dep. Leg. B. 26100/84

PAGE 1 ABOVE *Bugatti Type 13 (provided by D. R. Marsh).* BELOW *DeLorean (provided by the Patrick Collection).* PAGES 2-3 *BMW 315/1 (provided by BMW AG).*

PAGES 4-5 *Lancia Stratos cars (provided by Nick Mason/Morntane Engineering and Ian Fraser/Car).*

Special photography: **Ian Dawson**

CONTENTS

Foreword by
JACKIE STEWART   6

INTRODUCTION   8

1885-1915
THE GOLDEN YEARS
OF INVENTION   10

1915-30
FAST AND FURIOUS   32

1930-45
ECONOMIC CROSSROADS   56

1945-60
BEGINNING OF A NEW BOOM 84

1960-75
THROUGH FREEDOM
TO RESTRICTION   108

1975-85
THE FITTEST SURVIVE   134

CHRONOLOGY   156

INDEX   158

FOREWORD
by Jackie Stewart

I consider it a great honour to be asked to write the foreword for a chronicle of such historic value. Nearly everyone today has, in some way, a dependence on the motor vehicle. There are some alive today who might read this book and be able to recall clearly the great happenings which were to be landmarks in the development of the 'horseless carriage' from the very beginnings. For those of us of more tender years, this book provides an insight, historic in its nature, technically educational and humorously enlightening.

One hundred years is a short time in historical terms but, in the evolution of the motor car, many things have happened during this short segment of history. From the crude beginnings of the motor car, this book documents the many developments and technological breakthroughs. It also deals with the men who were responsible for creating and developing what has turned out to be the world's largest manufacturing industry. Many of those men were pioneers and, as is often the case with pioneers, some were not able to reap the benefits of their labours. In other cases, they were able to lay foundations that were to carry their names forever in the annals of history.

This book also demonstrates the considerable difference in the motor car and its application between Europe and North America. The horseless carriage was to be the symbol of wealth, prosperity and daring in Europe for the limited and elite few who were to buy, ride and drive the revolutionary contraption. They were, to begin with, to be identified as eccentrics and devil-may-care speedsters, while in the United States of America it was soon seen that the motor vehicle could be adapted and sold to the masses. Equally contrary were the early beginnings of motoring sport, where Europe was to see its growth through the wealthy amateurs and playboys, mixing in competition with the creators and pioneers of speed. In North America, the sport truly developed only when the motor car was in the hands of the mass public and, perhaps for those reasons, never did emerge in the United States with the social acceptance that the sport has enjoyed in other lands.

This book typifies all of the elements of motoring through those one hundred years. It is only right that a book as colourful and descriptive as this is should mark this great centenary. One hundred years after its creation, the motor car has made a large percentage of the human race totally dependent on it. From the delivery of our goods, for our businesses, for our convenience and our leisure and pleasure, the car and the network of roadways that criss-cross our lands are a monument to progress, ingenuity, and ever-changing technical tenacity. I have not yet lived even half the age of the car – since the first internal combustion four-stroke engines were run in Germany – but the car has played an incredibly important role in my life. I am not too young to appreciate the work of the great men of the past, whose colourful triumphs and failures, whose innovation, success and competition are now legend. I am old enough, however, to have enjoyed seeing some of the marques while they still had their own personal identity. Sadly, many of them have now slipped away in this modern world, perhaps never to return. But they will not be forgotten.

I also have driven some of those early horseless carriages,

RIGHT *First big season: 1964 success in F3 in a Cooper.*

Scotland's (and the world's) most successful drivers, Jackie Stewart and Jim Clark.

having enjoyed the privilege of doing the London-to-Brighton run which every enthusiast of the motor car should do at least once.

From the golden years of the early creators who applied their skills to a new era, to the fast and furious days of Chapter 2 when heroes were born for the motor car, we were to see great names merge for survival between 1930 and 1945. Germany's Third Reich changed the landscape of their country by building roads that were to be known as *Autobahnen*, and were to change the dominant colours on race tracks from red and blue to the German national racing colour of silver.

The beginning of a new boom emerges in Chapter 4 when again the ever-changing world of the motor car was to shift nationalistic pride from one country to another. Germany was to get the title of producing the world's post popular car which, incidentally, is still made in South America today. In motoring sport, Britain, for a period, was to dominate sports car racing in the great Le Mans years, and the birth of the modern racer was to emerge with the revitalization of having a rear engine configuration which has stayed with us ever since, at least in Grand Prix racing.

A great British politician could have titled Chapter 5 by telling us 'we never had it so good' but all good things do come to an end, it seems, and the motor industry on a global basis had to accommodate the incredible pressures of the energy crisis of the '70s.

The final chapter on the last ten years brings us up to date and sees some of the cars that will take us well into the next decade; documents the increasing popularity of the Japanese motor industry; the electronics and aerodynamics; the return, perhaps, of the love affair with the motor car that had somehow evaporated in countries such as America.

All in all, this is an illustrious history offering many, many anecdotes. The author of this book has done well to catalogue the events within these covers. I have known Andrew Whyte since he was a Jaguar apprentice visiting the Scottish Motor Show in Glasgow's Kelvin Hall. My father had a small Jaguar dealership in Dumbartonshire. Andrew was a disciple of the illustrious leaders of Jaguar in these days – people such as Lofty England and Bill Heynes – in the halcyon days of Sir William Lyons. He has been a student and a devotee of the motor industry since the first time I ever met him, and I dare say before that. His enthusiasm and his deep knowledge are truly reflected in this work that he has so conscientiously created. Let us all now look forward with anticipation to the second Century of the Car.

Nürburgring 1973: Jackie Stewart's third title for Tyrrell is clinched.

The complete experience: the London to Brighton veteran car run.

1885

A mere century is an immeasurably small fraction of the time that has elapsed since people first travelled by road. Even the start of transport by wheeled vehicle cannot be judged with any accuracy.

Aerial surveys of the Sudan suggest that primitive roads or trackways existed at least 15,000 years ago. Archaeology provides some clues which show that long overland journeys were being made by 4000 BC; for example, Danish flint tools of that period have been found in central Germany. Likewise, pictures show clearly that the wheel existed in Central Asia in similarly ancient times. In later prehistory the amber traders established regular ways from the Baltic south through Europe; there were the jade and silk roads between China and mystic Samarkand; incense caravans trekked through Arabia. Throughout the centuries, man has provided legendary travel tales.

Time scales have telescoped. Even the amazing network of Roman roads, which stretched virtually from Scotland to the Sahara and from Spain to Asia Minor, took little more than five centuries to complete. The contrast between the great ancient civilizations of (say) China or the eastern Mediterranean and the dark ages that prevailed in other territories for so long is as mysterious as the speed of subsequent progress. Four million road miles have been laid in North America since the first colonial route (now US-40) struck westward in 1651.

The greatest modern roadbuilder was Napoleon. His opening-up of Europe included construction of the magnificent Simplon and Mont Cenis Alpine roads and the revival of the ancient Riviera highway, the Grande Corniche. As first consul in 1802, young Bonaparte had even inspired the first Channel Tunnel project. The state into which Europe's roads had deteriorated before Napoleon's intervention is a fact that makes the feats achieved by his engineers in less than a decade more amazing than Hitler's *Autobahnen* or any other similar wonders.

Of course, the coming of the railways dissipated the effort, and when the vehicle we call the motor car made its appearance from 1885 few people took it seriously. Those who saw road locomotion as a threat to peace (or to the railways) were protected, in general, by legislation – but not for long.

Although the first motor car was made in Germany, it was in France that the practical pioneering work took place. Steam as a means of propulsion had been known to ancient China's Chou dynasty, and interpreted (as a model and in writing) by the 17th-century Jesuit father, Ferdinand Verbiest. Nicolas Joseph Cugnot's two steam tractors of 1769 and 1771 were, however, the prototype self-propelled passenger-carrying road vehicles. For over a century, steam power was developed all over the world, Britain's first definitive roadgoing machine being Robert Trevithick's carriage of 1801. The eventual transition from steam carriages to modern motor cars is probably best illustrated in the ever-changing work of the Bollée family of Le Mans in France.

There were patents galore as the idea of internal combustion became a reality – and once again it was France to the fore. Jean Joseph Etienne Lenoir patented the gas-burning two-stroke in 1860; and it was another Frenchman, Alphonse Beau de Rochas, who devised the four-stroke principle a couple of years later – although it was not until 1876 that a four-stroke gas engine was designed and made in Germany by Nikolaus August Otto. Germany was to hold that automotive lead for barely a decade: but in that time the motor car was born.

The ensuing century has been fascinating. France's lead in producing and proving the motor car (by devising competitions

19th-century Benz. *By 1885, Carl Benz was well advanced with his car design work, and his patent was granted early in 1886. He and Gottlieb Daimler, and all the other pioneers, might be amused by today's many arguments as to who was first, with what, and when! This dos-à-dos dates from 1897, when the motor car was well and truly on its way to practicality.*

for it) was soon followed in other countries. By the end of the 19th century Britain and Italy had joined France and Germany as serious car makers, while Belgium, Switzerland, and other European countries promised more than they would fulfil. Even at the very beginning, it seemed possible to pick out the strong from the weak – and nowhere more so than in the United States.

The genesis of the North American automobile was rapid. Here it was translated almost immediately from a plaything of the rich to an adjunct of everyday life. The lessons of Ransom Eli Olds and Henry Ford were learned quickly. Simple, practical transport was the route of least risk; few manufacturers who aimed at exclusivity would survive the early days unaided, but they added to the fascination of motoring while they lasted.

Once established, the American industry became a major influence upon Russia's limited manufacture. That experience was passed on to China. Neither country has led any important development work in this field. Where freedom is restricted, and consumer goods have a low priority, the motor car remains the simple tool of the State, and is usually of obsolete foreign design. (Exceptional in the Communist bloc, thanks to its Austro-Hungarian background, is Czechoslovakia where some fascinating indigenous cars and commercial vehicles are still being made.)

This book celebrates the centenary of the motor car, from 1885 to 1985. It is not a book of statistics; rather it sets out to pay tribute to the great cars and the men who made them – and drove them, for the sport of motoring has contributed to the business of car manufacture in very many ways.

In such a book as this, it would be only too easy to overlook the most amazing single achievement of these hundred years, and that is the emergence in the last quarter-century of Japan as the world's most successful car-making nation commercially. In 1923 over two million Model T Fords were produced for world consumption. Japan had then made very few cars. In 1925 it exported for the first time – three cars for China. That year, Ford began assembling vehicles in Japan, shortly to be followed by General Motors. Britain and France were among the contributors to Japan's industrial recovery after World War 2, Austins and Renaults being built under licence. Today the British Triumph Acclaim – BL's Honda – represents that wheel's full circle. Japan's achievements not only ensured the death of the British motorcycle industry, but were also a major factor in the trimming-down of the once-supreme car-making groups of North America and Europe. Japan has earned its success. The ideas may come from other countries; Japan's secret weapon is near-perfection in manufacturing techniques. The best example is, perhaps, Japan's ability to make an economic proposition of the Wankel rotary engine – one of the few totally new concepts since Panhard and Levassor established the classic layout for the motor car nearly a century ago.

Traffic and technical legislation may rule the customers' and the makers' lives nowadays. It is the price that must be paid for the motor car's dominant role. Yet the modern motorway is balanced by the leafy lane. The 'look-alike' saloons have not ousted the car for the individualist.

Of all life's daily chores, motoring seems to me to be the one that can be tackled in a spirit of enjoyment and even adventure. Every motor journey is a little bit of modern history in the making. That history began in Mannheim – at the heart of Europe's present-day road system – a century ago and therefore is surely worthy of special celebration.

Andrew Whyte

1985

20th-century Mercedes-Benz. The marque has a great tradition, and lives up to it. There are few car manufacturers who would not want to emulate Daimler-Benz's consistent achievements. This is a typical coupé of the 1980s. The origin of the name 'Mercedes' is described in chapter one.

1885

The story of these first 30 years must begin with the work of Carl Benz and Gottlieb Daimler in Germany: it was they who put internal combustion on to road wheels. Steam propulsion had already been in use in several countries for more than a century, first in France, then in Britain, America, and elsewhere. It was the big agricultural steam engines that inspired the motoring pioneers. Henry Ford, born and bred on a Michigan farm, was typical. By the time a Benz car reached the United States in 1895, he was already in a position to criticize it in engineering terms as too heavy. By then, however, the French pioneers had retaken the initiative. Panhard, Peugeot, and de Dion-Bouton were in business; and races on the excellent French roads were bringing motoring to public attention.

Soon the other major nations, like America, Britain, Germany and Italy, were catching up and ideas were being exchanged. Thus Daimler's sale of his engine patent rights led indirectly to Panhard and Levassor producing the first cars with the familiar engine-first layout. In Britain, time was lost in speculative antics but the first British production car bore the name Daimler. In the courts in 1911 Henry Ford finally put paid to the notion that one company could have the sole right to manufacture cars in America. And while Europe went to war, Ford's Model T became the toast of the motoring world. For him, those first 30 years were just a beginning. Today, too, the name of Ford is synonymous with road transport everywhere.

THE GOLDEN YEARS OF INVENTION

1915

There will always be arguments over which event or invention represented a particular landmark in the history of road transport. Some of the more significant ones have been referred to in the introduction to this celebration of the motor car's first hundred years. Few people, however, dispute the identity of the very first motor car, which moved falteringly, yet under its own power, on the streets of Mannheim in 1885. Others had pioneered and patented the gas engine itself. Carl Benz now applied it to a passenger-carrying vehicle.

It had three spindly-looking wire wheels and a seat wide enough for two adults. The single water-cooled four-stroke 1.7-litre cylinder was mounted horizontally on the tubular chassis frame, and fed from Benz's design of surface carburettor. The huge horizontal flywheel spun beneath a vertical crankshaft. The power – not more than one horsepower – was transmitted to the twin rear wheels via a belt (to provide start and stop control, with the engine running) and chains. Valves were operated mechanically, ignition was electrical, and there was even a neat differential. True, there was just one front wheel, for sophisticated two-wheel steering had not yet been developed – nevertheless, the overall concept showed not only great originality, but Benz's clear picture of the basic essentials of the self-propelling personal vehicle so important in our lives today. The patent for the Benz 'carriage with gas engine' was dated January 1886.

In 1888, further history was made when Benz's wife Berta drove two of their children the considerable distance from Mannheim down to Pforzheim (not far short of Stuttgart) and back, thus completing the first successful journey by car, and with relatively little trouble *en route*.

In 1892 Benz produced his first four-wheeler. By this time he had a French agent, Emile Roger, who had been selling Benz's stationary engines; France was to be particularly quick to take the initiative in automobilism. In 1896, August Horch joined the expanding Benz organization but left after only a few years to make cars himself. He was the first of several engineers who would earn more fame with other companies. Benz had always needed sponsors, of course, but by the turn of the century – still pursuing outdated designs – he fell out with them. Crisis followed crisis and, although the name would survive, the Benz marque on its own was never to find true greatness again – despite some racing successes in its later years, and even the world land speed record.

As a marque, the Daimler is essentially British and an exceptionally fine car. The Daimler-Benz company (maker of Mercedes-Benz cars) is German through and through; it, too, produces some of the world's very best vehicles. It would be wrong to begin any history of the motor car without mentioning the name of Daimler alongside that of Benz; yet the two great men never worked together – although they must, surely, have met at some of the big exhibitions they attended.

Gottlieb Daimler was 10 years older than Carl Benz and was therefore over 50 years of age by the time his first vehicle, a form of motorcycle, was built at Bad Cannstatt in 1885. At this stage Daimler and his loyal colleague Wilhelm Maybach were essentially developers of engines, and they left it to another German partnership, that of Heinrich Hildebrand and Alois Wolfmüller of Munich, to create the first production motorcycle in 1894. Daimler and Maybach made no more such vehicles, but the patented Daimler four-stroke engine was used in a converted four-wheeled carriage in 1886, then in sledges, boats and other vehicles. In 1889 Maybach's inspiration led to a purpose-built steel-framed Daimler car, which had four wheels with steel wire spokes similar to those of Benz's original three-wheeler (by now four years old). This machine was displayed at the World Fair in Paris that year.

France takes the lead

Germany was still very restrictive for the would-be car manufacturer, whereas Daimler (like Benz) found France open-armed. He sold the French Daimler engine patent rights to Edouard Sarazin, a Belgian by birth. Soon after Sarazin's death, his widow married Emile Levassor. This event, and the excitement created by Daimler's Paris show car and its V-twin engine, put France ahead in world motoring for many years:

ABOVE *1886 Daimler carriage*. Rendered 'horseless' by the fitting of Gottlieb Daimler's internal combustion engine (patented three years before in December 1883), this carriage can, with justification, be considered the world's first four-wheeled car.

FACING PAGE, TOP LEFT *Steam before petrol*. The Frenchman Amédée Bollée made steam carriages of all sizes. This miniature example dates from 1885 – but that was the year in which the internal combustion engine made its indelible mark.

PRECEDING PAGES *1905 Gordon Bennett Cup*. The sixth and last of this famous series, consisting of four laps of a 137-km (85-mile) circuit in the Auvergne, with three spacing controls per lap to prevent baulking. Vincenzo Lancia (FIAT), seen here at the Laqueuille village control, held a 13-minute lead at half-distance; then the radiator failed and victory was handed once again to France (see photograph of winning car on page 22).

Carl Friedrich Benz (*1844-1929*)

Benz was the son of a Karlsruhe railwayman who died in 1846. Frau Benz moved their home from Mühlberg to Karlsruhe itself, where her resolve overcame poverty and enabled Carl to receive a full period of technical education; it followed directly upon the filing of Lenoir's 1860 gas-engine patent, which inspired him greatly. After spells with several firms, including the railway company and the Karlsruhe foundry and machine works, Benz formed his own company with a partner. A decade later, however, he was still struggling to make ends meet – but he did develop his own gas engines. First he followed the two-stroke principle; then he adapted Otto's four-stroke system.

In 1885 he built the world's first definitive motor car at his Rheinische Gasmotorenfabrik in Mannheim. For that alone Carl Benz must be considered the father of mechanical road transport as far as internal combustion is concerned. Few cars followed, however, most Benz production consisting of engines for use in stationary applications.

With financial help came some further development in cars and commercial vehicles. During the company's ups and downs there were even some notable racing successes, despite Benz's personal dislike of the sport. Always, though, crisis lurked.

Benz was over 80 years old when the company merged with its rival, Daimler, in a necessary act of survival.

TOP RIGHT *The car takes shape.* The 'Système Panhard et Levassor' was characterized by the placing of engine and gearbox over the steered wheels, as in this early 1890s Panhard, one of the first 'production' cars. LEFT *1885-type Benz.* First run in 1885, Carl Benz's purpose-built vehicle was granted a patent (January 1886) as a 'carriage with gas engine' – in other words, a complete entity, a true 'motor car'.

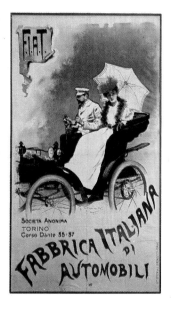

LEFT **The first FIAT.** Designed by Aristide Faccioli, the 1899 rear-engined 3¹/₂ hp model heralded the company's rapid growth under the brilliant Giovanni Agnelli.

ABOVE **Peugeot goes motor racing.** The 1894 Paris to Rouen Reliability Trial was the immediate predecessor of other inter-city races, and was dominated by Peugeot and Panhard petrol-driven cars. This one driven by Lemaître averaged 18.5 km/h (11.6 mph). Although it had its gearbox and Daimler-type engine from the Panhard, the early Peugeot was otherwise very different, featuring a lower, tubular chassis through which the cooling water flowed. The 3¹/₂ hp engine was at the rear.

Peugeot and Panhard were the joint winners. With Lemaître in the front seat (nearest camera) is Adolphe Clément.

certainly for the 30-year period covered by this chapter.

Emile Levassor and René Panhard were partners in a Paris company that made woodworking equipment. Use of the Daimler engine patent from 1889 led them to concentrate upon cars, but the Panhard car did not go into production until 1891; this was because designer Levassor wanted to take the Benz concept a stage further, that is to say, to create a technical entity rather than a confusion of odd components. Thus was born the classic bonnet, to house the front-mounted engine, behind which the gearbox was attached. The back wheels were driven by chain at this stage; shaft drive would come later.

Only a little behind Panhard in the use of Daimler's narrow-angle V-twin for production vehicles came Peugeot. Armand Peugeot, ironmonger, had been a customer of Emile Levassor, machine maker. The Peugeot family had been making bicycles for several years and, in 1889, produced a steam car. Levassor soon sold the internal combustion principle to Peugeot, who adopted it in 1891. Peugeot was one of the few really early marques to grow steadily, through every phase of the new industry, and is still in existence today.

The power unit for Peugeot's original steam car had been supplied by Léon Serpollet, the most successful of many engineers who saw steam as the long-term motive power for the road as well as the railway. His system of instant vaporization (by passing water through hot tubes) was the most important development in this form of locomotion. Serpollet was also the only European seriously to challenge the internal combustion engineers in competitions, once sport for motor cars got under way.

The most famous early French steam vehicles were the huge carriages of Amédée Bollée the elder, and of Georges Bouton, as sponsored by *Le Comte Mécanicien* Albert de Dion. Bollée's sons were quick to change to internal combustion. Léon Bollée christened his little two-seat three-wheeled air-cooled machine of 1895 the voiturette. This led Decauville to call its 1898 four-wheeled miniature the Voiturelle. In fact, voiturette remained part of the vocabulary of motoring and motor racing right up to World War 2. The Decauville was to prove one of the most effective light cars of the late 19th century, when it was driven by some of the great, although as yet unknown, racing pioneers. Its simple design, rather than any shortcomings in its construction, was to be a factor in the decision of an Englishman, Henry Royce, to design motor cars himself.

Like so many early motorists, Royce graduated to his first car from a de Dion-Bouton quadricycle. De Dion and Bouton made the switch from steam with confidence, and graduated via tricycles and quadricycles to proper cars. They also took a leaf out of the Benz and

Daimler books, and ensured their prosperity by selling their engines to other manufacturers. In the London–Brighton and other veteran car runs, the de Dion-Bouton continues to be the most popular and reliable of the small cars – just as it was in its heyday. The marque's system of universally jointed half-shafts, separate from the axle, is still very much in use, and keeps the great name of de Dion alive.

The story of 19th-century motoring in France is not complete without reference to a few of the other brave men who risked their all for the newfangled machine. Emile Delahaye switched from builders' machinery via stationary engines to cars based on the Roger-Benz as early as 1894. Louis Renault's road to fame began in 1888 when he lit his bedroom electrically; he was 11 at the time. Ten years later he modified his second-hand de Dion-Bouton, thus setting out on a journey that would lead to the world's first major nationalized motor corporation, Régie Renault. Alexandre Darracq was on the verge of 'mass production' at Suresnes, and innumerable folk of less astuteness had similar aspirations.

The birth of motor sport

France led the way in racing, and indeed in the odd motor competitions that preceded it. The most significant of these was 1894 Paris–Rouen Reliability Trial, the brainchild of Pierre Giffard, editor of *Le Petit Journal*. The criteria of safety, ease of handling, and economy cannot have been easy to apply in practice. Peugeot and Panhard were the leading contenders, and they shared the 5000-franc first prize. The best Peugeot's average speed of 18.5 km/h (11.5 mph) brought it to the finish some 30 minutes ahead of the leading Panhard, but the result took into account Giffard's observation that Panhard made complete cars and Peugeot's engines, too. Quickest of all, at 18.7 km/h (11.6 mph) for the 127 km (79 miles), was the remarkable steam car, with a semi-trailer for passengers, driven by Count de Dion, but it was placed third because it needed a riding mechanic as well as a driver. Out of a speculative entry list of 102, including one claiming 'gravity' as its motive power, 21 machines came to the start. The internal combustion engine's potential was well demonstrated with a 100 per cent finishing record for the 13 competitors with these units, whereas 4 of the 9 'steamers' failed to complete the course.

It was the enthusiasm of the Count de Dion that took racing on to its next stage, when he arranged a meeting of interested parties at his home in 1894. Among those present were the other French pioneers, Roger, Levassor, Peugeot and Serpollet. A road race from Paris to Bordeaux and back was conceived; virtually simultaneously came the idea of the

Gottlieb Wilhelm Daimler
(1834–1900)

Daimler, the son of a Württemberg baker, was born in the little town of Schorndorf. That his destiny lay in creative engineering was apparent from his workmanship as a gunsmith's apprentice. He left that particular trade and, after three years at Stuttgart Polytechnic, spent a period at Sir Joseph Whitworth's engineering works in Britain. In 1872 Daimler was given a senior appointment with the Deutz gas-engine company at Cologne, financed by Eugen Langen to exploit the skills of Nikolaus Otto. The latter, who had designed the first effective four-stroke engine, did not always see eye to eye with Daimler who left (after nearly a decade) to set up his own company to create the petroleum-fuelled four-stroke engine. With the help of his friend and colleague Wilhelm Maybach, Gottlieb Daimler adapted his engine for many uses, including the first motorcycle (1885).

Daimler patent rights were sold to other countries, and French cars with Daimler-type engines were the world's very first production vehicles.

Gottlieb Daimler's name is perpetuated in Britain's longest-established current marque, although he himself had nothing to do with its production or design at any stage.

Soon after his death, in March 1900, the German Daimler car became the 'Mercedes'. The merger that led to today's Daimler-Benz organization took place in 1926.

world's first real motor club, the Automobile Club de France.

The 1178 km (732-mile) Paris–Bordeaux–Paris race of June 1895 was an even clearer victory for the petrol engine, Emile Levassor's Panhard averaging 24 km/h (15 mph) and leading three Peugeots home. Behind came two Roger-Benzes and two more Panhards. Ninth and last (out of 22 starters) came the steam bus of Amédée Bollée the younger. One interesting vehicle that nearly made it was André Michelin's Peugeot. This pioneer was using pneumatic tyres, which kept failing, so he ran out of time at Orléans on the return journey; but such dedication meant that the modern tyre was on its way.

The first British cars and the 'Red Flag Act'
It may have been 1895 but Britain was still in the dark ages. The motor car was already ten years old, and indeed several Britons were well advanced in developing it. Samuel Brown had been the first Londoner to obtain brief propulsion by burning coal gas in a form of combustion chamber, back in 1824 at Brompton. At nearby Erith, in 1888, Edward Butler built a two-stroke petrol-engined tricycle. It was not until very late in 1894 that Frederick Bremer, who had no pretensions to becoming a manufacturer, took his home-made single-cylinder car chassis on to the road.

By then, however, Dr Frederick Lanchester was well on the way to becoming the British motor industry's first inventor-manufacturer. With his brother George, he built the 1895 Lanchester car as a design exercise. It had a single-cylinder air-cooled engine, replaced in due course by an air-cooled twin which had two flywheels; these rotated in opposite directions, and gave the engine a smoothness never previously achieved in internal combustion work. Other early developments included a change from chain to worm drive. Epicyclic gears, tangent-spoked wire wheels, pneumatic tyres and mechanical operation of valves were specified from the start. (In an epicyclic, or planetary, gearbox, small pinions revolve around a 'sun' or central gear, meshing with an outer ring gear.) Here was precisely thought-out automotive engineering at a time when it could not be put to good use, for Britain's lawmakers, having seen their fellow countrymen pioneer the railway locomotive, were completely out of touch with the motor car's possibilities. Did they still believe that the French were having fun and nothing more?

The first great promoter of the motor car in Britain was Selwyn Francis Edge, then London manager for Dunlop – and he had to go to France to experience motoring for himself! Cycle racing was an international sport and, naturally, brought people of different lands together. Edge himself had worked for Rudge and had taken part in

many cycle races, including the 1891 Paris–Bordeaux, and had made the acquaintance of the French ace Fernand Charron, who shared his inborn flair for salesmanship. Charron represented Humber bicycles in Paris for some time, but he had gone into partnership with a couple of fellow cyclists, Girardot and Voigt, and now dealt in the leading French car makes. (Later the partners raced Panhards and, from the turn of the century, produced their own make of car, the CGV.) In the winter of 1894–5 Edge, desperate to learn all about motoring, wrote to his friend Charron who promptly invited him to Paris to try a car. Charron's demonstration left Edge fascinated, and even more determined to plead the cause of the car at home.

The need for such action was simple. Back in 1865, by Act of Parliament, it had been decreed that all self-propelled road vehicles must be manned by three people, one of whom should walk ahead carrying a red flag of warning. Moreover, no such vehicle should exceed 4 mph on the open road or 2 mph in a built-up area. The steam road carriage had been overtaken by the railway train, and the car had not yet been invented. So the only likely target for such restrictions would have been the traction engine which hauled (and drove) heavy farm equipment.

Any kind of mechanical vehicle had an aura of danger about it; after all, there had been occasional boiler explosions in the steam-bus period. A modified Act of 1878 failed to anticipate progress, and when consultant engineer Frederick Richard Simms met Gottlieb Daimler and acquired his engine patent rights for Britain, the 'Red Flag Act' still applied. In fact, Simms even had difficulty with the authorities from 1891 when he wanted to demonstrate Daimler's engine in a boat for the first time. It was Simms who coined the terms 'motor car' and 'petrol'.

The first person to import a motor car into Britain was a Henry Hewetson of Catford, who had been to Mannheim, seen a Benz in action, and bought one himself. It arrived in December 1894, and soon Hewetson began trading in Benz vehicles. It was, however, in a Panhard

ABOVE **Stanley Steamer, 1904.** *The internal combustion engine did not kill the steam engine stone dead. Most famous of all the 'steamers' to live on into the motor car age was the Stanley, built in Massachusetts for 30 years, until 1927. Steam was a reliable enough form of motive power, but the engine's many adjuncts and the need to stop frequently for water became serious disadvantages as motoring progressed.*

Emile Levassor *(1844–1897)*
Levassor shaped the motor car as we know it: that is to say, he put the engine in front of the driver, a cover, or bonnet, over it and the gearbox behind it. He and his partner René Panhard had only just taken over the Périn et Pauwels machinery company in Paris when a friend, Edouard Sarazin, died; Sarazin had acquired the right to manufacture the Daimler engine in France and had wanted Panhard and Levassor to undertake this for him. Levassor married Sarazin's widow. Panhard cars were made from 1891, and Levassor won the first real motor race with one: Paris to Bordeaux and back single-handed in 1895. A year later he was leading the Paris–Marseilles–Paris race when his car overturned after hitting a dog. His co-driver, d'Hostingue, carried on and they came eighth. But Levassor was evidently quite badly hurt, for his untimely death in 1897 was attributed to the accident.

ABOVE **Lanchester, 1901.** Frederick and George Lanchester were Britain's equivalents to Benz and Daimler in that they produced their country's first real motor car (although they did so just a decade later than the Germans). The first Lanchester of 1895 showed great originality, much of it retained when the marque went into production at the turn of the century. This well-preserved example shows the unit construction of the lower body with the frame. Cantilever springs gave a soft ride.

RIGHT **Lanchester engine.** This view shows the thorough engineering of the 10 hp Lanchester. The air-cooled engine had an individual crankshaft and flywheel for each of its (opposed twin) cylinders; these shafts rotated in opposite directions, giving great smoothness. The three-speed epicyclic gearbox featured preselection of the two lower gears; there was automatic lubrication of engine and gearbox, and silent wormdrive to the rear axle. In many ways, this Lanchester is still a modern car.

Frederick William Lanchester (1868–1946)

Lanchester was more an inventor than an industrialist. Everything he did was original, and his first car (1895) was also the first that could be described as entirely British in concept. With the help of his brothers George (the manufacturing expert and designer of later cars) and Frank (a born promoter), Frederick Lanchester was producing cars commercially by the turn of the century. He was also a consultant to Britain's first series producer, Daimler of Coventry, whose owners (BSA) were ultimately to buy up the Lanchester company. Daimler continued to use the Lanchester name, but rarely for top-of-the-range models. This did not stop all three Lanchesters being highly respected, for they remained active throughout their lives: George lived to over 90, and was a consulting engineer until he was 88!

that Edge rode when he went to Paris; and it was a Panhard that Simms's Daimler Motor Syndicate Ltd imported for the Hon. Evelyn Ellis in the summer of 1895.

Shortly afterwards, Peugeot found its first British customer, Sir David Salomons. He was the mayor of Tunbridge Wells and organized the first British 'motor show' there on 15 October 1895, to emphasize the urgent need to repeal the 'Red Flag Act' by showing that motor vehicles were not too noisy or dangerous. In addition to his Peugeot, Salomons got Ellis to bring his two Panhards (one a fire engine); de Dion-Bouton exhibited the company's articulated steam wagon and, in contrast, a lightweight tricycle – so there were five machines to demonstrate.

This event was followed by a petition, published as a supplement in the new magazine *The Autocar* in February 1896, when the Prince of Wales was given a demonstration, by Ellis and Simms, in the latter's Cannstatt-built Daimler. That summer, there was a real show of French vehicles in London's Imperial Institute, and soon a new 'Locomotives on Highways' Act was passed, allowing vehicles weighing less than three tons to travel at 12 mph on Britain's roads – without a 'red flag' man in attendance. (From 1903 to 1930, the limit was 20 mph; 1935 brought the introduction of the 30 mph limit for built-up areas.)

Motoring was now generally feasible if not affordable, and the first celebration (or 'emancipation') run from London to Brighton took place on 14 November 1896. Although never active in the British Daimler company, Gottlieb Daimler did come to Britain for the event, driving down to Sussex with F. R. Simms.

Britain copied France unashamedly in its first series production cars, the introduction of which was held up to some extent by the attempts of Harry Lawson to establish a total monopoly on the manufacture and importation of all motor cars. The Lanchesters were above all this, but their first five years with cars were to be experimental ones. The Coventry-based Daimler company was more commercial than technical in its early days, and its primitive Panhard-style products began to appear from what had once been a cotton mill in 1897; the first private owner of a British car was Major-General Montgomery of Winchester.

In July 1897 the indefatigable enthusiast Evelyn Ellis and Daimler's works manager J. S. Critchley drove to the top of Malvern Beacon and were photographed there; and *The Autocar* editor Henry Sturmey (also a Daimler director) made the first John O'Groats to Land's End journey that October. Primitive it might be, but Britain's Daimler did work, and very soon it would acquire a character of its own – and become the marque of Royalty.

S. F. Edge had bicycled to the Tunbridge Wells motor show of 1895, and was now actively engaged in putting his interpretation on the Panhard theme. France's long-distance race of 1896 from Paris to Marseilles and back had been another Panhard benefit, and Merkel's car (the runner-up) was brought to Britain afterwards. Edge managed to acquire it, and it became the subject of major modification by D. Napier & Sons, a London engineering firm noted for the accuracy of the weighing machines it made for use in banks.

Montague Napier, a former cycling club colleague, fitted Edge's Panhard with worm-and-nut steering, controlled by a wheel rather than a tiller. Solid tyres were replaced by pneumatics; the water-cooling and lubrication systems were redesigned, and before long Napier had fitted his own design of engine. The outcome, in 1899, was Britain's first sports car, the Napier, which Edge made it his business to race, promote and sell from the dawn of the 20th century.

Car making spreads through Europe

Britain was not alone in the race to catch up with France in the development and production of motor cars. The Lanza of 1895 was the first all-Italian car; but it was the formation of FIAT in 1899 that put Italy on the map as a producer for the people.

Vienna was the technical as well as the cultural hub of Central Europe. It was there, in 1898, that 23-year-old Ferdinand Porsche began his career with Jacob Lohner, who had already been making vehicles for a couple of years. The Lohner-Porsche, used mainly as a commercial vehicle, was the first application of the petrol-electric drive-train system. Porsche's outstanding and original work has continued to influence car design ever since.

Whereas Porsche came originally from Bohemia, Austro-Hungary's other two great pioneers of motor-engineering – Edmund Rumpler and Hans (or Jan) Ledwinka, born 1872 and 1878 respectively – were Viennese, by birth at least. Both men's careers began in the Moravian village of Nesselsdorf (now Kopřivnice), near Ostrava, where Ignác Šustala had founded his coachmaking business in 1853. Thirty years later this firm had expanded to make railway trucks and carriages, and in 1897 the Nesselsdorfer Wagenbaufabriksgesellschaft, as it was then called (for German was the official language before the republic of Czechoslovakia came into being after World War 1), made its first Benz-based car. Rumpler left in 1898, and won fame in Germany; Ledwinka was to leave later, although he would also return to the scene of his apprenticeship to create some remarkable machines. Two 19th-century makes from what is now East Germany deserve particular mention. Friedrich Lutzmann of Dessau began his work along Benz

ABOVE **Dealer advertisements and posters** were already commonplace in France by the early 1900s. The car has a distinctive Renault look.

LEFT **Nesselsdorf bus, 1908.** The town of Nesselsdorf in what is now Czechoslovakia gave its name to Central Europe's first motor manufacturer of note. Here Ignác Šustala made wagons from 1853. The first Nesselsdorf motor vehicles followed in 1897. Like many manufacturers, this one produced commercial vehicles as well as cars. Today Nesselsdorf is called Kopřivnice, and this bus would be called a Tatra.

LEFT *1907 Darracq.* *This famous French make, with close British connections, was founded at Suresnes in 1896. Alexandre Darracq is sometimes described as the father of mass production.*

ABOVE *1907 de Dion-Bouton. The partnership of Count Albert de Dion and Georges Bouton began in 1883. Bouton and his brother-in-law had been making steam engines in Paris for over a decade when de Dion became the venture's sponsor. A steam-driven vehicle was built in 1883; 10 years later came the modern high-speed petrol engine. Up to the outbreak of World War 1 the company and its output mushroomed, but the momentum was never recovered afterwards.*

lines in 1893, and was producing in series by 1896. With Benz and Daimler, Lutzmann was the only exhibitor at the first German motor show in 1897. His design was acquired by Adam Opel and so, in 1898, as one marque died another was born.

Eisenach in Thuringia had its own *Fahrzeugfabrik* from 1898, when it began making the rear-engined French Decauville Voiturelle under licence, calling it the Wartburg after the castle that stands over the town. Eisenach was the name given to the company's other early products, including electric cars. Today's BMW is the indirect legacy of this obscure but historically important car-making centre.

Scandinavia and the Low Countries were also making cars in the 1890s, but there was no production in series. Probably the earliest, and certainly the oldest surviving, among the North European prototypes is Denmark's Hammel, of about 1887, which has completed a London to Brighton run in modern times. This is certainly the longest trip it has ever made!

Early days in America

Before turning to the new century, the influence of the United States must be put into perspective. Europe may have been the originator of the motor car, but America was never very far behind. If Britain lagged for reasons of road legislation, America's car makers were held up by a form of red tape through which only Henry Ford could cut – but not for many years to come.

Henry Ford was not yet 10 years old when, in 1872, George Brayton patented a crude two-stroke internal combustion gas engine. It was tried

out in a tram and a bus; it was also shown at an exhibition in Philadelphia in 1876. There, a clever attorney called George Baldwin Selden, who specialized in patent law, took his inspiration.

Very quickly Selden, whose hobby seems to have been engineering, schemed a complete vehicle to be powered by a theoretical engine that was different enough from Brayton's to enable him to file a patent of his own – and by keeping it pending while he made modifications, Selden managed to have it granted as late as November 1895, by which time the motor car concept was well established. However, there was still no Selden motor car.

John Lambert of Indiana (and others) may have been a little earlier, but it is generally considered that the true birth of the American car industry took place in Springfield, Massachusetts, in 1892 when the Duryea brothers made a gas-powered buggy – the first of several. Built in various subsequent locations, and even assembled in Belgium and the United Kingdom for a time, the products of Charles Duryea appeared regularly from 1895, when his brother Frank won a race from Chicago to Evanston and back. This was America's first official road race. It was sponsored by the *Chicago Herald-Tribune*, and should have continued along Lake Michigan's western shore as far as Waukegan; but snow fell and narrow wheels sank through the already poor road surfaces. Duryea's main opposition came from imported Benz machines, although several electric-powered vehicles took part; and all the entries were laboratory tested. This was the first time that comparative performance and specification had been noted in detail, to the extent of calculating running costs. This information is tabled in Gerald Rose's remarkable *Record of Motor Racing, 1894-1908*, which also mentions that the Haynes prototype had a motor of the two-cycle type and 'gave off a very foul exhaust'.

Electrically driven road vehicles have never become commonplace, except for short-haul work; but innumerable attempts were made in America, as in Europe, to produce a practical owner-driver vehicle with the blissful smoothness and silence afforded by electric traction. More than five hundred makers are on record around the world. The shadow of the Selden patent did not hang over them.

Not many drivers of electric cars ever won races. The first of the few was Andrew Riker, who beat Duryea and others in a series of one-mile sprints at Narragansett organized as part of the Rhode Island state fair in September 1896.

There was an alternative to electricity. The inaugural (1899) 'Climb to the Clouds', the 13 km (8 mile) timed ascent of Mount Washington, New Hampshire, was won by Freelan Stanley in the most famous

ABOVE **American race, 1895.** The first organized motor car competition in the United States took place in Illinois in November 1895 in wintry weather. Frank Duryea, the winner, is seen at the tiller of the car which led to the creation by Frank and his brother Charles of one of America's first motor companies. This race was sponsored by the Chicago Times-Herald.

LEFT **The pneumatic tyre.** André Michelin used the first-ever long-distance road race (Paris–Bordeaux–Paris) to test this new type of tyre publicly in June 1895. The tyres let him down, but their principle did not. Soon solid rubber tyres were to be the exception rather than the rule. Here a slightly pneumatic lady helps Michelin's German agency to promote these tyres on the basis of their success in the 1904 and 1905 Gordon Bennett Cup races.

'steamer' of them all. In the same year the Locomobile company bought the right to manufacture the Stanley brothers' steam cars.

Of the 19th-century American car makers employing internal combustion, Alexander Winton – a Scot who had settled in Cleveland, Ohio – was the first to demonstrate the performance potential. In May 1899 he managed an average speed of over 27 km/h (17 mph) between Cleveland and New York.

The growth of international racing

Simultaneously, on France's largely straight and infinitely superior roads, Edge's tutor Charron was the undisputed king of 19th-century motoring. On the very weekend of Winton's New York run, Charron's Panhard was charging from Paris to Bordeaux at an average of close on 48 km/h (30 mph). This event was run even faster than the famous 1898 Paris–Amsterdam–Paris, which had been highlighted by a race-long dual between the Panhards of Fernand Charron and his business partner Léonce Girardot (known as 'the eternal second').

Despite the lack of a yardstick for comparison, Winton reacted to Charron's Paris–Bordeaux victory by challenging the Frenchman to a 1000-mile duel. The latter responded with alacrity, going as far as

placing a deposit of 20,000 francs with the *New York Herald* in Paris. The French edition of that famous newspaper was run by James Gordon Bennett, an American publicist with an eye for a strong story. It was he, for example, who had masterminded Henry Stanley's search for the explorer David Livingstone in Africa.

The Winton–Charron challenge never materialized, but was followed very quickly by the announcement of a new *Coupe Internationale* – better known as the Gordon Bennett Cup – an annual motor race to be fought out between teams nominated by national motor clubs, and run under the rules of the Automobile Club de France.

Not many countries had clubs in 1900, and fewer still were ready to go racing. Britain had nothing suitable (the Napier was not yet ready), nor did Italy or Switzerland. At one stage it looked as if Nesselsdorf might represent Austria, but in the end the first Gordon Bennett race, from Paris to Lyons, produced only six contestants. Germany's entrant – Carl Benz's son, Eugen – had tyre problems before the start, and did not take part. The single American and Belgian competitors, Winton and Jenatzy, retired with tyre and other troubles; and two (out of three) French Panhards were the only finishers, with Charron leading Girardot home once again.

Because the first event had proved something of a damp squib, the Gordon Bennett Cup contests of 1901 and 1902 were incorporated into other road races. Thus Girardot was awarded the prize in 1901 as the first of the Gordon Bennett entrants, although he was well down the overall list of finishers in that year's Paris–Bordeaux. Edge had brought the new Napier, fitted with French tyres which (the French decided) made it ineligible to compete for the trophy on behalf of Britain. Poor framing of regulations and unreasonable interpretation of them seem to have dogged motor racing and rallying ever since. In 1902, however, S. F. Edge got his revenge, defeating the French and bringing the Gordon Bennett Cup to Britain for the only time.

By then, touring and racing cars had begun to acquire clear identities of their own. The power and weight of racing cars had increased dramatically. Panhard had started with tiny 3 hp models in 1894/5, and by 1902 was staying ahead of the game with 70 hp from 13.7 litres; but other makers were joining in.

The major race of 1902 was from Paris to Vienna, and it was significant for the introduction of a maximum weight limit of 1000 kg (2205 lb) for the big cars. However, the overall winner – Marcel Renault, Louis's brother – was competing in the light car class, yet averaged 62.6 km/h (38.9 mph) to beat a group of Darracqs, also weighing in under the regulation 650 kg (1430 lb). Henri Farman's

LEFT **1903 Gordon Bennett Cup.** *This was the first major race to be held in the British Isles, a result of victory the previous year by S. F. Edge (pictured overleaf). This time the Britons – Edge, Jarrott and Stocks with Napiers – were out of luck. Camille Jenatzy of Belgium won with a 60 hp Mercedes, which replaced the 90 hp cars destroyed in a factory fire. This picture shows the Belgian Baron Pierre de Caters (Mercedes) who retired with rear axle failure while well-placed; but his team mate*

Jenatzy's fine victory ensured that the 1904 race would take place in Germany. The Irish event of 1903 was run on a complicated double circuit, centred upon Ballyshannon.

Panhard was fastest of the big cars, coming second overall at 61.8 km/h (38.4 mph) after a battle with the privateer Count Louis Zborowski, who was placed fourth in his Mercedes.

Success for the new Mercedes

Mercedes was a new marque which had made its competition début at Pau in February 1901 and won the Nice–Salon–Nice race a month later, driven by Wilhelm Werner.

Shortly after Gottlieb Daimler died, Wilhelm Maybach, his close colleague of so many years, had responded to Emil Jellinek, one of the Daimler Motoren-Gesellschaft's most ardent (and wealthiest) admirers, and designed a new car for him. Maybach designed many special features for it, too, including a positive gear-change gate, a more efficient honeycomb (as opposed to tubed) radiator, and mechanical instead of automatic inlet valve operation. The last feature meant that the internal combustion engine could now produce its power in an efficiently controlled manner. The car had a pressed-steel chassis frame. Jellinek entered it at Nice for Werner to drive – but in the name of his daughter, Mercédès. The name was retained after that success, and the Mercedes was widely copied.

If design had tended to stagnate since the motor car's general shape had been settled by Panhard and Levassor over a decade earlier, Maybach's 35 hp Mercedes from Cannstatt changed automobile engineering from a hit-and-miss affair into a precise science.

Nevertheless, motor racing in the pre-World War 1 era would continue to be a battle of giants. Because Edge's Napier had won the 1902 Gordon Bennett Cup (although by default) the Automobile Club of Great Britain and Ireland gained the right to organize the fourth race of the series, in 1903; but mainland Britain at least was still opposed to racing on public roads. The Paris–Madrid race in May had been halted in Bordeaux, where Fernand Gabriel's big Mors led at an astounding 105.1 km/h (65.3 mph), because of the toll it had already taken in human life. For the first time, organizational weakness had led to many fatal accidents – including that to Marcel Renault – and inter-city racing was now at an end. The answer for the Automobile Club of Britain and Ireland was to run July's Gordon Bennett race on an enclosed circuit made up of country roads in the quiet central Irish countryside.

It was a good race, a four-way contest between America, Britain, France and Germany, each entering three cars. The American cars – two Wintons and a Peerless – failed to finish and, although Edge and Jarrott were running second and fourth after one lap, all three British Napiers were unclassified at the finish, two having crashed and the third being

disqualified when Edge received a push start at a control.

Determined to regain the trophy for France, Michelin chartered a ship to bring two Panhards for René de Knyff and Farman, plus Gabriel's Mors, and these cars were very fast; but second, third and fourth was the best they could do, for this was Germany's year.

Despite losing his new 90 hp cars in a fire at the Cannstatt works, Jellinek substituted 60 hp touring models and the fiery Belgian driver, Camille Jenatzy, led for most of the 530 km (330 miles) in one of them.

So the Gordon Bennett Cup went to Germany for 1904. There it was won back by France. The sixth and final race of the series took place in the Auvergne in 1905 when Léon Théry (Brasier) won for the second year running: although FIAT of Italy nearly did it both times.

The Gordon Bennett race format was not satisfactory and attempts to manipulate it to give the proliferation of French marques an advantage helped to bring the series to an end. Already the manufacturer had taken over from the wealthy individual as the dominant force in the new sport. There was no challenge from Britain or Germany for 1906 and James Gordon Bennett turned his attention to balloon racing; here, he felt, commercialism had not yet tainted sport.

Bennett had started something, however. 'His' event led to Grand

LEFT *Grand Prix racing begins.* The 1906 Grand Prix was won for Renault by the Hungarian Ferenc Szisz; this picture of him was taken in 1907 when he came second to Felice Nazzaro (FIAT). Bulkhead radiators were a feature of early Renaults. The marque would re-emerge in Grand Prix racing 70 years on.

ABOVE *1905 Gordon Bennett Cup.* Having lost the race for two years running, the French won in Germany in 1904 through the brilliant and consistent driving of Léon Théry. When the event returned to France in 1905, he won again. Here Théry takes his 11¼-litre 96 hp Brasier through one of the tight Auvergne bends.

Prix racing which, in its many forms, has lived on as the world's premier contest; and commercialism has taken an even more dominant role, as we shall see.

Monsters, miniatures and the quest for speed

A fascinating feature of the opening decade of the 20th century was the monstrous size of the cars permitted by the race regulations. The first recognized world speed records had been established in 1898 and 1899 in France, as a duel between electric-powered cars. Then, in 1902, Léon Serpollet's steamer had bumped the record up from about 105 to 120 km/h (65 to 75 mph) before the race for this particular honour became the preserve of the internal combustion engine.

Mors was the first; then came the amazing Gobron-Brillié which, in 1903, took the record past 130 km/h (80 mph) for the first time. The Gobron-Brillié did not follow the orthodox pattern of engine development, although the car itself was indeed a monster. Each cylinder had two pistons, which parted to draw in the fuel charge, then came together to fire it. Moreover, the cylinders were paired. The lower pistons operated orthodox short connecting rods on a common crankshaft bearing; the upper ones were coupled to diametrically opposed bearings, via extra-long connecting rods. The company retained the opposed-piston system for all its pre-war engines; for their complication was said to be outweighed by the smoothness with which they ran. In 1904, Louis Rigolly became the first person to exceed 160 km/h (100 mph) in a four-cylinder, eight-piston Gobron-Brillié.

Two other great marques, Delaunay-Belleville and Lorraine-Dietrich, remained more orthodox but benefited from the design skills of former Benz engineer Marius Barbarou. The more foresighted manufacturers were realizing that the car must not go on getting bigger and bigger, but many were already too late.

At the other end of the scale, French flair showed in the development of simpler, cheaper designs. The motorized tricycle and quadricycle did not remain popular once the light motor car had proved itself. The Sizaire-Naudin, with its sliding-pillar independent front suspension (inspired by Decauville's Voiturelle) was quite a sophisticated and very sporting little car. France's most prolific engine manufacturer, de Dion-Bouton, supplied the motive power. De Dion-Bouton, like other pioneers such as Panhard, was already losing the impetus it had been given when helping to create a new industry.

Exceptions to this tendency were Renault and Peugeot, whose growing empires moved with the times, even if not every venture was a complete success. In 1906 one of the Peugeot brothers, Robert, established a second marque called Lion-Peugeot and moved (with Sizaire-Naudin) to the forefront of light car racing. The last product of this factory at Beaulieu-Valentigney – a bought-out design known as the Bébé – was one of the most delightful of all miniature cars.

More typical of the era, however, was the cyclecar. The first of these spindly but economical creations was the 1910 Bédélia, in effect a four-wheeled, two-seater tandem. The central-pivot steering was controlled by the rear occupant. Belt transmission was used instead of the shaft drive that was rapidly becoming the accepted system. Indeed, that Bébé Peugeot of 1912 had *two* propeller shafts; but then it was designed by that legendary eccentric Ettore Bugatti, whose story comes in later chapters.

Famous Italians

In Italy (where Bugatti was born) the early years of the 20th century saw the rapid encompassing of the motoring spectrum by FIAT. Although this organization would remain the biggest, other companies now began to give Italy a reputation for automotive artistry.

FIAT's top racing driver, Vincenzo Lancia, left to form his own company, which has been making interesting cars ever since 1906. The

ABOVE **1904 Napier L48.** *Better known as the Samson, this was the fastest British car of its day, capable of well over 160 km/h (100 mph). The lamps indicate that promoter S. F. Edge is driving it in 'long-distance' trim at the newly* opened Brooklands track in 1907. This remarkable car was 're-created' in Australia in the 1980s.

ABOVE **Peugeot's baby.** *Designed for Peugeot by Ettore Bugatti, this car was a beautifully proportioned miniature, with an 856 cc four-cylinder engine. Little more than 2.4 m (8 ft) long, the Peugeot Bébé looked very modern when* introduced in 1912 – ten years before the Austin Seven, for example.

first Lancias were given the type name Alpha, and the Greek alphabet is still associated with the Lancia marque. Alfa, on the other hand, derives from the initials for Anonima Lombardo Fabbrica Automobili, which was set up in 1909 after licence-assembly of French Darracqs had proved unsuccessful; the bank in charge brought in a new man to run the concern – and his name was Nicola Romeo.

Italy's most splendid white elephants of those days were the Itala and the Isotta-Fraschini. An Itala won the first Targa Florio race – Italy's own replacement for the Gordon Bennett – in 1906, but the biggest claim to fame was the marvellous performance by Prince Scipione Borghese in winning the unique Peking to Paris trial of 1907.

Isotta-Fraschini followed Itala and FIAT in winning the Targa Florio. For his technically advanced marque, Oreste Fraschini devised one of the first four-wheel brake systems. In an early takeover bid, Lorraine-Dietrich acquired the firm, only to hand it back within a couple of years.

Central Europe and the Low Countries: engineering excellence
The Austro-Hungarian motor industry was developing rapidly at this time, and it was a combination of Isotta-Fraschini, Charron and Renault designs that got one important marque, the Praga, off the ground in 1907. Slightly earlier Laurin-Klement had introduced Bohemia's first regular production car. At about that time, too, Hans Ledwinka returned from Vienna to Nesselsdorf to design a new car for his old Moravian employers. In Vienna, Lohner was closing his business, whereas Austro-Daimler was developing. In an 'all change' (probably precipitated by Wilhelm Maybach), Ferdinand Porsche moved in as design and engineering chief at Austro-Daimler when Paul Daimler returned to Germany to do that job at his late father's firm. This followed a decision by Gottlieb Daimler's former partner, Wilhelm Maybach, to leave the Daimler Motoren-Gesellschaft and go into business with his son, making aero engines for Count Zeppelin at Friedrichshafen from 1907.

Another German on the move at this time was former Benz man August Horch. He had made cars since 1900, only to fall out with his backers, so he resigned. In 1910 he started another great marque, which has returned to fame in the 1980s. Horch used for it the Latin translation of his own name, calling his new car the Audi.

Ledwinka's old tutor at Nesselsdorf, Edmund Rumpler, joined Adler in 1903, giving that marque a character of its own before pursuing aero-engineering. His activity in this field overshadowed his work on swing axle suspension until after World War 1, which would take so many engineers in new directions, and help some of the more canny

firms survive through the wilderness years of 1914 to 1918.

Of Switzerland's national motor industry, three great names have survived – but only as high-quality commercial vehicles. Berna, FBW, and Saurer have all been closely linked for many years. The last-named was founded by Adolphe Saurer in 1897, and Joseph Wyss's Berna company was taken over in 1929. The superb handbuilt FBW trucks and buses of more recent years took their initials from the Yugoslav Franz Brozincevic, who built his original car in Wetzikon in 1898. Switzerland is better known for the motor engineers who worked beyond its frontiers. Ernest Henry made his name with Peugeot; Georges Roesch became chief engineer with the British Talbot company during the war; and in Barcelona in 1900 the most celebrated of Swiss engineers, Marc Birkigt, began his illustrious career. First he produced a few cars for La Cuadra, then for the company's principal creditor, Castro. In a second financial rescue, in 1904, the Castro became the Hispano-Suiza. Such was its artistry that the marque caught the eye of King Alfonso XIII. There was no question of Birkigt making a people's car, which might have been more appropriate for Spain. Instead, a Paris factory was opened in 1911 to produce confections for France's automotive gourmets. That Hispano-Suiza should become one of the great makers of all time, in the country where the motor car was king, simply confirms Birkigt's brilliance.

Before World War 1, Belgium and the Netherlands were excelling in the top echelons of motoring; Britain's J. T. C. Moore-Brabazon (later Lord Brabazon) and the Hon. Charles Stewart Rolls were among the most successful people to race Belgium's elegant Minerva. Spijker (or Spyker) of Holland was among the original experimenters with four-wheel drive, four-wheel brakes, and six-cylinder engines.

Progress in Britain and the founding of Rolls-Royce
Britain had lagged, but with the coming of the 20th century it leaped forward with excitement. S. F. Edge's enthusiasm was infectious, and he developed the Napier's action image through car and motorboat racing. In 1904 'his' marque became the world's first six-cylinder production car.

Other stars were in the ascendant. Daimler of Coventry, as the country's first regular producer, soon established itself as purveyor to royalty. The Birmingham Small Arms Company (BSA) began making cars in 1907; it bought Daimler in 1910, shortly after the latter firm had made a brave (but possibly ill-conceived) switch to sleeve-valve engines. Metal sleeves moved inside the cylinders, and suitably located holes did the work of inlet and exhaust valves; the result was silent if sloppy

ABOVE **What's in a name?** Soon after Gottlieb Daimler's death in 1900, although the company kept his name, the marque became Mercedes.

LEFT **Spijker, c. 1907.** Like the British Napier, Holland's Spijker (or Spyker) was one of the first marques to utilize a six-cylinder engine. Its lifespan (1899–1925) was similar, too. Ladies' motoring attire at this time tended to be fashionable or practical, but rarely both.

ABOVE RIGHT **Morris Oxford, c. 1914.** The 'Bullnose' Morris was Britain's first popular light car and its story is told in more detail in the next chapter. Robert Jones built the first bodies for Hollick & Pratt of Coventry, a firm that (like other suppliers) was eventually acquired by William Morris. Jones went on to found Carbodies, today's London taxi makers.

LEFT **Hispano-Suiza, 1912.** *This is the 1912 Alfonso model (its name reflects the patronage of the Spanish monarch), the sportiest of the early Hispano-Suizas designed by a Swiss, Marc Birkigt, and built in Spain. Hispano-Suiza also manufactured in Paris from 1911.*

RIGHT **By jingo, we'll win.** *Sadly, the Napier car never regained its former glory after World War 1 but Napier engines would keep the name famous.*

smoothness, and a long bluish vapour trail behind.

The Lanchester brothers trod their own furrow, putting their fascinating cars into production in 1900 after more than five years of experiment. More orthodox British cars sprang from older bicycle-making companies: Humber, Rover, Singer and Sunbeam were the most famous. The Vauxhall took its name from the London district where it was first made, formerly the Falkes Hall, or Faukeshall, estate. (Falkes de Bréauté, an early 13th-century soldier of fortune, included a wyvern in his coat of arms; this fabulous creature became the main feature of the Vauxhall badge.) Laurence Pomeroy senior was the fine engineer who moved in shortly after the marque went to Luton in 1905, to give the Vauxhall a flair that made it the Napier's natural successor as Britain's premier sports car of the immediate pre-war period. The most celebrated examples were the Prince Henry models, named after the German trials in which they competed.

'The pursuit of perfection' has been the aim of most good manufacturers. Two of them – Porsche and Jaguar – have been using that very alliteration in their 1980s slogans for English-speaking markets. In 1904 it was the be-all and end-all of one man in particular: F. H. Royce.

From 1884 Frederick Henry Royce had built up an electrical engineering business in Manchester, based upon skills he had gained at evening classes. He had put in £20 as capital, to go with £50 from his friend and partner Ernest Claremont. They had worked hard, and now, 20 years on, they were beginning to see some reward for their labours. The partners bought themselves motor vehicles, but Royce could not come to terms with what he regarded as primitive machines – so he decided to make something better. The first three Royce cars were made for the use of Claremont, Royce himself, and another director called Henry Edmunds: the only member of the trio already in the motoring 'set'. A member of the Automobile Club of Great Britain and Ireland, Edmunds was well acquainted with the dashing drivers of the day; one of them was the Hon. Charles Stewart Rolls who had bought his first Peugeot in 1896 and was now in business selling Panhards, Minervas and other good cars. He also spent much of his own time racing and (with the present Lord Montagu's father) was actually the first Briton to race a car in France, in September 1899. So, when Edmunds pressed Rolls, the high-class London motor trader, to make the journey to Manchester to see a new lightweight, two-cylinder car, the invitation was accepted more out of courtesy than enthusiasm.

Face to face for the first time in May 1904, Rolls and Royce found themselves in accord at once, despite a 14-year age gap. Royce was

RIGHT *Austin Ten, 1913.*
By this time, there was a proliferation of models in the Austin range. This typical Ten has an atypical two-seater body with luggage rack – 7s 6d (37½p) extra when new – and is one of many Austin cars displayed in Britain's newest motor museum, the Patrick Collection, Birmingham.

ABOVE *Vauxhall Prince Henry, 1914.* Fine engineering and discreet, distinctive styling typified this Vauxhall, named after the German trials in which these models took part, which took over (from Napier) as the British sporting man's car in the years before World War 1. Laurence Pomeroy Sr was the man who made it a classic. No marque would change its character so drastically as Vauxhall of Luton did when General Motors took over in the 1920s. This beauty, which was provided by Reg Long, was once owned by Pomeroy Jr. The characteristic flutes along the bonnet remained until quite recent times.

RIGHT *The Dieppe races.* Three pre-war Grands Prix took place at Dieppe, in 1907, 1908 and 1912. The first two were won by FIAT (Nazzaro) and Mercedes (Lautenschlager); but in 1912 the French crowds went wild when their own Georges Boillot won for Peugeot. The A.C.F. of the poster is the Automobile Club de France, the first of them all.

ABOVE **Rolls-Royce 40/50, 1924.** First seen in 1906, the Silver Ghost continued well into the 1920s. This limousine has coachwork by Joseph Cockshoot of Manchester, where Rolls-Royce itself originated. One of the last Silver Ghosts, this car went back to the works for conversion to four-wheel brakes. Provided by Rex Sevier and photographed at Tiddington Hall, Derby.

RIGHT **Christie, c. 1906.** Over half a century before the Mini-Minor, the Christie Front Drive Motor Co of New York was fitting its power units transversely across the chassis; indeed the crankshaft replaced the front axle. Note the huge V4 engine, the complex cooling system and the extra offside front wheel for traction at take-off. A similar car, if not this very one, displacing a claimed 19 litres, took part in the 1907 GP at Dieppe, driven by J. Walter Christie.

happy with his first attempts at making cars, and wanted to build something bigger, smoother, nearer to perfection. Rolls wanted to improve the turnover of his sales company, and to justify his name on a motor car. In next to no time, the Rolls-Royce was born.

At first there were two-, three-, four- and six-cylinder cars, all with dimensions of about one litre per cylinder. Then, in 1906, came a 3½-litre V8, partly inspired by Sir Alfred Harmsworth, the man behind the *Daily Mail*, who had already contributed his own piece on 'The Choice of a Motor' for the *Badminton Library of Sports and Pastimes*. 'Few undertakings require more care and caution than the choice of a motor car,' he had written. 'Of the three or four hundred types and varieties now in existence [i.e. in 1902] many are of no practical use, some are extremely complicated, not a few dangerous, and many more or less faulty in construction.' As the owner of eight cars – three petrol, three steam, and two electric – he had already reached the conclusion that the petrol engine would be a customer's 'wisest choice'.

Only three of those early V8s were built, but the conventional six-cylinder set Rolls-Royce on course to become the greatest prestige marque the world has known.

Britain did not have speed events like those on the Continent. There were reliability trials, sprints, and hill climbs; but the kudos gained from winning was small for anyone seeking publicity. Then came the Isle of Man TT – the Tourist Trophy, the oldest car race still on the international calendar. Its first winner, in 1905, was a Scottish Arrol-Johnston; a Rolls-Royce came second. Rolls himself won outright in 1906, and the marque's name was made.

A new company was formed to keep the business separate from the partners' previous interests. Sadly, Royce was in poor health and, more and more, acted as the reclusive consultant on the design of Rolls-Royce cars and aero engines. Rolls died in an air crash in 1910, and it was his colleague Claude Johnson who ensured that Royce's perfectionist approach continued to find expression in cars for the next generation of motorists to appreciate.

Meanwhile, in Birmingham, the dawn of everyday motoring was being anticipated by Herbert Austin. He had been with the Wolseley Sheep Shearing Company and had created its first car in 1895, basing it on the Léon Bollée tricar. Later came a variety of designs, including a horizontal four-cylinder racing model in which drivers of the calibre of Jarrott and Rolls proved capable of beating the Napiers (if not the best of the foreign opposition) in the 1904 and 1905 Gordon Bennett races.

Austin left Wolseley after an argument on matters of design. Orthodox but varied, the Austin range grew quickly, much of the inspiration coming from the United States where motoring was breaking out of its self-imposed cocoon.

Individuality and cars for the people in the USA

In America, the electric and steam-driven cars had persisted. One battery charge would take the Baker Electric 80 km (50 miles), and that satisfied the majority of customers for this, the most popular vehicle of its kind.

The Stanleys regained control of their marque from the Locomobile company, and continued to sell their wares for longer than most steam car makers – helped by some remarkable speed demonstrations.

True mass production came to America in the form of the single-cylinder, curved-dash Oldsmobile runabout produced in Lancing, Michigan, by Ransom Eli Olds. Output went up from 2000 in 1902 to 5000 in 1904, when Olds moved out and set up a new company, using his initials for its name, Reo, which has lived on into the modern truck world. Oldsmobile was to become part of the biggest of the new automobile empires – General Motors, the convoluted story of which comes into the next chapter.

America was not all pure commerce and, ever since the first Duryea,

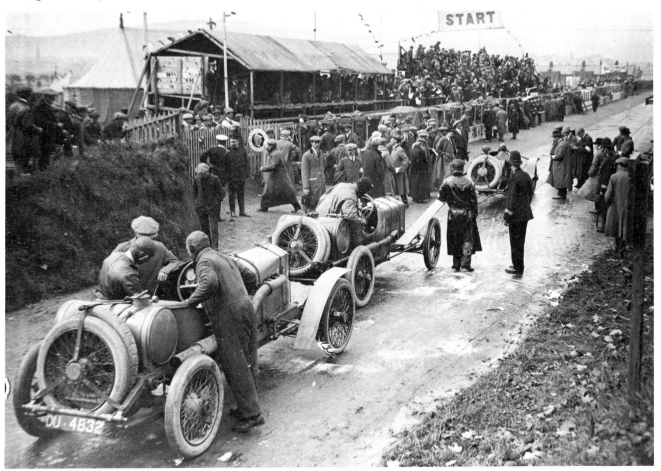

LEFT *Tourist Trophy, 1914. Held within a few weeks of the outbreak of war, this great 970-km (600-mile) event for cars of up to 3.3 litres took place on the Isle of Man. That year it was won by Kenelm Lee Guinness in a Coatalen-designed Sunbeam, with Walter Owen Bentley sixth in a French DFP.*

some delightful oddities have peppered its motoring history. John Walter Christie's front-wheel-drive cars of 1904 to 1910 anticipated the Mini with their transversely mounted engines; his four-cylinder monster for the 1907 Grand Prix displaced nearly 20 litres. Shortly afterwards, Lee Chadwick introduced supercharging, which has met with intermittent favour over the years as a means of producing extra power.

It is, however, in bringing the car to the people that America has made history; and that history is incomplete at any stage if the name of Ford is not included. Henry Ford was born on a farm at Dearborn, Michigan, in 1863 but did not choose to be a farmer. He thought farming inefficient and later, in *My Life and Work*, he recalled how he had been attracted to the mechanical world:

The biggest event was meeting with a road engine about eight miles out of Detroit one day when we were driving to town. I was twelve years old. I remember that engine as though I had seen it only yesterday, for it was the first vehicle other than horse-drawn that I had ever seen. It was intended primarily for driving threshing machines and sawmills and was simply a portable engine and boiler mounted on wheels with a water tank and coal cart trailing behind. The engine was placed over the boiler and one man standing on the platform behind the boiler shovelled coal, managed the throttle, and did the steering. It had been made by Nichols Shepard & Company of Battle Creek. I found that out at once. The engine had stopped to let us pass with our horses and I was off the wagon and talking to the engineer before my father, who was driving, knew what I was up to . . .

How many other youngsters of the period must have had similar experiences – and similar dreams? Ford left school at 17, and served his apprenticeship as a machinist at the Drydock engine works. In the evenings he repaired watches and got close to making them, reckoning he could sell them at 30 cents apiece. Later he worked for Westinghouse,

servicing steam-driven 'road engines'. In his own words: 'What bothered me was the weight and the cost. They weighed a couple of tons and were far too expensive to be owned by other than a farmer with a great deal of land.' Ford was already having thoughts about light steam cars and tractors.

Ford's experience with Westinghouse led him to conclude that steam power was not the answer for light road vehicles; by now the principles established by Otto had been published. In 1885 – the 'year of the car' in Germany – Ford worked on an Otto four-stroke, and in 1887 built one himself, 'just to see if I understood the principles'. After a period back on the farm, he took his skills to the Detroit Electrical Company, but set up his own workshops at home, too, and made a car for himself. In 1895 a Benz arrived at Macy's store in New York. ('I travelled down to look at it but it had no features that seemed worthwhile . . . it was much heavier than my car.')

In 1899 Ford joined a group of speculators, but did not like their idea of making cars to order, and getting the highest price for each. That was why finally, in 1902, Henry Ford decided to set up the Ford Motor Company as his alone.

There remained one problem: the Selden patent, which would-be monopolists had purchased for 10,000 dollars. Henry Ford's first race-track rival, Alexander Winton, had already lost in a test case; but Ford was determined to break the system of licensed manufacture. For years Ford fought the Patent Office ruling that a 'combination patent' covering a complete road vehicle could be valid. It took him until 1911, and cost him a great deal of time and money – but in the end he won.

In proving that there was no limit to the motor car's future, Henry Ford opened more eyes and gained more favourable publicity than he could have imagined. ('It appeared that we were the underdog; we had the public's sympathy.')

Despite the lawsuit, Ford had already worked on the principle that he would win his case. He put his Model T on the market in 1909, and suddenly the world was awheel! Mass production of a simple machine also meant consistent quality. The reliable Model T Ford, or 'Tin Lizzie', was original and sophisticated, too. Production went up, and the price came down. In 1913, over 100,000 were made. A year later the figure was double – and so it went on while Europe, suddenly, became involved in war.

Both sides in World War 1 profited from the experience of the motor car's first 30 years, in terms of basic mechanization. It also taught many firms how to produce in quantity; but Henry Ford knew how to do that already and had more than a head start.

LEFT ***Oldsmobile, c. 1903.*** *The story of the single-cylinder, curved-dash Oldsmobile runabout is something of a legend. Like many other motor manufacturers of the pioneering days, Ransom Olds had tried a variety of projects: steam-, electric- and petrol-powered. Then in 1901 his Lancing, Michigan, plant was burned down. Just one car was pushed out before the ceilings caved in: an experimental light car with a curved dash. The decision was taken to go ahead and produce the model in quantity. In* *1904 the annual production rate of these delightful and practical little cars was around 5000. Olds left the company, which was to have a key role in the formation of General Motors.*

LEFT **Buick racer, c. 1909.** *It was the troubled Buick company that William Durant took in hand and used as the basis for his incredible GM-forming schemes. Swiss-born Louis Chevrolet (seen here) was an established racing driver and the two men created Chevrolet as a marque. Chevrolet, more of a racer and a tuner, was not involved in the company when it was sucked into the GM maw in 1917. The Chevrolet car would become Ford's biggest rival.*

ABOVE **Ford Model T, c. 1914.** *Production of this amazing machine averaged nearly one million units a year for close on 20 years.*

1915

For some, World War 1 meant the end of business, perhaps the end of everything. Yet the war hastened certain technical developments, particularly through the demands of military aviation. Not just engines and carburation, but materials and structures, improved speedily.

In America, the interruption to civilian production was minimal and, while Europe's industry struggled to catch up, Detroit forged ahead. From the outset, America wanted to prove that the car was for everyone. Ford had one way of showing it, General Motors another. And the United States could also show itself to be quite capable of making super-cars for road, Hollywood Boulevard, or race track.

Europe's super-cars were many and varied, but it soon became clear that Hispano-Suiza had taken over from Delaunay-Belleville as the top Continental rival to Rolls-Royce. Benz and Mercedes were both struggling; their merger would bring them back into contention for top honours in many spheres.

The new nation, Czechoslovakia, started a trend in 'people's cars' with the Tatra 11/12; but world markets were not really opening up for anyone. Finance was going out of control, leading to the 1929 crash; some companies got through it by merging, others by changing their model policy.

Austin went into receivership and weathered a General Motors takeover bid, and went on to produce the 'motor for the million': the Austin Seven, a simple but much-sought-after design.

On the circuits, the Sunbeam was Britain's most successful Grand Prix car; but the star of the new 24-hour Le Mans races was the Bentley sports model: a classic machine, typifying the vintage years.

FAST AND FURIOUS

1930

Long before the North American states were created, let alone united, French trappers and colonists in the Great Lakes territory felt their local fur trade to be threatened. The English had a good foothold on the eastern seaboard and were beginning to make inroads, so the French commander of the narrows between Lake Michigan and Lake Huron was sent downstream to set up a new fort on the strait (*étroit*) to Lake Erie. The year was 1701, and that commander's name was Antoine de la Mothe Cadillac. The fort he established became known as D'Étroit. Two centuries later Detroit, by then the most important inland city of America, was rapidly becoming the centre for the world's biggest motor businesses.

The United States did not become involved in World War 1 until 1917, and in that year the founder of the biggest of all the motor giants, William Crapo Durant, was having his finest hour.

Durant and the building of General Motors

The Detroit newspaperman Malcolm Bingay once wrote: 'To compare Billy Durant with Napoleon is to transcend the usual cliché . . . With him all superlatives were understatements. The world for him was just a hickory nut which he, and he alone, knew how to crack . . . He never thought in dollars and cents. Always it was millions.' In 1917 Durant organized the deal that brought Chevrolet and General Motors together, and thus he returned to power – for a time, at least.

The story of William Durant and General Motors is as complicated as Henry Ford's is simple. Indeed, for a brief period Ford himself had been a part of its background, designing a car for the shortlived Detroit Automobile Company. Ford's Detroit featured planetary transmission (as would his own Model T a few years later). When Ford left to start his own company in 1903, Henry Leland, a precision machinist who had been supplying the main mechanical components for the curved-dash Oldsmobile, took over the Detroit Automobile Company, renaming it and its subsequent products Cadillac after the city's founder.

Durant was born in Boston in 1861, and in the 1890s he was a leading maker of horse-drawn carriages, with Joshua Dallas Dort at Flint, Michigan. Then, when he saw the potential of the motor car, he decided that he would control the whole industry. The venture began in 1904 when he took over the new but already bankrupt company that had been founded by an immigrant Scot, David Dunbar Buick. Basing himself with Buick, Durant began a series of takeovers and attempted takeovers which would include many obscure and long-forgotten makes.

The most important names he brought together initially were those of Buick, Cadillac, Oldsmobile and Oakland (predecessor of the Pontiac).

These were the mainstays of the first General Motors Company, registered by Durant in September 1908. In effect it was a central office with only a few of its numerous and largely autonomous satellites making any money. Within two years the company was struggling and Durant lost control; but he remained quite undeterred. He got together with William Little, a manager he had known at Buick, now a car maker in his own right. More significant was Durant's association with former de Dion-Bouton trainee Louis Chevrolet, who came to the United States and joined the New York motor trade in 1900. Ten years later Chevrolet was a respected racing driver for Durant's Buick team, and in 1911 he designed the first Chevrolet car. In 1914 Chevrolet moved on to build and race his own specials, leaving Durant the right to use his name for a

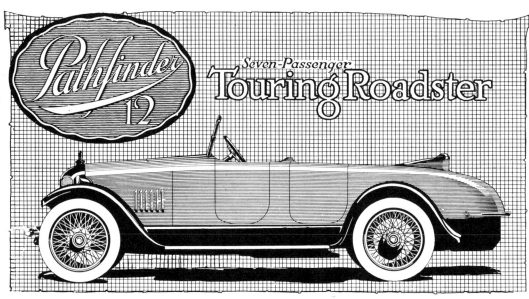

PRECEDING PAGES *Longbridge, c. 1930.* The Austin production line.
RIGHT *Pathfinder, USA, 1917.* For every marque that ever made the grade, dozens disappeared within years or even months of their announcement. This modern-looking 6.4-litre 12-cylinder car from Indianapolis was the last of its particular line.

TOP *Oldsmobile Model 37-B, 1920.* Within General Motors, Oldsmobile has always been something of a specialist marque, representing about one tenth of the corporation's output. The slanting windscreen suggests an urge to start streamlining.
ABOVE *Chevrolet c. 1920.* The Chevrolet name, which was acquired by GM in 1917, became the corporation's challenger to Ford. Annual production of the marque was to soar from 100,000 in 1919 past one million within a decade.

product and for a holding company. Durant had continued to buy shares in the bank-held GM company. In 1917 he was able to prove that his Chevrolet Motor Company had 450,000 of the 825,589 shares in what would become the biggest business in the world: the General Motors Corporation.

Years later, GM Chairman Alfred P. Sloan Jr summed up Durant as:

a great man with a great weakness – he could create but not administer, and he had, first in carriages and then in automobiles, more than a quarter of a century of creation before he fell. That he should have conceived a General Motors and been unable himself in the long run to bring it off or sustain his personal, once dominating, position in it is a tragedy of American industrial history.

'Brilliant, daring, reckless' – Sloan used these words to describe this man he obviously admired; yet, once again Durant let himself down by taking new business risks that could have brought General Motors to its knees very easily. Some projects were to be successful, notably the tiny Guardian Frigerator Company of Detroit. (GM reimbursed Durant for his personal cheque of $56,366.50 in 1919; in return the corporation had acquired what we now know as Frigidaire.) On the other hand, his ventures in the agricultural engineering field were failures. It was the vast empire of Pierre DuPont that bought out Durant, who resigned as GM's president in November 1920. After this, General Motors got down to consolidation.

It was not the end for Durant, but his third attempt at empire building was still very shaky when, in 1929, the Depression came. From 1921 to 1932 there was even a Durant car, of which over 50,000 examples were made in the first full production year. Durant was also the last owner of the distinguished Locomobile marque, and of the Eagle, the Flint, the Princeton and several other makes with which he tried to stretch his wings again: but this time it was to no avail. In 1932 Durant moved into the supermarket business. He was not a wealthy man when he died 15 years later, but there are many who owe their wealth to him.

American variety and quality
Ford and General Motors were the top volume manufacturers of the 1920s, but they were not on their own; not everyone in America would fall by the wayside.

Charles W. Nash had been with Durant in his carriage-building days and was brought into GM in 1910 to run Buick; steady and reliable, Nash was made president of GM two years later. In 1916 Nash left, having acquired the Kenosha, Wisconsin, works of Rambler. This famous marque was begun by Thomas B. Jeffery in Wisconsin in 1902, but was now to become the Nash.

Charles Nash's works manager at Buick from 1911 had been Walter Percy Chrysler. He, too, decided to go it alone and took over Maxwell and Chalmers to enable him to do so. The first Chrysler car of 1924 was supplemented in 1928 by the DeSoto and Plymouth, designed to stretch the range and compete with Ford and Chevrolet. In 1928, the Chrysler Corporation expanded greatly by acquiring Dodge Brothers. In their early days, John and Horace Dodge had supplied engines to Ford, and since 1914 had been making worthy cars in large numbers, pioneering all-steel bodywork and rustproofing on the way.

So many makers were stretching their wings in the post-war period that it is possible to mention only the biggest or the best of them.

Clem and Henry Studebaker were blacksmiths and wagonbuilders in South Bend, Ohio, at the time of the American Civil War and their company was still pursuing those skills at the time of World War 1. In the meantime, the name Studebaker had become synonymous with quality cars, and the 1920s saw them (with GM Oldsmobile) pioneer the use of chromium plating for embellishment. In 1928, Studebaker took control of the famous Pierce-Arrow company of Buffalo.

By coincidence, Studebaker's later partner Packard had also begun as a brotherly partnership in Ohio. J. W. and W. D. Packard, in fact, had a similar experience to that of Henry Royce, in that they bought a car (in their case a Winton in 1898) and decided they could do better themselves. At first the brothers followed form, but in 1915 Packard introduced the world's first production V12: ultimately the inspiration for a certain Enzo Ferrari. Ralph DePalma raced a special Packard Twin Six (as it was called) and an even fiercer version was timed at 240 km/h (150 mph) on one occasion: well above the official land speed record of the day. The Packards thus set a quality standard for the 1920s – and the big guns of the industry fired back.

GM development: shaping up in a competitive market
At General Motors, the Buick continued to be the advanced, middle-price model, but a restyling in 1924 gave it a distinctly Packard look. At the top end of the GM range Cadillac reigned supreme, maintaining the reputation for precision bestowed upon it by Henry Leland. Cadillac had adopted Delco electric lighting and self-starter (the work of Charles F. Kettering) in 1912, and a de Dion-Bouton power unit inspired Cadillac's first V8 of 1915. So important was Cadillac's niche at the top end of the market that a 'junior V8 Cadillac' was added to the lists in 1927 and given a separate marque name: LaSalle, after one of the French

LEFT *1928 Miller, Indianapolis.* *America's most celebrated race is the 'Indy' 500, which has been run regularly since 1911. The name of Miller dominated it in the 1920s and 1930s. Brilliantly engineered, Miller cars had a strong influence upon Ettore Bugatti. This photograph was taken on the occasion of the first of Louis Meyer's three 'Indy' wins.*

explorers who had hoped to colonize the lower Mississippi territory in the 17th century. (Chrysler's DeSoto of the following year was a bit of one-upmanship, since the Spaniard Hernando de Soto had done his exploration in the 16th century and is credited with the actual discovery of the Mississippi.) Undeterred, GM picked the name of another Mississippi adventurer, Marquette, from Durant's bag of dead businesses, when labelling its 'down-market' 1929 Buick.

The LaSalle was a prime example of the tendency, which began in America and has been followed in more recent times in other parts of the world, to create a marque in order to fulfil a particular marketing purpose. As their businesses grew and competition between them became stronger, the big American manufacturers were doing everything in their power to occupy every possible price sector. The closed body was now taking over from the open one as the most popular type. In 1924, for example, the proportion of closed to open cars produced by GM went up from 40 to 75 per cent. GM's first major new marque, the Pontiac, announced in 1925, was intended by Alfred Sloan to be 'the lowest priced six-cylinder car that is possible, constructed with Chevrolet parts'. (The independent Hudson company had created the Essex to attack the Chevrolet market from the top, and the Pontiac was Sloan's reaction.) The LaSalle was the other concept. It profited from the prestige of its Cadillac background – and it shared the Cadillac V8 engine – but was priced lower. Moreover, it broke new ground in being designed by a stylist.

In 1926 Lawrence P. Fisher, general manager of Cadillac and a member of the Fisher bodymaking family, visited Don Lee, a Los Angeles dealer who had developed the custom body business for domestic and foreign chassis. This included the lengthening of chassis, thus giving cars exotic proportions in keeping with their potential Hollywood occupants and their bank balances. Lee's chief designer was Harley J. Earl, the son of a carriage maker from whom Lee had bought

the business. Fisher saw the way Earl redesigned cars as entities, using modelling clay to create shapes – something Detroit had not got round to – and offered the stylist a special contract to come east to design the new LaSalle. Such was its success that Sloan invited Earl to run a new department (called the Art and Colour Section) for the use of all GM's divisions. This 'beauty parlour', as GM folk called it, also served the purpose of retaining some individuality for the different GM marques as the threat of technical uniformity increased. Earl's department was later renamed the Styling Section: possibly the first use of the term.

In those heady pre-Depression days, technical advances under Charles Kettering were considerable, too, and by 1929 the Cadillac and LaSalle lines were being fitted with synchromesh gearboxes and safety glass as standard: one up to GM again. Then, in the winter of Wall Street's discontent, 1929–30, came a truly exotic inauguration to keep Cadillac at the top of the tree: the world's first V16 production car. Depression or no, pure luxury would still find a way.

Fords by the million

As others grouped and regrouped, Henry Ford's autocracy marched on, the Model T reaching the magic million-a-year mark in 1922. A two-million-plus peak was reached in 1923. Originally priced at $850, the 'Tin Lizzie' was down to $260 by 1925. From 1914 to 1925 the only colour *was* black: yet during its life span, from 1908 to 1927, 16,536,075 examples of the Model T were produced. (That figure was surpassed only by the Volkswagen 'Beetle' in the mid-1970s. Still being assembled in Brazil and Mexico in the early 1980s, the VW was to become the first basic model of any car to pass the twenty million mark: which makes the Ford achievement all the more incredible.)

In May 1927 Henry Ford sprang a surprise. He shut down his huge plant at River Rouge and spent the rest of the year retooling. This left the mass market clear for GM and Chrysler's fours, the Chevrolet and

LEFT *1929 Cadillac 341-B.* GM's standardbearer, the Cadillac, would soon be offered with V12 and V16 engines. The car in this picture is the bread-and-butter V8. Cadillac-LaSalle production represented a tiny fraction of GM's total output, which approached two million vehicles in 1929.

ABOVE *1929 Ford Model A.* In 1927, the Ford factory in Detroit was closed down for several months while the last of the Model Ts were being sold and a completely new (if more orthodox) Ford was tooled up. The four-cylinder $450 Model A was a worthy workhorse, like its predecessor. Photographed quite recently in Italy, this example still appears to be in a working environment. The Ford has always been a car for all the world.

Henry Ford (1863–1947)

Without doubt, Henry Ford's great contribution to motoring was to bring the car to *more* people, *more* quickly than anyone else in the business. On 31 May 1921, the Ford Motor Company produced its five millionth car. When the Model T went out of production in 1927, over 16 million had been made.

Ford made his first 'gasoline buggy' in 1893 and, after working with the Detroit Edison and Detroit Automobile companies, started experimenting full-time. His two specials, Arrow and 999, helped bring his name into the news, particularly after he got the latter to exceed 145 km/h (90 mph) on frozen Lake St Clair in January 1904: a world record speed.

The Model T (1909 to 1927) proved the wisdom of Ford's decision to follow a one-model policy; later he and his sons would be just as wise in their broadening of the range and extending of manufacturing facilities at home and abroad.

Today the name of Ford remains strong.

the Plymouth: but not for long. A comeback with the modern, attractive, Model A soon put Ford on top, that is, ahead of Chevrolet again, although General Motors had now established its overall production lead.

Part of the new Ford's success was the unhesitating introduction of another new concept of car. For years, the basic Model T had trundled between small railway stations and scattered homesteads, carrying people, luggage and goods with utter reliability and some discomfort. Now that the enclosed sedan had established itself as the most popular choice of family car for the city dweller, surely there should be a more sophisticated vehicle to deal with passengers and packages at the same time? Ford's answer was to acquire thousands of acres of north Michigan woodland, filled with birches, maples and other suitable trees, and 'invent' the station wagon.

Nor had Ford overlooked the luxury market. Back in 1902, when Henry Ford struck out on his own, Henry Martin Leland had changed the Detroit car into the Cadillac. Through the early GM years Leland, who had been a Federal arsenal toolmaker in the Civil War, contrived to influence the new corporation. GM chief Alfred Sloan himself admitted that, in his younger days with the Hyatt company, he had had trouble selling roller bearings to Leland: 'Quality was his god. He taught me the need for greater accuracy to meet the exacting standards of interchangeable parts.' Leland was well over 70 when the Cadillac V8 was introduced, and he retired shortly afterwards. Then in 1920, with his son Wilfred, he set up in business again to make another quality V8 – and again he chose the name of someone he admired, President Abraham Lincoln.

The 1921 Lincoln had a 5.8-litre engine with full pressure lubrication, and at over 80 bhp was powerful for its day. Almost at once the business side ran into trouble, but in 1922 Ford came to the rescue; the Lelands resigned within a few months. Henry Ford was now nearing 60 himself, and it was his son Edsel who developed the Lincoln as Ford's super-car, beloved of police and escaping hoodlums. President Calvin Coolidge started the fashion for White House Lincolns in 1924, and the marque's reputation soared.

American dreams: the great specialists

Literally hundreds of car makers had fallen by the wayside since the birth of American motoring, yet still there were many splendid specialists in the 1920s, usually sustained by sporting achievement. (Pierce-Arrow suffered from a lack of this kind of action and, from 1928, lost its way under Studebaker.)

In 1900, the Eckart Carriage Company had begun working on cars named after its home town, Auburn, Indiana. Auburn made beautiful-looking cars with proprietary engines. From 1924, Lycoming engines were used at the instigation of Erret Lobban Cord, the company's new chief, and the 1928 eight-cylinder boat-tail speedster broke the stock-car record for the famous Pike's Peak hill climb in Colorado.

Since 1911, through the Indianapolis 500, Indiana had been the great centre of American motor racing and another of its home marques, the Marmon of Ray Harroun, was the classic's first winner. The Stutz, too, came from Indianapolis, although it never won the big race there. In other respects Harry Stutz's cars were consistent winners, and his Bearcat probably spelled the death knell of its great rivals, the Kissel, the Wills Sainte Claire, and the Mercer, which did not enjoy such success in racing. Stutz left, however, and later Stutz cars had a European flavour. They were designed by the Belgian engineer Paul Bastien, and one of his overhead camshaft straight-8s actually took second place at Le Mans in 1928: the best American car performance there until after World War 2.

The USA's biggest surprise for European racing, however, occurred in 1921 when James Murphy won the French Grand Prix in a Duesenberg – revenge, perhaps, for five successive Indianapolis victories achieved by European cars. Back home he bought the car, put a Miller engine in it, and won the 1922 Indianapolis 500. Duesenberg and Miller were by far the most important American racing cars of the 1920s, each taking top honours at Indianapolis and elsewhere.

Frederick Samuel Duesenberg and his brother August had come to America from Germany as children. They worked for others before setting up their own engine business, supplying quality car makers such as Biddle and Roamer (the latter was an unabashed Rolls-Royce copy car). In 1920, in Indianapolis, the Duesenbergs introduced hydraulic brakes on the first of their magnificent straight-8 production cars, which soon caught the eye of empire builder E. L. Cord. In 1926 Cord bought the Duesenberg Motor Company, giving Fred Duesenberg *carte blanche* to make a dream car, fabulous in performance, specification, and price: and he was not to be disappointed. Duesenberg stuck to his straight-8 format, but this time it was a 6.9-litre, twin-overhead camshaft unit with four valves per cylinder; and it was built in Cord's Lycoming factory. Announced towards the end of 1928, the Model J Duesenberg was, at well over 200 bhp (no matter if it was not produced efficiently), the most powerful production car the world had seen. The chassis price of $8500 was doubled by the fitting of bodywork from one of the exclusive coachmakers including Dietrich, Judkins and LeBaron. Now, half a century on from the building of the last of those great cars with their

LEFT *1930 Auburn. On acquiring Auburn in the mid-1920s, E. L. Cord had the entire range restyled. By 1930 the Auburn had discarded its earlier artillery wheels and looked really elegant. This is the 8-95 phaeton sedan. Keen pricing helped the marque through the Depression.*

ABOVE RIGHT *1929 Cord. The L-29 reflected Harry Miller's genius in many ways, including the front-wheel drive and hydraulic braking systems. E. L. Cord, who named it, came from used-car selling to presidency of his own corporation very quickly, only to emigrate temporarily in 1934 rather than face an investigation. Three years later he came home and axed three of America's greatest marques – but not before a final stunner had been created (see page 82).*

RIGHT *1929 Duesenberg. When the Duesenberg J was launched in December 1928, E. L. Cord declared it to be 'the world's finest motor car' This particular dream machine was made in Pasadena by the Walter M. Murphy Co, specialists in convertible coachwork.*

380 mm (15 in), vacuum-servo assisted hydraulic brakes, automatic chassis lubrication and – in later, supercharged form – 210 km/h (130 mph) capability, the Duesenberg is probably once more the most expensive car to buy. There are still a good many of the 500 Duesenberg Js and SJs in existence, but not as many as there are folk who would covet one. Crowned heads of Europe, multi-millionaires like William Randolph Hearst and Howard Hughes, top film stars like Gary Cooper and Clark Gable: all were captivated by the most exciting car of its day; yet for Cord it was not enough to run Auburn and Duesenberg. His dream car, the L-29, bore his own name.

Launched in 1929, the low-slung Cord was the first front-wheel-drive car in America to reach production in series (although its competitor, the Ruxton, would follow it closely). This front-drive system, incorporating a de Dion-type axle, was manufactured under licence from Miller, the celebrated racing car maker.

The Miller influence

Harry Armenius Miller made cars to order, although they did not always bear his name. Some were made to the order of Clifford Durant, son of GM's founder. (Most of these were called Durant Specials, although in

1925 Miller sold a front-wheel-drive car. Durant named this the Junior 8 to promote the Locomobile of the same name, which, ever-optimistic, he was now hoping would compete with Chrysler. This was, in fact, the end of the Durant dream.) Miller, whose cars were victorious at Indianapolis a dozen times, was to some extent inspired by Bugatti. But Miller inspired Bugatti in turn. Indeed, in 1929 Bugatti acquired a pair of front-wheel-drive, twin-overhead camshaft (ohc) straight-8 Millers in exchange for three roadgoing Bugattis. Soon afterwards came the first twin-ohc Bugatti, the Type 50.

The sharing of technical knowledge and insight cannot be dismissed as mere copying when it takes place between the most brilliant brains in a particular field. Where there has been interchange of ideas this can give rise to endless historical research as later generations try to assess influences and track down the sources of developments. The man who bought the historic Millers from Bugatti 20 years later, Griffith Borgeson, indicated the relationships between the greats – Miller, the Duesenbergs, Ernest Henry of Peugeot and Ballot, and many more including, of course, Ettore Bugatti – in his book *Bugatti by Borgeson*. His work seems to make the Atlantic much narrower. It is time now to cross that ocean and examine the Europe of the Vintage years.

European vintage

The Vintage period of motoring is clearly defined, by Britain's Vintage Sports Car Club, as the period from 1919 to 1930 inclusive.

While America experienced a mere dip in civilian vehicle production in 1917 and 1918, the European industry had been totally disrupted from 1914 until well into 1919; and what happened then depended very much upon the circumstances of the country in which a particular company happened to be, or the war contracts that had kept it going.

Although it was essentially French in character, the legendary Bugatti provides the best illustration of Europe's moving frontiers. The Bugatti was made in the heart of Alsace, not far from Strasbourg – itself famous for its engineering wonder, the ancient astronomical clock, still a

fascinating adjunct of the great Gothic cathedral. It was in Strasbourg in 1904 that Ettore Bugatti teamed up with Emile Mathis. Their partnership lasted for a couple of years, during which they produced the Hermes-Simplex car which showed Bugatti's ingenuity to good effect; but the two men argued and parted. Mathis was to stay in business until taken over by Citroën in 1954, having failed to utilize the opportunity to consolidate while Fords were being made in his plant. Bugatti as a marque vanished soon afterwards, too, but what a heritage it left!

Ettore Arco Isidoro Bugatti was born in Italy in 1882. His first employers were the cycle makers Prinetti & Stucchi of Milan, for whom he rode in competitions. He designed a car in 1901, and Baron de Dietrich (who saw it at a Milan exhibition) took him on as a designer on

Ettore Bugatti
(1881–1947)

Carlo Bugatti of Milan designed and made furniture. His eldest son was christened Ettore Arco Isidoro and, following in his father's artistic footsteps, began training at the Fine Arts college.

Ettore Bugatti was fascinated by motorcycling, however, and when the Prinetti & Stucchi sewing machine company started making bicycles in 1898 he joined as an apprentice. His design work won a prize at an exhibition in 1901; this caught the eye of de Dietrich, and in 1902 Bugatti went to Niederbronn in Alsace, only to be sacked in 1905 because the cars were proving unreliable. His friend Emile Mathis (de Dietrich's local agent in Strasbourg) came to his rescue with a contract to make Hermes cars; but these were not a success,

and only when he moved on to join Deutz in Cologne did his prototypes show signs of the special character of the Bugatti car. Deutz never went into serious car production, and Ettore Bugatti returned to Alsace in 1909 with finance to start making cars in his own name at Molsheim.

In the next three decades, the Bugatti was to acquire a reputation equalled only by that of Ferrari in more recent times.

Ettore Bugatti's son, Gianoberto (1909–1939), usually known as Jean, was responsible for many of the later designs of bodywork and for much of the administration, although he never took over the whole business. He was killed while testing a car shortly before the outbreak of World War 2, a war from which the Bugatti company could not recover fully. The name remains a legend.

ABOVE ***Bugatti T.41, La Royale.*** *Bugatti made magnificent motor cars, but the gargantuan La Royale was not the best of them. In 1926 or 1927, the body from Ettore Bugatti's Packard was transferred to a massive chassis with a wheelbase of more than 4.25 m (14 ft), and a straight-8 engine of great size. Later that chassis was rebodied several times. This photograph* *shows it with its Packard body when it was the prototype T.41 in the late 1920s. Ettore Bugatti is at the wheel. He may have dreamed of turning this creation into the ultimate motor car; certainly, it will never be forgotten.*

the strength of it. Up to that time, the baron's company had made Amedée Bollées under licence. Bugatti introduced bigger models to his design, but making cars at Niederbronn, Alsace, did not pay, and from 1904 only the Lunéville, Lorraine, branch of de Dietrich was kept. In fact, from 1908 the marque name was Lorraine-Dietrich.

Bugatti, meantime, stayed in Germany (Alsace-Lorraine was German at this time). After the Mathis period, Bugatti spent what must have been an interesting few years in Cologne, with the Gasmotorenfabrik Deutz AG, for this was where Otto, Daimler and Maybach had worked a generation earlier, although they had not built cars. It was Bugatti who designed the first Deutz car; but Deutz did not pursue car making, and the later Deutz designs became the first Bugattis. These were made from 1909 in an old dye works in the small wine town of Molsheim, and the early cars were well received – as were Bugatti's other designs, including the previously mentioned Bébé for Peugeot.

Alsace had been part of France since the French Revolution, but was ceded to Germany in 1871 after the Franco-Prussian war. When the German authorities occupied his factory in 1914 Bugatti, a Francophile, moved to Paris and undertook government aero-engine work. In 1919, Alsace was restored to France under the Treaty of Versailles, and at last Bugatti was able to get down to making a succession of sporting cars, each detail of which seemed to possess as much artistry as engineering brilliance. In many ways Bugattis were the ultimate.

Other men to take their skills into the wartime aircraft industry and then back to quality motor cars included Gabriel Voisin, René Fonck, Maurice Farman and Marc Birkigt. All sought perfection, and Birkigt's Paris-built Hispano-Suizas, as dressed by the *haute couture* coachbuilders, got nearer to it over a longer period than the others. Once again, France was the showplace of motoring. Some of its great roads had suffered in the long, weary battle, but it did not take long for the grandeur to return. For the true Vintage years at least, Delaunay-Belleville, Brasier, de Dion-Bouton, and other great names lived on, only to be killed by the Depression. The Le Mans 24 hours, instituted in 1923 as France's new race for production cars, was to become a classic, as were two of its early winners, the Chenard-Walcker (1923) and the Lorraine-Dietrich (1925 and 1926), but these makes were swallowed up in the difficult years ahead.

French innovation

Several French names made history almost without finding a customer. Sensaud de Lavaud, for example, showed a low-built coupé with infinitely variable automatic transmission at the 1927 and 1928 Paris exhibitions. The Bucciali brothers, Angelo and Paul-Albert, tried the de Lavaud transmission on their TAN of 1928 which had front-wheel drive and all-independent suspension, too. Both these shortlived makes combined fabulous looks with fairy-tale specifications.

Front-wheel drive had, in fact, been around since the birth of the car, but it was in France that it took hold, thanks to a typically adventurous soul, Jean Grégoire, who had tried oil prospecting on Madagascar before buying a Paris garage with the last of a dwindling inheritance, and help from a friend, Pierre Fenaille. Grégoire specialized in Mathis cars (like Bugatti, Emile Mathis escaped from Alsace and then returned after the war). Fenaille and Grégoire enjoyed competition motoring, and it was Fenaille who persuaded Grégoire not only to make a car himself, but to give it front-wheel drive. They had admired the work of the Buccialis, but noticed how the brothers squandered their inherited fortune upon cars that were too idealistic to sell, or even run.

Grégoire was a cautious businessman, but he had learned of the 1925 racing achievements of Harry Miller's driven de Dion front end. In 1926 he built the first of his Tracta competition cars. Like the early Buccialis, it had a SCAP (Société de Construction Automobiles Parisiennes) 1100 cc engine. This was turned back to front with the gearbox ahead of it; and it had a Cozette supercharger. This low, long-bonneted machine was built for several years as an attractive coupé or saloon, and bigger engines by Continental or Hotchkiss were to be had. In 1927, it was the one genuinely available front-wheel-drive car in commercial production (although Grégoire did go on record as saying that he thought no car of his had been sold for more than its actual cost).

Grégoire developed a particular application of the Hooke joint, to overcome the problems of adhesion, snatch, and excessive wear. He was to spend a lot of time trying to establish patents for his Tracta constant-velocity joint in different countries, often with indifferent success. Jean Grégoire was a humorous and philosophical man and later

RIGHT **Hispano-Suiza H6-B.** *The Paris-built Hispano-Suiza H6-B was introduced almost immediately after World War 1, and was the most desirable Grand Tourer of its day, being the product of Marc Birkigt's recent aero-engineering experience. In the mid-1920s, the aluminium (but steel-lined) overhead camshaft six went up from 6.6 to 8 litres' capacity; the latter size offered a 160 km/h (100 mph) maximum speed. From 1919 the Hispano-Suiza had servo-assisted brakes to all four* *wheels; this feature alone put it ahead of Rolls-Royce. This Hibbard & Darrin-bodied car dates from 1929, shortly before Hispano-Suiza's mighty V12 was introduced.*

he went on to create further fascinating vehicles.

Of France's three great Ds – Darracq, Delahaye and Delage – it was the last that shone in the Vintage period. In 1920, Darracq merged with the British combine of Sunbeam and Talbot and, during a period of baffling nomenclature, the name Darracq became linked with Talbot, pronounced the French way. Delahaye stayed out of trouble but the cars he made at this stage were dull.

By contrast, the flamboyant Louis Delage always made interesting machines. From light cars, effective in racing, he turned to fairly large, luxurious sporting models. In the Vintage period, however, it was the Grand Prix Delage that achieved most of the fame, as we shall see later in this chapter.

In the 1920s the 'big boys' of France, Peugeot and Renault, were joined by a newcomer to car making, André Citroën, once the technical chief of Mors. He went into business making double helical gears, thus originating the Citroën 'chevron' symbol. His first cars, from 1919, were tough, simple and suitable for mass production. The 5CV, also built as an Opel in Germany, was endearing as well as enduring; and a special Kégresse half-track model became famous for its successful crossing of the Sahara in 1923.

German motorways and mergers

In Europe, road improvements began everywhere – and nowhere more quickly than in Germany. Back in 1907, an *Automobil-Verkehrs- und Übungs-Strasse* was proposed for the Grünewald, near Berlin, but the war had intervened soon after the work had begun. This 'Motor Traffic and Practice Road', known ever since as the AVUS, was completed in 1920 in time for the first post-war German motor show. Now split between East and West Berlin, it consisted then of adjacent parallel roads, joined by looping bends at each end. The next important road created purely for motoring was in Italy, the Milan-Varese *autostrada* opened in September 1924. Apart from the AVUS there was a fascinating scheme drawn up by Professor Robert Otzen, a German civil engineer, to link major cities by highway. The first of these, dated 1926, was given the project name 'Hafraba', for it was intended that it should link the old *Ha*nsa ports of Lübeck, Bremen and Hamburg with *Fra*nkfurt and *Ba*sel. It was in 1929 that work actually began on the Cologne–Bonn *Autobahn*, a genuine motorway, replacing the usual road junctions with bridges. Even at that date there was no disputing the need (the old Düsseldorf–Cologne–Bonn road, for example, was already carrying 1800 vehicles per hour at peak times) but still the Hafraba plan met with no support from the Reichstag. Hitler, in fact, caused some surprise on his accession to power several years later by announcing his plans for the *Autobahn* network.

The AVUS circuit was used for racing, and the first winner there, in 1921, was Fritz Opel in one of his own cars at nearly 130 km/h (80 mph). Opel of Rüsselsheim had progressed a long way from its Lutzmann System and Darracq-making days, and had remained a family business; soon the company was making more cars than anyone else in Germany. In 1925, however, Ford set up in business at Cologne. General Motors was going international, too, and in 1929 negotiated the purchase of Adam Opel AG.

Among firms in German ownership, much the biggest news of the 1920s was the merger of the two oldest motor vehicle makers: Benz and Daimler. Gottlieb Daimler had died in 1900 and Emil Jellinek had instigated the name Mercedes in 1901. That name had identified the marque ever since. Daimler's son Paul had maintained the family reputation, however, by undertaking the Mercedes engineering design work.

Rapid aero-engine development during the war influenced cars to some extent, and the first supercharged vehicles ever to go on public sale were two new Mercedes models exhibited at the 1921 Berlin show. In 1923 Paul Daimler left to join the Horch company at Zwickau, where he

ABOVE *Citroën Type A, c. 1920.* At the same time as, and in similar manner to, William Morris, André Citroën learned about car production from the Americans. This photograph was taken in the early days of his Paris factory when the design was still uncomplicated. Later Citroëns have been notable for technical innovation and futuristic styling.

RIGHT *French GP, 1923.* From 1922 to 1925 a 2-litre formula led to some interesting machines in which speed was sought through aerodynamics. For the 1923 Grand Prix at Tours, Bugatti and Voisin fielded full teams of streamliners but could not do better than third and fifth respectively. The race went to Britain's Henry Segrave in a British-built (but Italian-designed) Sunbeam. All Voisin's products were unusual to look at – even the sleeve valve-engined GP car seen here.

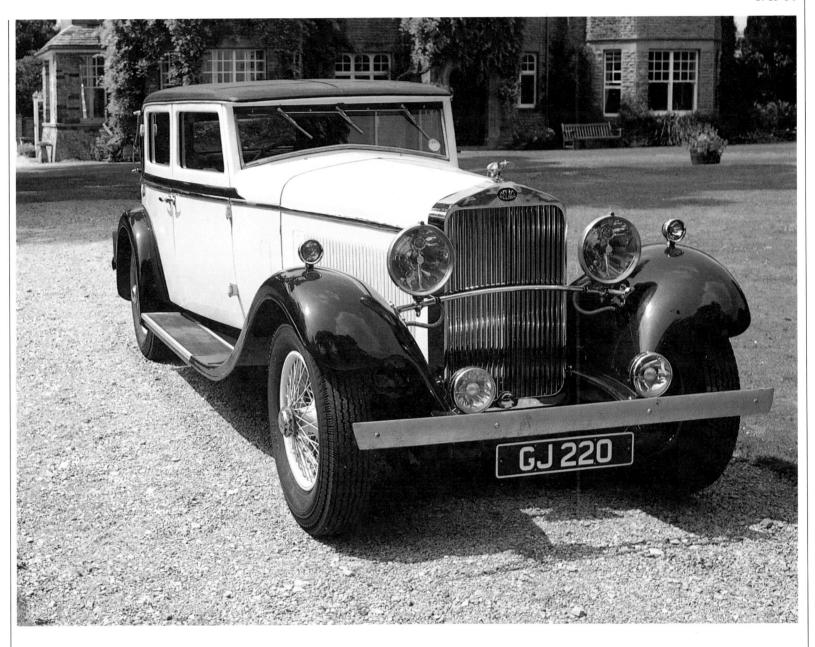

ABOVE **Delage D8, 1930.** Henri Chapron of Paris specialized in making clean-lined, elegant coachwork for Delage and Delahaye, both before and after these great French marques combined. This photograph of a Chapron-bodied 4-litre straight-8 Delage D8 in an English setting tells all.

RIGHT **Italian Grand Prix.** Italy followed France in establishing a premier race, and the famous Monza circuit was built for this purpose in a once-royal park near Milan in 1922. FIAT won that year, and again in 1923.

was chief engineer for some five years. There he concentrated on twin-cam straight-8 engines.

Daimler's successor at Mercedes was Ferdinand Porsche, whose top engineering post at Austro-Daimler went to Karl Rabe. Porsche's first new car for the Daimler-Benz combine in 1926 was the Mannheim, an orthodox model so called after Benz's home town: as a diplomatic move, since Mercedes-Benz (in that order) was to be the new marque name for the group's products.

Benz had done well in racing, often as opponents to Mercedes, but the road cars had remained more old fashioned. Both firms had worked on the heavy oil engine known as the diesel, after Rudolf Diesel, who developed its system of ignition by air compression. (His achievement tends to overshadow the early work by Priestman and Stuart in the United Kingdom.) In fact, Benz and Daimler cooperated on diesel research in the early 1920s and, ultimately, a Mercedes-Benz was to be the first diesel-powered production car.

Radical engineering and economy cars

Thanks to Porsche's opposite number, Hans Nibel, a fascinating final Benz racing model appeared in 1923, although it ran only once in a major race: the 1923 Grand Prix of Europe at Monza, where examples came fourth and fifth. This car pointed the way to the future with its mid-engine layout. It was streamlined, and incorporated swing-axle independent suspension and inboard rear brakes. Its concept dated back to that first post-war Berlin show of 1921, when Edmund Rumpler startled the world with an amazing car which had been forming in his mind while he was working on aircraft. This 'teardrop'-shaped saloon had its six-cylinder engine (three banks of cylinders in pairs, to make a 'W' shape) at the rear of its streamlined body. Only a few were sold. Rumpler did some front-wheel-drive experiments before returning to aviation. The 1922–3 London-built North-Lucas prototype was an unsuccessful copy of the Rumpler; and, at about the same time, the independently sprung, rear-engined San Giusto light car made its brief appearance on the Italian market. Earlier still, in 1913, a Michigan engineer, Howard Blood, had introduced a car called the Cornelian with swinging live axles – and Louis Chevrolet drove one of them at Indianapolis in 1915. Who is to say for certain who was first in this field – or in almost any sphere of invention?

One definite first goes to Rumpler's former pupil, Ledwinka. He had been with Steyr in Austria during the war, and designed that company's first car before returning for a third spell to Nesselsdorf, which was now called Kopřivnice, for Moravia was part of the new republic of Czechoslovakia, formed in 1918. The old firm had been busy on armaments; now it was being financed by Baron Ringhoffer, and the facilities expanded. There was a new name for the vehicles, too: Tatra.

The first Tatra was a direct attack on the popular car market. It was called the Type 11 and featured swing axles at the rear (soon the Tatra acquired independent suspension all round). The 1100 cc flat-twin air-cooled engine was cradled at the front, and drove the rear wheels via a central tubular backbone which replaced a conventional chassis. (The French-domiciled researcher Griffith Borgeson has pointed out that the magazine *La France Automobile* depicted a Simplicia backbone chassis as early as 1909, but subsequent development remains obscure.) The Tatra 11 was announced late in 1922 and was followed by the Tatra 12 (which had four-wheel brakes) in 1926. It may not seem a lot now, but Tatra's own records show 14,610 examples were made of this, the world's first modern economy car; and, although a surprise class win in the 1925 Targa Florio brought publicity, few were sold abroad. They were durable and light, and very accessible, with a modern one-piece opening bonnet. In Czechoslovakia, enthusiasm for early Tatras has meant that a remarkable number have survived.

An early German people's car

In Germany the contemporary 'people's car' was even simpler. In 1924, the Hannoversche Maschinenbau AG made a dumpy all-enveloping rear-engined single-cylinder two-seater known as the Kommissbrot ('army loaf'); but it was just too basic, and Hanomag had to change its tune in order to survive.

At the other end of the scale Wilhelm Maybach's son Karl moved into the luxury car business. He had built aero and car engines but the latter did not find many takers; thus the magnificent Maybach car was born.

Unitary construction and luxury from Italy

Retired racing driver Vincenzo Lancia produced Italy's most revolutionary post-war production car in 1922. This was the ohc V4-engined Lambda, which had a basic body-cum-chassis frame of great

ABOVE **Rumpler, 1921.** Edmund Rumpler, formerly with Nesselsdorf and Adler, produced this rear-engined oddity for the 1921 Berlin motor show.

Only a few of them were ever sold but Benz acquired the rights to adapt the format for an equally unusual competition car.

ABOVE **Hanomag 2/10PS, 1926.** This forerunner of the Volkswagen idea, nicknamed the Kommissbrot ('army loaf'), had a rear-mounted single-cylinder 500 cc engine. Over 15,000 were built in Hanover between 1924 and 1928.

RIGHT **Mercedes-Benz SSK, 1928.** As great a contrast as could be imagined with its diminutive compatriot (above), the supercharged 7-litre SSK ruled the roads and the racetracks in thunderous celebration of the coming together of Germany's two most renowned marques.

LEFT **Bosch poster.**
*Dramatic, stylish
advertising, even from the
component manufacturers,
was all part of making
motoring acceptable if not
fully understood from the
outset. Electrics were,
perhaps, still somewhat
magical.*

RIGHT **FIAT Tipo 805
supercharged, 1923.**
*This was the first
successful 'blown' GP car
and it dominated the
Italian GP at Monza in
1923. Carlo Salamano
was the winner from
Felice Nazzaro, who is
seen here at a pit stop.*

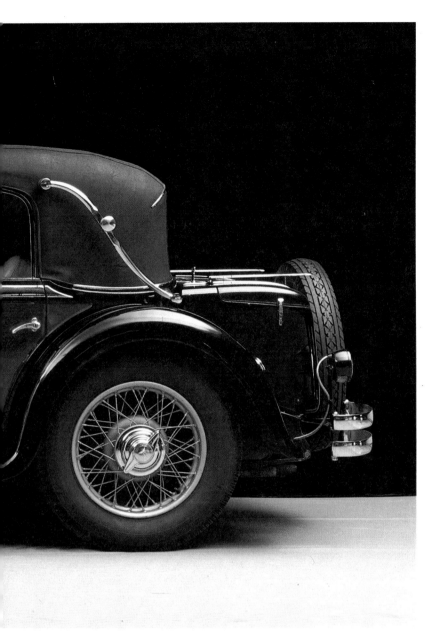

rigidity, as well as sliding-pillar independent front suspension. The unit-construction idea would eventually become standard practice, but not for many years.

In terms of Italian luxury, chief designer Giustino Cattaneo kept Isotta-Fraschini at the top of the tree with his 6-litre straight-8. The star engineer in post-war Italy was, however, Vittorio Jano. He was with FIAT for several years, then moved to Alfa Romeo to design a succession of winners.

International racing in the Vintage era
The Vintage years were strange ones for motor racing, and its development during the period should be described. The makings of a 'premier league' or Grand Prix Formula series, later to be known as Formula One, appeared in 1921 when France, previously the only organizer of a European Grand Prix race as such, was joined by Italy. Jimmy Murphy's remarkable one-off victory for America in the 1921 French GP at Le Mans has been mentioned already. Runners-up Ballot then won the first Italian GP, with Jules Goux driving.

For 1922, a subcommittee of the Association des Automobile Clubs Reconnus rewrote the rules. Already, the monsters of old had become dinosaurs. Now the maximum engine capacity went down from 3 litres to 2, with a drop in minimum overall weight from 800 to 650 kg (1765 to 1435 lb). This formula lasted four seasons in which Italy's FIAT and Alfa Romeo vied for honours with Delage and Bugatti of France. Sunbeam's French chief designer, Louis Coatalen, hired two Italian (ex-FIAT) men to provide Britain with its first-ever Grand Prix winner. Henry Segrave gave the Wolverhampton marque its greatest victory – a lucky one – at Tours in 1923; but Sunbeam had less success than it deserved in the long run.

For 1926 and 1927 a 1½-litre formula was adopted, and in these seasons, Delage emerged as the most effective team with a beautiful supercharged 'eight' designed by Albert Lory. Friction losses were minimal, due to extensive use of ball or roller races instead of shell bearings, and eventual power output was more than 180 bhp. Robert Benoist was Delage's great driver; later he was a hero of the French Resistance, executed by the Germans in 1944.

The Grand Prix Formula rather lost its way after 1927, and most organizers in the 1928 to 1930 period chose to run a free-for-all. Alfa Romeo and Bugatti showed the most consistent winning tendencies, and thus made sporting reputations for themselves that would be exceeded only by the man who formed his own Alfa Romeo racing team in 1929: Enzo Ferrari.

LEFT *Bugatti and Delage GP cars.* These were France's outstanding GP cars of the late 1920s and early '30s; then Italy took over, followed by Germany. Louis Chiron won the 1932 Dieppe GP in a twin-cam T.51 (developed from the T.35) from William Williams and Guy Bouriat, also in Bugattis. Earl Howe's already obsolete ex-works 1926-7 Delage (no. 1) was later sold to Richard Seaman. He proved that great 10-year-old car was still a winner!

ABOVE LEFT *Mercedes-Benz Mannheim.* After the merger of Benz with Daimler, to create the Daimler-Benz company and the Mercedes-Benz marque, came the first range of orthodox sixes with a choice of 100 mm or 115 mm stroke engines. These were called the Stuttgart and the Mannheim respectively (after the homes of Mercedes and Benz). They were mechanically mundane but, as this 370S (3.7-litre) illustrates, they could look absolutely superb.

The quest for the world land speed record

Although Britain was not in the forefront of motor racing, a particularly British type of heroism was developing as three men, Malcolm Campbell, Henry Segrave and John Parry Thomas vied with one another in the mid-1920s to be the fastest men on earth. Thomas died at Pendine Sands, Wales, in 1927 when his antiquated Liberty-engined special, *Babs*, went out of control. That year Segrave took a 1000 hp Sunbeam streamliner to Daytona, Florida, to beat 200 mph (320 km/h) for the first time.

In 1928, Campbell won the record back with his *Bluebird*, to be beaten almost at once by the brute power of *three* 27-litre Liberty engines and the bravery of America's Ray Keech, whose totally unsound machine (called the White-Triplex) was to kill another driver at a later attempt. Segrave returned to Florida in 1929 with the beautiful *Golden Arrow*, which averaged over 370 km/h (230 mph). Back in England, Segrave was knighted and then, in June 1930, he became the fastest man on water. At that moment, his craft, *Miss England*, hit a partly submerged log and Segrave was killed. Although alone in the field for several years, Sir Malcolm Campbell (he was knighted, too) continued to push the record up, his feats undoubtedly providing good publicity for Britain's motor industry.

The wartime development of Napier and Sunbeam aero engines had provided Campbell and Segrave with the power to achieve great things; but somehow, Napier and Sunbeam cars never quite made the grade again. S. F. Edge and Montague Napier had parted company, and Napier's ensuing decline as a car maker served to indicate just how much it had depended upon Edge's campaigning. Edge, who went to AC Cars in the 1920s, was an unpopular figure in the industry and his early work to promote motoring in Britain was overshadowed by his tendency to take advantage of public ignorance of the motor car when making claims for it. Criticism is easy at this distance.

British luxury cars

Parry Thomas, the enigmatic Welshman, was the designer of Britain's most expensive and powerful car of the immediate post-war period, the Leyland Eight. However, Leyland pulled out of the project after only a few had been sold and went back to commercial vehicles, while Thomas

TOP **Isotta-Fraschini Tipo 8A, c. 1926.** *In 1919, the Tipo 8 was the first straight-8 to be produced for public sale. This model was essentially a high-class touring car and had a 7.4-litre 120 bhp engine.*

ABOVE **Lancia Lambda (V4), 1922.** *Many other racing drivers have gone in for manufacture but few as effectively as Vincenzo Lancia, whose marque was born in 1906 when he was still FIAT's star driver; the first true Lancia landmark was the Lambda, of unit construction not unlike that of the early Lanchesters. This example, provided by Gerald Batt, is one of the earliest made during a 10-year lifespan.*

RIGHT **Leyland Eight, 1920.** *At over £3000, the Leyland was the most expensive British car. Nineteen were built so it was not quite such a flop as Bugatti's six-off La Royale (see page 40) of a few years later. Leyland's isolated venture into private motoring was designed by Parry Thomas, seen at the wheel.*

ABOVE RIGHT **Ards TT, Ulster, 1929.** *The race got under way only after hoods had been lowered in, clearly, dangerous circumstances. Even greater danger was caused by a subsequent cloudburst through which the great Rudi Caracciola* (Mercedes-Benz) *charged to beat the handicappers. Many cars came to grief, including the rare 2.4-litre sleeve-valve Arrol-Asters (nos 60 of Norman Garrad and 61 of Eddie Hall), the Dumfries-built descendants of the Arrol-Johnston that won the* first TT in 1905. *The merger of Arrol-Johnston with Aster did not work out, and the joint company closed in 1931.*

LEFT AND RIGHT **The record breakers.** Ultimate speed has always been a British speciality, often with help from Castrol. To the names of John Parry Thomas, George Eyston, John Cobb, Henry Segrave and Malcolm Campbell (depicted here) must be added that of Richard Noble who, in the spring of 1984, was awarded the coveted Castrol Segrave Trophy. In October 1983, Noble's Thrust II broke the World Land Speed Record at over 1010 km/h (630 mph).

concentrated upon his ill-fated record cars. In retrospect both decisions seem unfortunate, to say the least.

Among the others in the British luxury market, George Lanchester's Forty, an ohc six-cylinder 6.2-litre, with epicyclic gearbox and underslung worm drive, was the outstanding design. The senior Lanchester brother, Frederick, had become an engineering consultant many years earlier, and his advice to the bickering board of Daimler had helped the Coventry marque stay in business and retain Royal patronage. Knight sleeve-valve engines were still used throughout the extensive Daimler range, which reached its most exotic peak with the 1927 Double-Six. Even 12 cylinders and more than 7 litres failed to give this vast Daimler a performance better than adequate; but Britain did have a fine new marque, to take on the role of leading sports car. To most Britons, the Bentley is *the* classic Vintage sports car.

Walter Owen Bentley had imported DFP cars from France before the war. In 1919, the first Bentley 3-litre sports car was shown at Olympia, but it was not until 1923 that the marque began to establish its legendary reputation.

In 1923 the Grand Prix d'Endurance was inaugurated at Le Mans: a 24-hour race for production touring cars, and today the most famous single annual motoring event in the world. Thirty-three cars, representing eighteen manufacturers, took part in the first of these great marathons. All were French, except for a pair of Belgian Excelsiors and one of the new London-built 3-litre Bentleys, driven by John Duff and Frank Clement, which finished fourth. They returned in 1924, and once again they found their car was the only British marque in the race. This time there were 40 starters – and the Duff/Clement Bentley was the winner! Duff later emigrated to the United States, where he drove at Indianapolis; but his performances in France in 1923 and 1924 led to a

racing policy that was to bring Bentley four more outright victories at Le Mans in 1927, 1928, 1929 and 1930: three of them by financier Woolf Barnato. Legend has Ettore Bugatti and others describing the big, solid Bentley as the 'fastest lorry in the world', but the fact remains that it did its job, and is still to be seen being put to work on road and track. Although Bentley was later taken over, it is the only *current* marque name to be found in the first five Le Mans 24-hour race finishers' lists.

While Bentley thrived on its racing, Rolls-Royce had made a conscious withdrawal from the sport. Rolls was, of course, long gone; he had been the sporting partner. Claude Johnson was now running the company that manufactured 'the best car in the world'; a claim that has never been disputed – not loudly, anyway!

In 1919, a Rolls-Royce-powered Vickers Vimy aircraft made the first non-stop transatlantic crossing piloted by Alcock and Brown, shortly before assembly of Rolls-Royce cars in America began: not a successful venture, as it turned out, although nearly three thousand were made during a ten-year stay. After the immediate post-war years in Europe, Rolls-Royce wisely abandoned its one-model policy, introducing the Twenty for 1922. In 1925, the top car, the 40/50 or Silver Ghost, became the New Phantom with dual ignition and overhead valves for its impressive six-cylinder engine – bigger than ever at 7.7 litres and still as smooth as silk – and the welcome if overdue feature of four-wheel brakes (five years after the Hispano-Suiza, which Royce had studied).

Claude Johnson's sudden death in 1926 came as a great blow. The first Phantom was not as modern as it should have been, at a time when industrial competitiveness was essential. However, by the end of the decade, with former Napier man Arthur Sidgreaves now in charge, Rolls-Royce achieved a lower look with its new Phantom II, which supplemented the more mundane Twenty admirably.

ABOVE **Bentley Speed Six, Le Mans 1930.** *The 6.6-litre six-cylinder cars from Cricklewood, North London, prepare for their one-two finish. For Bentley financier Woolf Barnato this was to be a hat trick; his co-driver in no. 4 was Glen Kidston.*

The runners-up were their team mates Frank Clement and Dick Watney (later of Lagonda) in no. 9. This was Bentley's fifth and final victory in the French 24-hour Grand Prix d'Endurance: the 'fastest lorries in the world' won

in 1924, 1927, 1928, 1929 and 1930. Originally, W. O. Bentley was against competing at Le Mans, but privateer John Duff, whose car won in 1924, made him change his mind.

ABOVE RIGHT **Rolls-Royce New Phantom, 1928.** *The 40/50 was updated in 1925, with overhead valves and four-wheel brakes. This example carries Hooper coachwork more characteristic of the Coventry Daimler.*

Americans in Britain

Although no British make seriously challenged the Rolls-Royce, many people consider the Vauxhall 30/98, largely the creation of Laurence Pomeroy Sr, to be the Bentley's superior among the sporting machines. It was undoubtedly a more sophisticated and much less aggressive touring car than the Bentley. Vauxhall was forward-looking, too; the company was experimenting with the Wilson preselective gearbox (see the next chapter) when it was taken over by General Motors in 1926.

This was not the American giant's first attempt to buy its way into Europe. In 1919, William Durant had sent over a study group including the brilliant Charles Kettering and Alfred Sloan; the result was a period of serious negotiation for half of the new Citroën organization, but in the end the French connection was not made. The next GM effort was directed towards the United Kingdom, where American cars already had a following. Indeed, Ford had established a plant in Manchester's Trafford Park complex as early as 1911; but the British taxation system measured horsepower in a way that favoured small, long-stroke engines. Operating costs for a typical Austin would be little more than half those for, say, a Chevrolet touring model in Britain – and the British car would be cheaper to buy in the first place. In 1925, GM came quite close to buying Austin and an offer was made, only to be withdrawn after a disagreement on the value of the assets.

So it was that General Motors made its next approach to Vauxhall. A much smaller project than Austin or Citroën would have been, the

Charles Rolls (1877–1910)
Frederick Royce (1863–1933)

The name Rolls-Royce has come to mean The Best In The World, even if the claim is no longer made without qualification. The names that go so well together are those of two very different men.

Frederick Henry Royce was a brilliant, perfection-seeking engineer who made his first car largely because he had found those he had bought unsatisfactory.

A son of Lord Llangattock, the Hon. C. S. Rolls was, with S. F. Edge and Charles Jarrott, one of the leading British sporting motorists in the early days of motoring. It was his natural salesmanship that made Rolls the ideal partner in promoting Royce's cars, and he drove one to victory in the 1906 RAC Tourist Trophy race. Rolls died when his Wright aircraft crashed during the 1910 Bournemouth Aviation Week. His former business colleague

Claude Johnson built up the name and success of Rolls-Royce cars after that.

F. H. Royce was the same age as Henry Ford; and there were other similarities. Both were 'naturals' at car making, rather than qualified engineers or scientists, having taken the 'apprenticeship' route to success. It can also be argued that each marque made its name through the rigid application of a one-model policy over virtually the same period. Ford *and* Rolls-Royce have become household names at opposite ends of the motoring spectrum.

OVERLEAF *Bentley 4½-litre, supercharged, 1929.* Like the Napier and the Vauxhall before it, the Bentley was Britain's leading sporting marque for several years. These photographs show just why, where words cannot. This particular car, from the Nigel Dawes collection, was a works 'demonstrator' road-tested in 1930 by The Motor.

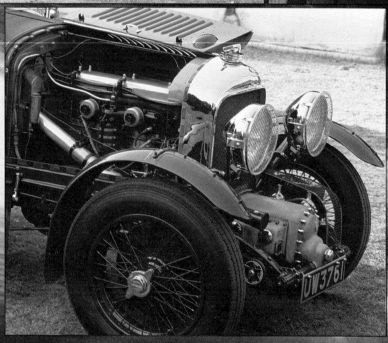

'Americanization' of Vauxhall was regarded by GM president Sloan as 'an experiment in overseas manufacturing'.

Two of the earliest customers for the new American-looking Vauxhalls were William Walmsley and William Lyons, partners in the Swallow Sidecar and Coachbuilding Company. It was the first time they had bought full-sized family cars, but they were not yet making them themselves. Their SS was yet to come.

They had started working together in 1921, making and selling Walmsley's streamlined Swallow sidecars in a small way, and forming a company when Lyons, the businessman of the two, reached his majority in 1922. From 1927 they made special bodies for light cars, and this led in 1928 to a move from the seaside town of Blackpool south to bigger premises in industrial Coventry. Walmsley and Lyons did not often share the same opinion or taste, and this was to lead to a parting of the ways; so it is all the more interesting, in the light of subsequent events that, when Walmsley appeared at the works one day with a brand new Vauxhall 20/60 Kingston coupé in his favourite brown and beige colours, his younger but more ambitious colleague went out and bought one, too, albeit in plain black and white. At £600 or so the Kingston was, in its way, the epitome of upper middle class motoring. Nevertheless, it spelled the death knell of the top-bracket Vauxhall; never has a marque's character changed so radically in so short a time, as when GM came to Luton. Only as the motor car was approaching its centenary would the name Vauxhall return to being one of the most admired on the British market – still thanks to General Motors.

British coachbuilders and mass producers

Truly, the 1920s were the years of the small car in Britain. The Budd-type all-steel body was slow in coming to Britain (see chapter 3), where the Weymann system of covering a wooden framework with fabric was being copied by all and sundry. The Weymann body flexed as the chassis flexed, and kept the magnification of mechanical noises to a minimum. Many of the traditional coachbuilders worked hard to improve their alloy panelling, but bodies still creaked a lot unless they were properly mounted on a really stiff chassis. The Weymann style could make a closed car look like a drophead coupé, and for a long time it was fashionable to fit dummy hood irons at the rear quarters.

In Britain, therefore, it was not just the more expensive chassis that received individual coachwork. Even the cheapest or most mundane of chassis could be made to look very special.

Of all Britain's early mass-producers – although they were never on the American scale – the greatest names were those of Morris and Austin.

William Richard Morris (later Lord Nuffield) had made his first car just before World War 1, and was Britain's first 'assembler'. He started building his cars with Coventry-made White and Poppe engines in 1913; then he introduced a second model with a Continental engine from Minnesota. War brought a link with Hotchkiss, whose Coventry engine factory was soon acquired by Morris. At £175 in its early guise, the 'Bullnose' Morris led the light car field, and its success enabled Morris himself to take control of Wolseley (and create M.G.), thus starting Britain's own shortlived 'General Motors in miniature'.

In the meantime (Sir) Herbert Austin was trying, unsuccessfully, to follow a one-model policy with his workaday single-valve four-cylinder Twenty – only to go into receivership. Two new cars changed the policy and Austin's fortunes. First came the tough Twelve; it would live on to World War 2 as a taxi. But the most brilliant and famous of all Austins was the ubiquitous Seven, born in 1922. Small and simple, with four cylinders displacing 747 cc, the Austin Seven went into production at £165 with the slogan 'The Motor for the Million'. Within five years, with the basic price down to £135 for the Chummy and £99 for the chassis only, specialist coachbuilders could offer some of the million customers a really individual small car for under £200. The brightly painted Austin Seven Swallow was the most expensive special of all, at £190 with soft and hard tops.

Austin was not keen on selling his chassis to just any company; thus Lyons acquired his first Austin Seven chassis through a dealer. That was in January 1927. At that month's Berlin motor show, Austin came to an agreement with the Gothaer Waggonfabrik of Eisenach, enabling the Austin Seven to be made under licence in Germany, as the Dixi. That these simultaneous actions should lead to the making of two of today's greatest rivals in the world of the super-car, namely the Jaguar and the BMW, is something Austin could hardly have predicted.

ABOVE **Ards TT, Ulster, 1928.** *It was Harry Ferguson who got the Ulster Government and the RAC together, to run the TT (which had lapsed for several years) eight times from 1928 to 1936, on the Dundonald–Newtownards–Comber road circuit. The first winner was Kaye Don (Lea-Francis Hyper) who is seen here at the* Dundonald hairpin. The runner-up was Leon Cushman (front-wheel-drive Alvis). Third and fourth came a pair of steady and impressive Austro-Daimlers.

ABOVE **Service with a smile.** *By the 1920s, cars were part of everyday life. Servicing them became a whole new industry, with a vigorous line in advertising campaigns.*

ABOVE RIGHT **Austin Seven Ruby, 1937.** *First seen in August 1934, some 12 years after the original Austin Seven, the Ruby was priced at £120. For its final season (1938) it was listed at £131. This is one of many Austins in the Patrick Collection, housed close to the Longbridge works where they were made.*

RIGHT **Sir Herbert Austin (right).** *He was present at Boulogne in September 1923 when the fabric-bodied Austin Sevens made their overseas racing début as a team.*

Herbert Austin *(1866–1941)*

Like Henry Ford, Herbert Austin was born into a farming family at a time when agriculture was starting to be mechanized. At 18 he left his home in Little Missenden, Buckinghamshire, and joined an engineering company in Melbourne, Australia. He moved around, gaining experience. Soon he became superintendent for a company supplying parts to the Wolseley Sheep Shearing Company, and was advising Frederick York Wolseley how he could improve the reliability and serviceability of his products, which were selling well in the Australian outback. When Wolseley decided to transfer manufacture to the United Kingdom he kept in close touch with Austin, inviting him to join the company as General Manager. In the winter of 1893, after nearly a decade in Australia, Austin came back to England. In Birmingham he did much to help the company through a bad period during which, in 1899, Wolseley died.

Austin made his first car (on Bollée lines) in 1895, the year in which the Wolseley company took up general machine-tool manufacture. Several more experimental vehicles were made before Wolseley went into car production, soon after Austin had won his class in the 1900 Thousand Miles Trial.

Finance for the car project came from Vickers Sons and Maxim Ltd, and Wolseley cars were raced seriously between 1902 and 1905. Then Austin left

Wolseley, ostensibly disagreeing with Vickers over engine design (his place was taken by John Siddeley).

Austin began his own company early in 1906. He was so successful that by 1914 the Austin Motor Company was producing more motor vehicles than any other in Britain. After World War 1, a one-model policy (it did not work for everyone!) put Austin into receivership. The 1922 Austin Seven and other outstanding new models put the company on course again. Having been knighted, he was made a baron (he chose to be Lord Austin of Longbridge) in 1936. He did not live to see any of his company's post-World War 2 mergers.

1930

During the 1930s only the fittest manufacturers survived, many of them only by takeover or merger. The Bentley lived on, but only on Rolls-Royce's terms. The Lanchester was drawn into the British Daimler administration, by courtesy of the latter's owners, BSA. Nuffield and Rootes became groups, each marketing its range of wares as different makes, while all the time bringing in increasing rationalization.

In the '£100 war', Morris made the headlines first, but Ford's Y-type saloon, developed specifically for Britain, proved that more comfort and better value could be built at Dagenham using the latest American production techniques.

Although North America still led in terms of production, and lent its skills to emerging countries like Japan and the USSR, it was continental Europe that scored on technical originality. The car of the decade was, surely, the front-wheel-drive Citroën, so admired by its competitors throughout the world. Italy took the everyday car a stage further with its compact Lancia Aprilia and baby FIAT *Topolino*.

Variety remained the keynote in Germany, where economy through streamlining was part of the Third Reich plan to put the nation on wheels. Front and rear power packs were tried with equal success, both in road cars and in the Mercedes-Benz and Auto Union machines that virtually took over Grand Prix racing from 1934 onwards.

The war was shorter for the United States than for the European countries and this meant less disruption of its industry. On the other hand, there were just too many companies trying to make too many cars; there would be fewer names in Detroit when peace returned in 1945, and one influential new one: the Jeep.

ECONOMIC CROSSROADS

1945

There are sad and happy tales in every motoring era. Both are to be found in full measure in the 1930s, a period it is no longer fashionable to write off as one of automotive atrophy.

Britain was behind America in terms of production techniques, and behind continental Europe in technical advance. Road conditions and British conservatism meant that travel was slow. Even by 1939, few towns with their traffic bottlenecks had been bypassed adequately. Overall gearing of cars tended to be low; a characteristic that persisted for years. Road surfaces were good, generally, but there were steep hills to be coped with and this meant a low bottom gear, with the subsequent problems of upward spacing of ratios.

'Roadholding' was beginning to become a part of the motorist's language, but 'handling' is modern terminology by comparison. Few people drove regularly at over 65 km/h (40 mph); 80 km/h (50 mph) was considered a high cruising speed. For the most part, solid axles and semi-elliptic springs all round were the order of the decade. Yet in learning to produce more cars more cheaply, Britain's manufacturers did not allow their products to lose their character altogether, and today there is a healthy appreciation of the popular cars of motoring's 'middle period'.

As for the luxury cars, they did not all fade away. Rolls-Royce, for one, stood its ground and actually expanded through acquisition. The cars were old-fashioned, but the Continental version of the Phantom II was always beautifully proportioned.

In 1931, W. O. Bentley brought out his most magnificent monster of all, the 8-litre, which offered prodigious performance despite great weight. Mightier than the mightiest of Rolls-Royces, it could not prevent Bentley's business being wound up after little more than a decade of independent car manufacture.

The Bentley marque re-emerged as a sporting Rolls-Royce in 1933, when the latter company outbid Napier for its purchase in 1931. If there was any doubt about which name would take the top honours, it was dispelled in 1935 when the Rolls-Royce 7.3-litre V12 Phantom III, with independent front suspension, was introduced. Meanwhile, Bentley himself overcame the restrictions placed upon him through the sale of his own name by playing an active role in the revival of Lagonda, as we shall see later in this chapter.

The last true Lanchester

The other big merger of 1931 was between Lanchester of Birmingham and Daimler of Coventry; but this was an even more one-sided affair. Daimler had been taken over by BSA more than 20 years earlier. Now it was Lanchester's turn.

The top model in the Lanchester range was the 4.4-litre straight-8. Its quality and engineering integrity were beyond reproach. It was beautiful in an understated way; and, like all Lanchesters, it ran very smoothly and quietly, but it was not very glamorous. By now, it seemed, there had to be a touch of glamour in the high-price field, if sales were to be found. Daimler had glamour through its customers, for it was still the car of Britain's Royal household, King George V having maintained the tradition started by his father. The year 1931 brought not only the absorption of Lanchester into Daimler, but also the birth of a glamorous

item of Daimler specification. This was the combined use of preselective gears with a fluid transmission coupling, a system that Daimler would continue to use on cars for many years, and on buses for many more. With a preselective gearbox, the change is effected by dipping the gearchange pedal (which replaces the normal clutch pedal).

Earlier, Daimler's chief engineer, Laurence Pomeroy, had introduced the long-established Coventry company to the V12 engine, for which this new semi-automatic transmission was ideally suited: especially when it came to easing along London's Mall at a snail's pace behind slow-trotting ceremonial horses! His next move was the speediest possible return from sleeve- to poppet-valve engines, which had become much quieter and more efficient in the 20 or more years since Daimler had last fitted them.

Daimler's modernization made Lanchester's downfall even more inevitable, much to the chagrin of an enthusiastic (but too small) clientele. One man who stayed loyal was the Duke of York, soon to become King George VI; he continued to order Lanchester straight-8s. By 1934 Pomeroy had created such a power unit, so the Duke's cars were Daimlers with Lanchester radiator grilles! An Indian maharaja who had been buying fleets of Lanchesters (through the diplomatic activity of the youngest of the Lanchester brothers, Frank) showed where his allegiance lay, too, but it was to no avail. Despite this patronage (and the special radiator grilles it entailed) the Lanchester car was destined to become the poor relation of the Daimler. Even victory by a Daimler-built Lanchester in the first-ever RAC Rally (1932) could not prevent the sharp decline of Britain's pioneer marque. It was probably the only way to stay solvent, however, for Daimler, Lanchester and BSA together covered a wider price spectrum than any other car maker of the 1930s – and offered an easier gearchange than Rolls-Royce.

Cars were still distinguished largely by the shape and style of their radiators or radiator cowls. Rolls-Royce's brilliant Greek temple effect has been copied on many lesser marques, but never equalled for artistry. Daimler's fluted grille stems from the days of finned radiator tops for air-cooling purposes, and has always looked rather fussy. Armstrong Siddeley also had an instantly recognizable radiator, with a shapely, sculptured elegance and Sphinx mascot on top.

Back in 1909, John Siddeley (who had succeeded Herbert Austin at Wolseley) moved to the Deasy company of Coventry. Amalgamation of Siddeley-Deasy with Armstrong-Whitworth in 1919 resulted in the Armstrong Siddeley car, which now represented solid British workmanship at its best, but little glamour. Armstrong Siddeley offered the Wilson design of preselector gearbox shortly before Daimler, but

initially without a fluid coupling. Lanchester had had preselector gears as early as 1900 but, like so many experiments, it had not been followed up with any persistence. Convention was a selling point that could stultify the work of a designer.

Armstrong Siddeley kept production going at a steady but limited rate. Reliable cars for reliable people – that might well have been the slogan for one of the company's best years, 1932, when the economic situation was at its worst. A hint of sportiness appeared in 1933 with the elegant 5-litre Siddeley Special, but in the next five years it was made at the rate of less than one a week.

Not everyone in the luxury car business had other enterprises to fall back on when times were hard. For example, the Argyll and the Arrol-Johnston (renamed Arrol-Aster), Scotland's most revered marques, dating from the 19th century, were among many to succumb as the Depression set in. (But two other Scottish marques, Albion and Beardmore, were to remain famous for their trucks and taxicabs respectively.)

However, it is difficult to see why some cars failed. In some cases was it perhaps conservatism at work again? The London-built Talbot is a case in point. Swiss engineer Georges Roesch had been with Talbot for several years, and by the 1930s had revitalized the marque connoisseurs regarded as a car of Rolls-Royce quality and style, but on a smaller scale – and much more sporting. The Roesch Talbot could have been an all-time great, with its thoughtfully designed and properly developed six-cylinder overhead valve engine to give it a string of excellent results at Le Mans and in the Alpine Trial, under the aegis of Surrey agents Fox

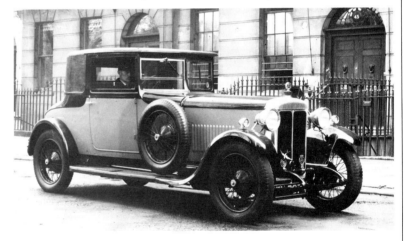

PAGES 56/7 *Rolls-Royce Continental Phantom II, 1933.* The Continental version of the 1929-35 7.7-litre model was slightly modified and tuned, and was approved by Sir Henry Royce at his Sussex retreat in August 1930. Its lowered chassis made the Phantom II one of the best-proportioned of cars. Tom Mason provided his Park Ward-bodied example.

LEFT *Lanchester Straight-8, 1930.* Introduced almost simultaneously with the Rolls-Royce Phantom II (and at £1325 nearly £500 cheaper on chassis price), this was the successor to the excellent Lanchester 40, which had challenged Rolls-Royce throughout the 1920s. Stuart Best provided this fine works-bodied example, which has been repainted just twice – at the age of 24 years and then again at 50.

ABOVE *Burney Streamline, 1931.* At the height of the Depression there was still room for eccentricity; somehow this oddity seemed to get worse rather than better when Crossley of Manchester tried to develop it. It had vanished from the lists in 1936.

TOP *Daimler Double-Six, 1930.* The Coventry Daimler was the original Royal car, and the first marque made in volume in Britain. It was taken over by BSA in 1910 and Lanchester joined the company in 1931, shortly after this sleeve-valve V12 coupé was made.

and Nichol. In view of the excellence of Roesch's designs, the quick decision by the Rootes brothers to annihilate them will always be seen as one of the biggest of many mistakes made in that era of ruthless industrial growth. Roesch himself would depart disillusioned, taking a job with the David Brown gear company shortly before the outbreak of World War 2.

Rootes rules

The Rootes story epitomizes the changing times. William Rootes, the elder, had begun selling cycles and cars in the previous century. His first son, also William (although always known as Billy), spent a brief, probably incomplete apprenticeship with Singer Motors in Coventry, bringing a Singer agency home to Kent afterwards. It was 1912, and Singer had just brought out its best model yet, a lightweight Ten which sold for £185 – excellent value in those early days – enabling Rootes to open a new garage. After the war, Billy persuaded his younger brother Reginald, a civil servant, to join the expanding business and Rootes Ltd soon moved into the big cities: London, Birmingham and Manchester.

For their particular purpose the Rootes brothers made a splendid team, though they were opposites in every apparent way. Their promotions man, Dudley Noble, once summed them up neatly: 'Billy saw the visions on the horizon and strode towards it with seven-league boots; Reggie surveyed the intervening ground with his keen and calculating eye, making sure no loose ends of any project were left untied.'

In 1928, having observed the General Motors system in action, they adopted it themselves, except for the divisional autonomy! The theory was that they should take over long-established but financially rickety makers of worthy motor cars and have them work together for mutual benefit. The first move, in 1928, followed William Hillman's death, and resulted in the merging of Hillman and its neighbour, Humber. By 1932, the Humber-Hillman plants at Stoke, in Coventry, were under the control of Rootes.

Talbot was already associated with Sunbeam (and with Darracq in France) but the Depression had placed the holding company, STD, in difficulties. Once-illustrious Sunbeam was in real trouble, and went into receivership. In June 1935, it was reported that Sir Alfred Herbert's famous machine-tool empire had acquired the Sunbeam car and trolleybus business, and that the former would be sold to SS Cars Ltd. Somehow, the deal fell through: presumably because the Rootes were prepared to take control of Sunbeam *and* Talbot.

Humber and Hillman were already thoroughly 'badge-engineered' (i.e. they produced the same basic cars, but gave them minor external, mainly cosmetic, differences to suggest that they were separate makes). Soon the same would happen to Sunbeam-Talbot, a combined marque from 1938.

With the arrival of the Hillman Minx, Rootes' output soared. In five years, from 1932 to 1937, over 100,000 Minx cars rolled off the production lines in Coventry where Rootes was, suddenly, providing steady employment: so arguments against the closure of the Talbot and Sunbeam operations carried little weight.

Coventry's other big car maker, Standard, was now being run more by John Black than by its ageing founder, Reginald Maudslay and, like the Rootes Group, it was getting bigger all the time. Black, an ex-army man, was married to one of William Hillman's daughters, and had been joint manager at the Hillman works until 1928. Now he was carrying out a determined restructuring of Standard's range and output: to the extent that annual production would increase sevenfold during the decade up to 1939, when over 50,000 cars were dispatched from the Canley, Coventry, site. Black's idea of the Union Jack badge helped popularize his cars, especially the Flying Standard range from 1935. These were distinctive cars, but Black wanted a prestige marque of his own.

The creation of the Jaguar

It is unusual for a manufacturer to bend over backwards to help a rival, unless there is an ulterior motive. Soon after moving to Standard, John Black became acquainted with William Lyons, who was separating the Swallow sidecar and coachbuilding businesses as part of a move to become a fully fledged car manufacturer. Swallow had its first stand at the motor (as opposed to the motorcycle) show in 1929, and one of the brightly coloured little saloons there was built on a Standard chassis. Up to that time Lyons had been making bodies for Austin Sevens almost exclusively. His team was modifying and adding weight to Austin

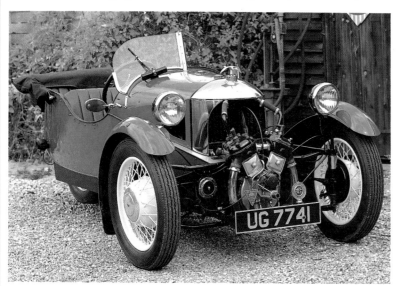

ABOVE *Morgan, 1933.* From 1910 to 1950, the small family business in Malvern, Worcestershire, led the world in sporting three-wheelers – and the firm is still going strong (see page 138). The cheapest models of the early 1930s were priced at under £100.

RIGHT *Morris Minor SV, 1933.* This was the car that in 1931 began Britain's £100 'price war' (see page 68). For £100 the specification had to be pared to the barest necessities.

Morris Minor Chassis

MORRIS
COWLEY : OXFORD

chassis and, understandably, Austin would not associate himself with Swallow's activities. Lyons therefore thought there was a risk of his supply of chassis running dry. So for 1930, Lyons hedged his bets by offering his Swallow coachwork on FIATs, Standards, Swifts and Wolseleys.

That 1929 Standard Swallow show car wore a high 1920s-style radiator cowl and this, combined with the low Swallow roofline, left the car with strange proportions and a slit-like windscreen. Early in 1930, Lyons launched the car again with a more modern cowl, which Black quickly adapted for his own range.

In 1931 the link became closer when Black agreed that specially modified Standard six-cylinder chassis 'to suit special body requirements' would be supplied to Lyons on an exclusive basis. All other aspects of the arrangement left Lyons free to do virtually what he wanted, including the creation of a new marque name – SS.

It was a rush to get the first SS to the 1931 Olympia Show on time. Lyons had to go into hospital with appendicitis; then when he returned, too late to alter it, he found that his partner, William Walmsley had raised the roofline of the six-cylinder model, the SSI.

Lyons resented the change and redesigned the coupé's shape for the London show of 1932, when the SSI looked truly sleek. 'Last year,' wrote Harold Pemberton in the *Daily Express*, 'I described the SSI as the car with the £1000 look. This year it might be called the car with the £1500 look. And it costs only £325.'

LEFT **Ards TT, Ulster, 1933.** *The works 'hack' M.G. K3 being driven to victory by Tazio Nuvolari.*

ABOVE **M.G. K3, 1933.** *Introduced in autumn 1932, the K3 was an 1100 cc supercharged six, with preselective gearchange. This example is part of the famous Californian collection of Briggs Cunningham, who built and raced his own sports cars in the 1950s.*

The regular Standard Sixteen saloon of the same year may have had that much-vaunted invention, the eddy-free roof (instead of the traditional peak above the windscreen), but it was a typical high, upright saloon just the same, and it was priced at £235. By contrast, nothing looked quite like the SS coupé, which is why Lyons's new cars found favour during the worst period of the economic crisis.

In 1934, Lyons and Walmsley fell out for good. Walmsley bought himself out at the end of the year, when Lyons became sole proprietor of the firm now called SS Cars Ltd. (He continued to produce Swallow sidecars until 1944 when that business was sold.) Early in 1935 a young Humber engineer, Bill Heynes, became chief engineer at SS, and in the autumn of 1935 a completely new range of overhead valve high-performance 'bargain-basement' SSs made its appearance under the evocative name of Jaguar.

Lyons made a new arrangement with Black to keep producing engines exclusively for him, but the Standard man was getting steadily angrier. Black had hoped that at least he would get a stake in the blossoming SS company, if not a place on its board: but Lyons responded blankly to both ideas.

Patrick and/or Jensen

Swallow was by no means the only specialist coachbuilder on popular chassis, but it was the only such firm to make a satisfactory transition to major motor manufacturer. Standard was, however, close to another coachbuilder in the 1930s. This was the Avon Body Company of Warwick, run by Reginald Maudslay's son, John, which produced the most attractive and luxurious coachwork for Standard chassis under its design chief C. F. Beauvais. The first Avon bodies were the work of the Jensen brothers. They left to work at the Edgbaston Garage Ltd in Birmingham, where Joseph Patrick was adding coachbuilding to his business. The open Wolseley Hornet sports they produced was given the name Patrick Jensen; but this led to trouble, since it was soon clear to Patrick that the Jensens were muscling in on his family business, which quickly became simply Patrick Motors. Their plan rumbled, in late 1931 Alan and Richard Jensen moved on again, this time to join a commercial vehicle coachbuilder named Smith in West Bromwich. From these devious beginnings eventually came the Jensen car of 1936.

The ever-upward clawing of its aspiring leaders is a fascinating aspect of this industry which has risen and fallen and risen again on many occasions during its first century. At every level, high, low or in between, vaulting ambition so often has been the crux of a company's success or failure. It is a pity that of the many great personalities whose

RIGHT *SS1 Airline, 1934. Many British manufacturers dabbled in streamlining in the early 1930s – more for styling than for aerodynamic purposes. This was William Lyons's only fastback model (apart from the E-type Jaguar, of course).*

ABOVE **SS Jaguar 100, 1939.** This shapely two-seater first appeared as the SS90 in the spring of 1935. It was completely updated mechanically that autumn, when the name Jaguar was used for the first time. At first it was overshadowed by the 2.7-litre overhead valve six-cylinder SS Jaguar saloon. A 3.5-litre engine was offered from 1937, making the SS Jaguar 100 (at £445, compared to the BMW 328's £695) the cheapest 160 km/h (100 mph) road car on the British market. The Jaguar 100 could not match the BMW on most race circuits, but it was a fine rally car and twice achieved best performance in the RAC and Alpine rallies. This example is from the Nigel Dawes collection.

LEFT **Rover 1389 cc P1, 1936.** The 'P' series of Rovers began in 1933 with the first of ex-Hillman director Spencer Wilks's 'Quality First' projects, which turned the Rover into one of Britain's proudest marques – deservedly so, for its origins lay in the early Midland sewing machine and bicycle industries. (John Kemp Starley had made Rover bicycles and tricycles in the 1880s.)

human traits have conditioned their business strengths – often with fascinating results – only a few can be mentioned here.

Back in 1928, John Black's co-chief at Hillman had been Spencer Wilks. He, too, had married one of the Hillman sisters; but with the coming of the Rootes brothers he made a dignified exit in 1929, promptly being invited to take the general managership of Rover, little more than a mile away from Humber Road. Rover had its origins in the early days of the bicycle and had made cars in the heart of Coventry since 1905. The excellent publicity from a 'race' with the famed Blue Train through France early in 1930 was not enough to prevent Rover falling on hard times. However, with the help of his brother Maurice (another Hillman refugee), Wilks soon hauled the Rover into an

enviable position. It became one of the smartest, most individual, yet least ostentatious of British cars, ideal for the doctor or businessman, with superb new four- and six-light body styles from 1937. With other fine cars such as Alvis, Riley and Triumph being made there, Coventry was the heart of Britain's motor industry: but it was not the centre for either of the country's two top producers of the 1930s, Austin and Morris.

Austin overseas

The Austin works at Longbridge, near Birmingham, recovered from its near bankruptcy and the famous Austin Seven was doing well everywhere: at home, in Germany (as the BMW Dixi) and in France

where, from 1928, Citroën's original engineer Jules Salomon teamed up with Lucien Rosengart and adapted it to suit French tastes. An American Austin Seven (later called the Bantam) was less successful, but to have made the attempt was brave. Nor could Austin rest on its laurels in the United Kingdom for there were constant challenges, some more successful than others. Output of the Seven had exceeded 26,000 in 1929, but dropped to 20,000 by 1933. Then, in 1934, Sir Herbert announced his 'jewels' for the 1935 season: the Ruby, the Pearl and the Opal. In the £120 Ruby saloon, the famous baby Austin was given a new look without any loss of charm or individuality, and in 1935 Seven production reached a new annual record at over 27,000. Aged 70, the old master was made a baron in 1936 – Lord Austin of Longbridge.

It was not just the Austin Seven that gave Longbridge its strength in the 1930s. The breadth and modernization of the range, with famous models such as the 10 hp Cambridge, helped establish real meaning for the slogan: 'Austin, you can depend on it'.

Announced in August 1936, the Cambridge at last gave external access to a split boot containing a horizontal spare wheel beneath a shelf for a reasonable amount of luggage. Only long-bonneted cars could take a side-mounted spare wheel comfortably and the British family car had had little option but to keep its spare attached vertically at the rear. If the wheel was hidden from view it occupied valuable space; any bulky load was lashed to the bootlid, laid flat to serve as a rack. So the new four-seater six-light Cambridge saloon at £160 (or £178 for the fancier version with a sliding roof) was just about the ideal family car of 1937. For most uses the luggage could be kept hidden, yet there was still a fold-flat bootlid. Moreover, thought was now being given to the damping of potential noise and vibration from the modern steel body. The family car was not just transportation – it was transportation in comfort.

Oxford v. Cambridge

The name Cambridge drew attention once again to the strong rivalry that existed between Austin and Morris. The latter had dropped the name Oxford and was concentrating on the idea of the 'series' in an effort to get away from the 'model year' principle, which was continuing to gain strength in the United States. The Series II Morris saloons had been much more modern-looking than their Austin counterparts when introduced in May 1935; but the Series II did not even have a bootlid, and loads had to be passed through the passenger compartment. In 1937 the Morris Series III with semi-integral body was introduced as a Twelve, at £177 10s, to redress the balance.

On the whole, Austin and Morris level-pegged, with the latter tending to be the market leader. The year 1937 was the best for Austin, and a good one for Morris, although their combined share of the British market, which itself achieved a record, had dropped. Production had more than doubled since 1930. The 1937 achievement was for Britain to build, in round terms, 300,000 cars for home use plus 80,000 for export. The main contributors were Austin and Morris with about 90,000 each, but Ford, Rootes, Standard and Vauxhall were all moving into the big league.

William Morris, ultimately made a viscount, is better known as Lord Nuffield. His Nuffield Group was, in its day, Europe's biggest motor empire. When Wolseley went bankrupt in 1926 it was Nuffield who

LEFT ***M.G. SA, 1938.***
Introduced at the same time and price as the first SS Jaguars, M.G.'s attractive 2.3-litre saloon was soon supplemented by a 2.6, the WA. This one was provided by Michael Turvill.

OVERLEAF ***Aston Martin Mark II, 1935.***
Beautiful and purposeful, this sports-saloon with the bulldog stance was one of the last of the famous 1.5-litre, dry-sump, ohc-engined models designed by A.C. Bertelli. By now, however, Aston Martin came under new management and the only really interesting new models to emerge were purely experimental – and bore fruit only after the war was over. Car owned by D. J. E. Proffitt, provided by the Nigel Dawes collection.

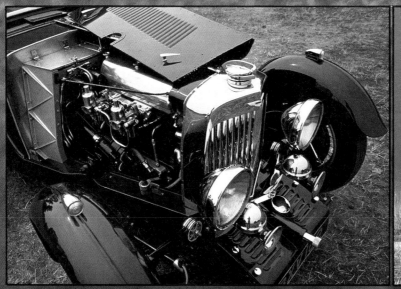

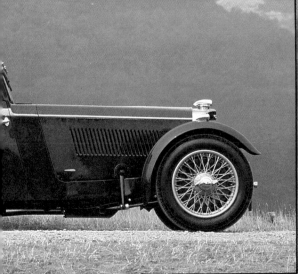

outbid Austin for it and he kept it in his own name until 1935, when it became part of Morris. M.G. was the sporting car of Morris Garages, also dating from the 1920s. Apart from a number of component makers, the other big purchase was of Riley, in 1938, the Coventry-based builders of a delightful variety of sporting cars. Even in the short time available before the outbreak of World War 2 in 1939, Morris managed to banish the Riley's individuality to outer darkness (although the 1940s would allow a brief reprieve).

The joint marketing of M.G., Morris, Riley and Wolseley did, at least, keep famous names going and permit the buyer to maintain his or her particular brand loyalty – a strong characteristic of Morris's chief rival, the Austin. With the setting up next to the Cowley, Oxford, works of the Pressed Steel Company in the late 1920s in conjunction with the American pressing pioneer Edward Budd it was inevitable that Nuffield should take maximum advantage of modern construction techniques regardless of purist criticisms.

During the 1930s, General Motors changed the face of Vauxhall as ruthlessly as any Rootes or Nuffield; by contrast, annual car production at Luton rocketed from less than 5000 to more than 35,000 within that period. With relatively little car importation (compared with the 1920s) few Britons noticed the similarities to the GM's American-German Opels. Vauxhalls retained their distinctive fluted bonnets but in 1937 they were, nevertheless, Britain's first cars to have fully integral body-cum-chassis structure and gave the economy motorist his first opportunity to try independent front suspension, albeit the soon-outmoded 'knee-action' type, which could behave strangely. As early as 1931 some Vauxhalls had had synchromesh gearboxes, allowing gears to be changed smoothly: another 'foreign' feature welcomed wholeheartedly in the long run. All the purist has to do is to think of pre-GM and post-GM Vauxhalls as different makes, and his problem is solved.

The £100 war

It was the American incursion into Britain that was to escalate the bargain-price war of the 1930s. And one particular battle – for the £100 car – was to be an American victory.

From 1911, Ford had assembled cars at Trafford Park, Manchester, and had been able to capitalize on the British industry's post-war inability to produce many cars by taking over 40 per cent of the United Kingdom market in 1919. A decade later, Ford was building a factory at Dagenham on the Thames Estuary marshes and was well on the way to taking the popular car market by storm.

Small firms like Jowett and Trojan offered cheap cars, but these were better suited to commercial use, although each had a cult following. Before Ford, however, the real price war was between Austin and Morris whose cheapest models in 1930, the Seven and the Minor, were priced at £130.

As the slump took its toll on everyone's pockets, desperate steps were taken. The most desperate were those at Cowley, where the new Morris Minor had been brought in as a Wolseley-inspired 850 cc overhead-camshaft challenger to Austin (it inspired the M.G. in turn). Determined to capture what he could in those hard times, Morris authorized the manufacture of an absolutely basic open tourer with no bumpers, a single windscreen wiper, side-valve engine and a painted radiator shell. (An amusing thought, perhaps, is that coloured radiator shells have, in modern times, become symbols of super-luxury.) This austere baby appeared in 1931 and its success was not in its actual sales – for the Morris Minor was too spartan to be attractive – but in the way people bought more expensive versions because its basic advertised price was £100. Austin pulled a similar trick a few seasons later; but it was

ABOVE **Triumph 2-litre Roadster Coupé, 1938.** *The car with the famous 'waterfall' grille.*

RIGHT **Ford Y-Type Popular, 1935.** *Conceived in the USA and built at Dagenham, Essex, from 1932, this was the only properly equipped family car ever to sell for £100 – a price that was held from 1935 to 1937.*

ABOVE **Morris Works, Cowley, Oxford.** *This was Britain's busiest car factory in the 1930s, producing 90,000 to 100,000 cars a year compared with an average annual UK total of 350,000 cars between 1935 and 1939. The photograph must have been taken in 1940, as civilian and utility Tens are being assembled side by side.*

Ford who made the only genuine £100 four-cylinder saloon car in Britain.

In 1932, Ford opened its new Dagenham plant and introduced its car for Europe, the £120 Y Type or Popular. So efficient was the Ford manufacturing system that this simple but endearing Tudor (i.e. two-door) was brought down to £100 in 1935 and held there for two seasons until an updated Ford Eight replaced it at the very acceptable sum of £115.

Morris copied Ford blatantly. The resultant Morris Eight was priced at £120 and was among the first British cars to be offered with steering wheel on the left for export. Singer's Bantam was almost identical in looks and cost £132 10s. For 1938 the Morris Eight was modernized as

the Series E, its built-in headlamps – unfamiliar in Britain – adding to its pleasantly chubby appeal for only £128. Austin got left behind in this particular race. The Big Seven of 1937–9 counted as an eight for tax purposes, but still looked like its smaller brother. The Austin Eight came out only just before the war.

Ford's swift arrival on the small car scene had been one of the wonders of the decade.

The record breakers

On the sporting front, Britons ruled in terms of sheer speed. Malcolm Campbell, knighted soon after the other great driver and record breaker Sir Henry Segrave, kept pushing the world record up until he took

LEFT *Lagonda LG6 4½-litre, 1937. W. O. Bentley was in charge of technical matters for Lagonda of Staines from 1935 and revitalized its image. He improved the Le Mans-winning six-cylinder Meadows engine for the LG6 and master-minded a completely new V12 of similar swept volume. Both models could be had with this superbly proportioned drophead coupé body. Even the Dinky Toys version was a cut above its fellows. This one is a star of the Patrick Collection.*

Bluebird through the 480 km/h (300 mph) barrier at Bonneville, Utah, in 1935, using a Rolls-Royce V12 aero engine. Sir Malcolm then turned to water speed record breaking. Between 1937 and 1939, George Eyston (*Thunderbolt-R-R*) and John Cobb traded records, Cobb's *Railton-Mobil* holding the honour until after World War 2 at fractionally under 595 km/h (370 mph).

Comparable achievements remained elusive for Britain in the top echelons of Grand Prix racing; and Bentley's 1930 Le Mans victory was followed by four years of Alfa Romeo domination. A surprise but well-deserved win at Le Mans in 1935 came too late to prevent Lagonda being disbanded, then brought to life again by Alan Good. Now that his old company was part of Rolls-Royce, W. O. Bentley himself joined Lagonda at this time and gave the Staines firm a new lease of life with his fine high-speed sixes and V12s.

AC, Alvis, Aston Martin, Frazer Nash, HRG, M.G., Riley, Singer, SS Jaguar, Triumph – all made fine sports cars that provided for the 1930s clubman, and each was typically British in its own way. Britain's only Monte Carlo Rally winner of the decade was Donald Healey, driving a big Invicta in 1931; Tom Wisdom achieved best performance of all in the 1936 Alpine Trial, driving the newly introduced SS Jaguar 100 2½-litre sports car.

It is to the Riley we must look to find *the* British racing car of the decade: for it was Raymond Mays's special 1933 supercharged Riley sprint car that inspired him and engineer Peter Berthon to create English Racing Automobiles Ltd to make ERA single-seaters. These won innumerable international races at Division Two level, the top driver being Mays himself, with 'B. Bira', Arthur Dobson, Pat Fairfield, Dick Seaman and, later, young Tony Rolt, Peter Walker and Peter Whitehead.

It was the heyday of Brooklands, the complex of high and low speed tracks near Weybridge, Surrey, originally built with great forethought in 1906 and 1907 but, in the end, unsuitable for Grand Prix-type racing. Through the 1930s, however, the banked concrete bowl attracted crowds to watch thunderous monsters from a bygone age attaining unheard-of speeds.

Britain's need for a 'natural' circuit was met in 1933 by Fred Craner and his Derby and District Motor Club colleagues, who were the first to arrange motorcycle racing in the grounds of Donington Hall on the Leicestershire–Nottinghamshire border. The site was improved for cars and, in 1937 and 1938, works teams from Auto Union and Mercedes-Benz brought Donington Park to life. These two marques were genuine competition for one another, but to the exclusion of everyone else – for

they were the standardbearers of the highly organized Third Reich motor sport programme overseen by *Korpsführer* Fritz Hühnlein.

In the early 1930s there was considerable variety in the Grand Prix results, with Bugatti starring for France; Alfa Romeo and Maserati for Italy; and sometimes the big Mercedes-Benz SSK for Germany. From 1934 to 1939 it was Auto Union and Mercedes-Benz all the way.

German diversity

Hitler's Germany produced the *Autobahnen* and the KdF car, or Volkswagen. It also produced a wide variety of fascinating machines from brilliant engineers. Some of them were orthodox. General Motors maintained Opel's position as market leader, whereas Ford's Y Type did

LEFT ***Douglas, Isle of Man, race, 1937.*** *Britain's outstanding single-seat racer of the 1930s was the ERA, the brainchild of Raymond Mays seen here leading eventual winner 'B. Bira' in the premier British light car international event of 1937.*

TOP ***Monaco Grand Prix, 1936.*** *The most successful driver of the 1930s, Rudi Caracciola (Mercedes-Benz, right) drove wisely and well to win. Achille Varzi and Hans Stuck (Auto Union) were second and third from Nuvolari (Alfa Romeo, centre). Chiron (Mercedes-Benz, left) and Rosemeyer (Auto Union, second row, right) were among the many who crashed in the wet.*

ABOVE ***Brooklands, 1936.*** *Walter Hassan was responsible for these typical Bentley-based specials.*

not have the same attraction for Germans as it did for Britons. In Germany there was less of a set development pattern than in, say, Britain or America, although certain common factors did emerge. One such factor is the frequency with which different manufacturers tried Paul Jaray's ugly aerodynamic bodywork on their chassis as part of the search for economical *Autobahn* motoring (after Edmund Rumpler, as a Jew, had fallen from favour).

The Horch, the *Grosser* Mercedes-Benz and the massive 8-litre V12 Maybach Zeppelin with its dual-range gearbox: these are the amazing machines that tend to come to mind for the particular time and place; but there were other extremes of design.

Hanomag had given up making its famous baby, the Kommissbrot, by 1930. Now the company turned its hand not only to sporting cars such as the Sturm, but ran Mercedes-Benz a close second in pioneering the diesel-powered car. The 1939 streamlined Hanomag 1300 saloon was to be the inspiration for Sweden's first 'international' car, the PV444.

From Austin Seven to BMW
In acquiring the Dixi factory at Eisenach in 1928, the Bayerische Motoren Werke of Munich had taken on the right to build the Austin

Seven, already under construction as the Dixi 3/15. This was rapidly updated and given the name BMW, already famous on motorcycles. As in Britain, Budd's patented pressed-steel coachwork had been introduced in the late 1920s, and BMW became one of many companies to rely heavily upon the Berlin factory (Ambi-Budd), the biggest German body plant of its day. The BMW quickly acquired technical individuality, under Fritz Fiedler who had already done good work for Stoewer and Horch. The 1936–9 BMW 328 proved to be the best of all German sports cars, and a strong rival for Britain's SS Jaguar 100 in rallies; the difference was that the BMW (sold as a Frazer Nash–BMW in the United Kingdom) was also an effective circuit-racing car. Here the 2-litre Aston Martin was its more direct British adversary.

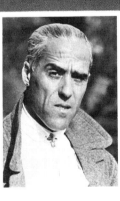

Auto Union 3-litre V12, 1938. Between 1934 and 1937 the straight-8 Mercedes-Benz and the V16 rear-engined Auto Union dominated Grand Prix racing, with more and more power. A top engine capacity limit of 3 litres was imposed for the 1938 season, but both marques were ready (each with a V12), and their domination continued. Tazio Nuvolari (LEFT) joined Auto Union and won the Grands Prix at Monza and Donington Park (TOP) with the new car, which had a novel Eberan-designed three- camshaft supercharged engine (FAR LEFT). By 1939 it had two-stage supercharging and developed 485 bhp.

ABOVE **BMW 327, 1938.** *All that was best in German styling, like its even sportier brother the 328 open two-seater. Indeed, the 328's 80 bhp engine was available for the 327. Fritz Fiedler's engineering was much appreciated by other manufacturers. (SS, later Jaguar, ran a BMW test car during the war.) The Eisenach factory was to find itself in the Russian zone after the war, and the 327 continued to be made there as the EMW from 1945 to 1955.*

Front-wheel drive comes to Germany

Front-wheel drive had not been seen much in Germany so far, although the Brennabor and the NAG-Voran (a last gasp for Berlin's old Nationale Automobil-Gesellschaft) did feature Richard Bussien's front-wheel system, first seen on his 1926 Voran.

Of the long-established marques, Adler was still a design leader, with Hans-Georg Röhr's front-wheel-drive Trumpf and Trumpf Junior, which came with all-independent suspension and rack-and-pinion steering. The Adler Trumpf was also built abroad, in France and Belgium, and was renowned for its worldwide customer service scheme. The streamlined coupé, which ran so well in 1937 and 1938, was Germany's most successful Le Mans representative, once the big Mercedes-Benz SSK was obsolete.

Röhr had resigned from his own company in 1930. The first Röhr car of 1928 had been brilliant technically but not financially. The company continued for a few years without him, making the Röhr Junior (a licensed Tatra 57: Ledwinka's 11/12 updated) and the 1933 supercharged eight-cylinder Olympier (a Ferdinand Porsche design) which looked as startling, if not as handsome, as a Cord when clothed by Autenrieth of Darmstadt. When Röhr folded in 1935, Stoewer of Stettin (now Szczecin in Poland) took on the Tatra 57, calling it the Greif Junior. Meantime, Röhr himself moved on from Adler to Daimler-Benz! The moves of those great engineers and their creations make fascinating study. Almost straightforward by comparison is the case of the DKW.

It was a Dane, Jørgen Skafte Rasmussen who, in his younger days, had designed a *Dampfkraftwagen* (German for 'steam car'); and from that name he extracted the initials DKW for the motorcycle business he started in 1919. In 1931, DKW made history by becoming the first mass-producer of front-wheel-drive cars. A year later the Auto Union was formed when DKW joined forces with the imperious Horch and two 'middle-class' makes: Audi (in which Rasmussen already had a big stake) and Wanderer.

Birth of the 'Beetle'

Most complex of all is the background story to Hitler's car for the people, the Volkswagen, with its air-cooled engine in the tail, swing-axle suspension and streamlined beetle shape.

The key probably lies in what happened at the Berlin Motor Show, which Germany's Chancellor of 12 days, Adolf Hitler, opened and inspected on 11 February 1933. Earlier, in Austria, Hitler had used one of Ledwinka's tough little Tatras; now (it is said) they met and discussed at length the forthcoming rear-engined Tatras. Another conversation took place with Joseph Ganz – editor of *Motor Kritik* and campaigner-in-print for a German people's car or Volkswagen – one of whose rear-engined designs (similar to Carl Borgward's baby Hansa) was about to go into limited production at Wilhelm Gutbrod's Standard works in Ludwigsburg.

Chief architect of the VW venture was, of course, Ferdinand Porsche who, after leaving Daimler-Benz in 1929, had spent a while with Steyr in Austria before setting up his own consultancy business near Stuttgart. Before the VW took its final shape, Porsche had worked closely with Zündapp and NSU on experimental cars, but the government decree, when it came, was that Daimler-Benz should build the 1937 prototypes. (There were, in fact, several Mercedes-Benz rear-engined cars on the market then but they were soon dropped.)

It is right and proper that Porsche should have the credit for devising the VW, which did not see the light of day until Hitler's own hostile activities had ceased, but then became the world's first model to exceed the 20 million production figure. Nevertheless, the work of other inventive men such as Borgward, Ganz, Ledwinka, Nibel and Rumpler has its place in the 'Beetle' saga.

Porsche's other great machine of the 1930s was the rear-engined V16 Auto Union Grand Prix car, built in the Horch works at Zwickau. Only the most talented drivers – first Hans Stuck then Bernd Rosemeyer – could extract anything like the car's full potential, yet they were Europe's top drivers for 1934 and 1936 respectively. By contrast, 1935 was a great year for the new straight-8 Grand Prix car from

LEFT *Tatra 12 saloon and Tatra 57 roadster.* The Tatra 11/12 (1923-34) was revolutionary in combining a 1050 cc air-cooled opposed-twin engine with a backbone chassis and swing-axle rear suspension, and led to the four-cylinder Tatra 57 (1932-47). These remarkable 'people's cars' are overshadowed historically by the later streamlined Tatras. They have a strong following today. These were photographed in 1983 in Kopřivnice.

RIGHT *FIAT 518, 1933.* Advertising to brighten the dullish image of the very middling family-sized FIAT Ardita. Its baby brother, the 508 Balilla, was more fun.

ABOVE *Maybach Zeppelin, 1932.* The dramatic coachwork is by Spohn. The attempt to make this V12 Maybach an Autobahn windcheater is interesting if not altogether successful aesthetically.

OVERLEAF *Alfa Romeo 8C, 1932.* The most successful competition sports car of the early 1930s. Its two in-line four-cylinder alloy blocks had a common crankshaft from the centre of which was taken the drive for the two camshafts: the engineering of Vittorio Jano at its glorious best. Provided by J. C. Bamford Excavators Ltd.

Mercedes-Benz, whose hero-driver Rudolf Caracciola won the European Championship (as he did again in 1937 and 1938). There was, as yet, no official world championship.

From 1938, a new formula brought to an end a four-year period of unlimited power, but the new Mercedes-Benz 3-litre V12 supercharged engine was soon delivering 500 bhp. Porsche was concentrating on the VW project and Auto Union's new car, also a V12, was designed chiefly by Robert Eberan-Eberhorst. Auto Union had lost Rosemeyer in a record attempt on the *Autobahn* near Frankfurt airport, but morale was raised when Tazio Nuvolari replaced him and proved that the rear-engined racer was still a winner. Between them, the German teams controlled Grand Prix racing until war intervened. The British did, however, take pride in the selection of Richard Seaman for the Mercedes-Benz team and of the underrated A. F. Agabeg ('Fane') for BMW's Mille Miglia squad.

This domination had come about through the German government's sponsorship of Auto Union and Mercedes-Benz racing programmes, following Hitler's visit to the AVUS circuit in 1933, when Bugatti and Alfa Romeo trounced the outdated Mercedes-Benz SSKL. The new Chancellor had reacted by approving a huge subsidy.

In the period leading up to this intervention, Alfa Romeo had acquired a wondrous reputation, through the work of Vittorio Jano. Following the success of his 1924 P2 Grand Prix car, Jano had been responsible for a whole series of marvellous sports cars which kept Italy's car-making reputation at a high level; for during the 1930s Alfa Romeo took *successive* victories in the Mille Miglia seven times, the Targa Florio six times and at Le Mans on four occasions.

Jano's 1932 Type B Grand Prix car (the *monoposto* P3 as it was termed) was yet another work of art from both visual and technical standpoints. It was the only car ever to beat the Germans on level terms; that was Nuvolari's dream win in the 1935 German Grand Prix. No one could stop the flood, however, so it was sad that Jano's later attempts to put Alfa Romeo back in contention should lead only to his departure.

Jano's new master, Lancia, continued to produce cars bristling with ingenuity. The compact, integral, thoroughly modern V4 Aprilia saloon would surely have been named Italy's 'car of the decade' had a vote been taken. It was in any case a lasting memorial to Vincenzo Lancia, who died in 1937.

Il Topolino

FIAT, as ever, dominated the Italian scene. The Depression hit hard and FIAT's reaction was to produce *Il Topolino* (Italian for Mickey Mouse). In 1936 it was the first of a series of miniatures for which FIAT is still famed. Even on the British market it was priced at a mere £120; at home it could be bought for the equivalent of a two-figure sum and did for Italy the job the Austin Seven had done for Britain a dozen years before. By putting its 569 cc four-cylinder engine ahead of the front wheels, Franco Fessia and Dante Giacosa were able to give their delightful little design the looks of a bigger car, and soon there were French and German versions from assemblers Simca and NSU.

Many of Italy's other great marques of the past were already on the way out, killed by heavy taxation which meant there were no new cars of over 3 litres' capacity being made after 1937.

French ferment

In France the situation was worse still, for there was high unemployment. A national strike led to an uneasy industrial peace in the late 1930s, when more satisfactory working hours and rates of pay had been achieved, but it was a decade in which much of France's old impetus was lost.

Hotchkiss, founded by an American and managed by an Englishman, maintained a balance between style and utility and – helped by a series of impressive Monte Carlo Rally victories – it stayed afloat. One day, soon after the war, it would absorb Delage and Delahaye (which came together in 1935) and continued to make beautiful cars; but they could not outshine Bugatti. This Alsace-based company produced some outstanding racing cars and won several Grands Prix in the early 1930s. Bugatti then concentrated upon sports cars, taking victory at Le Mans in

Vittorio Jano (1891–1965)

After working for a couple of years with the Società Torinese Automobili Rapid from the age of 18, Vittorio Jano took his skills as a draughtsman to nearby FIAT where promotion was quick. When World War 1 was over, Jano became well known as a designer, and he contributed to the brief success enjoyed by FIAT in GP racing in the early 1920s.

Young Enzo Ferrari recognized Jano's exceptional work on high-performance cars and talked him into joining Alfa Romeo in 1923. There followed a series of new Alfas, beginning with the FIAT-inspired P2. Probably the purest of Jano's creations at this stage was the famous *monoposto* of 1932 with twin propeller shafts.

Its twin-block eight-cylinder supercharged engine was both beautiful and effective – as indeed was the car itself. (Its designation was Tipo B, but it is more often known as the P3.) The sports cars were as successful as the single-seaters, with four victories in a row at Le Mans from 1931 to 1934.

Jano did all he could to meet the onslaught of the Auto Union and Mercedes-Benz teams, but other projects had priority. Old age was the reason given to him when the management of the recently nationalized Alfa Romeo organization dismissed him, after lack of development prevented his 4.5-litre V12 Tipo 12C-37 from putting up a good show in the 1937 Italian GP.

Too old, indeed! Vittorio Jano was appointed head of Lancia's experimental department almost at once, and he led the design and development work that produced the Aurelia and its competition GT variants of the early 1950s. From these came the race-winning V6 sports cars. Jano was also responsible for the 1954 V8 GP Lancia which, as the Lancia-Ferrari, brought Fangio his 1956 world title. (Fangio was champion five times between 1951 and 1957.)

In the arrangement that entrusted Ferrari with the responsibility for the future of the Lancia racing programme, Jano continued to work with his former colleague as a consultant, undertaking much of Ferrari's late-1950s design work.

It was said that Jano believed – mistakenly – that he had cancer; in any event, the greatest of all Italian car design engineers committed suicide in 1965.

ABOVE LEFT **Lancia Aprilia.** *Advanced, compact, sporting, this neat four-seater had the famous V4 engine configuration favoured by Vincenzo Lancia, who lived just long enough to see the Aprilia into production. It had integral construction and all-independent suspension, and paved the way for the Aurelia (see page 98).*

ABOVE **Bugatti T.57S, 1939.** *The influence of Ettore Bugatti's son Jean was considerable by this time, and Bugatti's 3.3-litre T.57 was Molsheim's ultimate expression of motoring delight. The S was quick, and the SC even quicker. Some of the coachwork was done at Molsheim, some by the great coachbuilding houses. This one, with body by Van Vooren of Courbevoie, Paris, was provided by T. A. Roberts.*

LEFT **FIAT 500, from 1936.** *While Lancia led Italy and the world in compact family-car design (see opposite), this little Topolino, which spanned the same 12-year period, met the needs of those who would not otherwise be able to afford a car. What a little gem it was, too! This ingenious design by Fessia and Giacosa filled a similar niche in their home market to the Austin Seven in Britain. As with the British baby, versions were produced abroad.*

1937 and 1939 with the streamlined 'tank', based on the Type 57. Much nicer – perhaps the most beautiful cars of the age – were the road-going Type 57 saloons and coupés. Here, in coachcraft, was one trade where French (and British) skill could not be overtaken by German finance.

Voisin and Hispano-Suiza kept their respective eccentricity and top-price quality going for as long as they could before pulling out. So many French marques had thrived in the carefree 1920s; now there was little space for them. Saddest to see was the original *grande marque*, the Panhard, shambling so awkwardly through the minefield of modernity, still wearing its valves in its sleeves and, from 1934, a body style – called the Dynamic! – more visually discordant even than that of the contemporary Chrysler and DeSoto Airflow. Now that Rootes ruled in Britain, the French Talbot was making a few beautifully smooth road and race cars, under the guidance of Antonio Lago.

Although it, too, took risks with streamlining, the Peugeot of the 1930s kept its position at the top of the popular motoring tree. Renault cut out the dead wood at the upper end of its range and modernized hard; the Juvaquatre looked like a copy of the Opel Kadett, however, which did not make it very popular in France as storm clouds loomed.

France's new revolution

French flair had not gone for ever, even if there was only one car to prove it: the *traction avant* Citroën.

What a design! It still looked acceptable in 1956 when it went out of production; on 15 April 1934, when shown in public for the first time, it seemed sensational.

Somehow, the *traction* combined brilliant styling with integral construction: and the rare feature of a wheel at each corner gave a muscular, bulldog stance. The character of this car was more than skin-deep, for it had torsion bar independent suspension and cornered beautifully. The four-cylinder overhead-valve engine was tough, if not very powerful at first. (A V8 version was discarded before going on the market; later, there was to be a 2.9-litre six.) The drive line worked well but wore quickly and needed frequent attention, as did the long control rods between the gearchange lever (sticking out of the dashboard) and the gearbox, which was mounted at the front of the car. There had been Citroën production in the United Kingdom since 1926 and soon a Slough-built Citroën *traction* could be bought for around £250. Introduction of the range put the Société Anonyme André Citroën in jeopardy, however, and so the vast Michelin tyre company came to the rescue. This, naturally, led to some very interesting joint development work which helped both parties stay ahead of the field.

TOP **French GP, Linas-Montlhéry, 1936.** *Because of German domination, France chose to hold its 1936 GP as a sports-car event, which provided a home victory for Bugatti's T.57G 'tank' over two Delahayes. (How modern the BMW 328 – the white car – looks at this, its foreign début.)*

ABOVE **Monte Carlo Rally, 1934.** *The most famous if not always the best rally in the world. The 'Monte' was first held in 1911 as a trans-European winter marathon, when 23 crews set out from four capitals. French Hotchkiss cars won it no fewer than six times; the drivers on this occasion were Trévoux and Gas, who had set out from Athens. Jean Trévoux would win four times in all – twice more for Hotchkiss, once for Delahaye. (In 1983 Lancia went one better, with a seventh win.)*

ABOVE RIGHT **Citroën traction avant, 1934-56.** *The protruding boot marks this 11 cc Normale (or 'Big 15') as a post-1953 example, but otherwise the front-wheel-drive Citroën looked much the same for 22 years without dating. The marque has remained famous for bold design. This French-built example was provided by Alec Bilney.*

Although France was trailing as a result of its internal problems (which had caused the 1936 Le Mans 24-hour race to be cancelled), it did at least manage to find a way of using the war period to continue to develop cars for the future, including economy cars that would become Citroëns and Panhards when peace returned.

America shows the world

When Hitler went to war in 1939 Germany was, as in the beginning, the engineering leader – although by no means all its top designers were themselves Germans. The world's *production* kings were, of course, the Americans. Besides their home and European bases, they were now taking their technology around the world: to Australia, to Japan, to South America and to the Soviet Union. The strides being made by other nations in the 1930s had been taken by Detroit much earlier.

Even so, the fascination of motoring was as strong after Wall Street crashed as it had been before. The producers settled down to produce; the specialists struggled to survive.

The consolidation of General Motors was countered in March 1932 by the world's first high-performance car to be offered at bargain price. Ford had done it again with its new $460 Model 18, the V8, which was soon on sale in Britain at an amazing £185.

Even though the Depression was biting deep, 10 per cent of the USA's working population was now reckoned to be earning its living, one way or another, from the motor car.

André Citroën (1878–1935)

A contemporary of William Morris, André Citroën learned early lessons of car manufacture as the man responsible for trying to reorganize the Mors company of Paris. Under his management, Mors made more cars than ever before; then Citroën left to start his own gear-cutting firm, in 1913.

Citroën saw that American production methods and French flair could make an excellent combination. The first car to bear his name, the 1919 Type A, was France's equivalent to the 'Bullnose' Morris. It was followed by the famous 5CV, and from 1925 (like Morris) Citroën adopted the Budd system of welded pressed-steel bodymaking, enabling the marque to join Peugeot and Renault at the top of the French market. Citroën also set up organizations abroad, including a British plant on Slough's new industrial estate in 1926. The small Citroën was tough and reliable. This reputation was to be emphasized in the ensuing years by some of the longest endurance tests ever run.

The key year in the history of Citroën's company was 1934, for it marked the arrival of modern styling combined with unit construction, torsion bar suspension all round, and front-wheel drive. The new car was offered initially as a four or an eight, but the latter version was dropped. The four-cylinder overhead-valve engine was later supplemented by a six-cylinder unit, however, and the remarkable *traction avant* models remained the staple product for more than 20 years. Indeed, the Citroën marque has eschewed convention ever since.

Launching the *traction* placed a heavy strain upon the company's resources, and in 1935 Citroën sold out to Michelin. He did not live to see the completion of the remarkable demonstration by François Lecot who covered 400,000 km (250,000 miles) in an 11CV in one year.

ABOVE ***Packard 1601, 1938.*** *This famous American straight-8 incorporated many alloy components and featured hydraulic brakes and independent front suspension.*

LEFT ***Franklin six-cylinder Airman, 1932.*** *These fine air-cooled cars were made in Syracuse, New York, for over 30 years. Unlike many American classics, the Franklin was not usually over-adorned and the white sidewall tyres seen here are unusual.*

With its acquisition of Dodge, the Chrysler Corporation had built itself into a strong force to complete America's Big Three. In the early 1930s its top models, 6.3-litre nine-bearing, straight-8s, were long, low and beautifully proportioned. They compared well with their V12- and V16-engined rivals, the Lincolns, the Cadillacs and the independent Packards. Everyone, however, was desperate for a share of the reduced market. The serious lull was only temporary, but its effects were to be far-reaching, not just for the specialists but for the big corporations, too. Chrysler would be the greatest sufferer, as subsequent history has shown. What Chrysler did in 1934 was very daring, even foolhardy.

Had not the investment been so great, the Chrysler and DeSoto Airflow project might not now seem so misguided. Commercially it was a failure: its revolutionary streamlined form did not appeal to the public. At the time, however, the world's industry did not query it. For example, in 1935, the first car to come from the Toyoda family's automatic loom-making works was a close copy. (The name of that car was changed to Toyota two years later, because in Japanese script this reduced the number of pen strokes from ten to eight.) In Sweden, Volvo had been producing high-quality American-style cars since 1927. When a new style was sought, local efforts to find one were unsuccessful and so the Airflow was copied. Only 500 examples of the Volvo PV36, or Carioca, were made. In Germany, where the streamline fad often went to dire extremes anyway, it did not seem too awful when Opel stepped out of line with GM by giving the Admiral an Airflow-style front end. But the 1936 Peugeot 402 was more of a surprise, proving that even France could forsake style for fashion.

Even Britain made its own version, which *Meccano Magazine* announced in December 1934 as 'an exceptionally handsome model which demonstrates excellently the principle of streamlining'. Dinky Toys, part of Meccano Ltd, chose the Airflow as its first one-piece diecast model saloon car, price 9d (just under 4p). Actually, the full-size Airflows for Britain were assembled at Kew from Canadian parts, which was normal practice.

The Chrysler and DeSoto Airflow have become collectors' favourites. In April 1934, a three-month lag from announcement to production (despite a relatively long design gestation period) was blamed for their poor reception. When they were dropped at the end of the 1937 season the Airflows had contributed nothing to Chrysler's growth. This came from the more orthodox types (like the Airstream) which fortunately Chrysler persisted with.

Having got everyone into the motor car, America was now developing the art of easing his or her lot behind the wheel, providing maximum comfort through soft springing and good sound insulation. All the major groups played a part in this process of evolution.

Meanwhile, the great individualists were on their way out. Abner Doble, the last of the true believers in steam power for the car, had to give up making his magnificent machines in 1932. As regal as any Cadillac, the Doble hid its flash boiler and its four cylinders beneath an impressive bonnet. The mighty V16 Marmon was to disappear soon after and others would tumble in a rush, including the splendid air-cooled Franklin.

Pierce-Arrow made headlines in 1933 with (only) five supposedly futuristic Silver Arrows, but these did not please the customer, who wanted his V12 to possess the patrician looks of yore – and he got them. Studebaker loosened the reins, however, and passed the Pierce-Arrow concern to a group of financiers who finally closed it down in 1938.

ABOVE RIGHT **Ford V8 'woodie', 1937.** *From 1932 the Ford V8 represented multi-cylinder motoring at bargain price. It was turned into a V12 for the 1935 Tjaarda-styled Lincoln Zephyr which, in turn, provided the clean front-end treatment for the 1937 model Ford V8s. Ford got it right where Chrysler (see lower picture) got it wrong.*

FAR RIGHT **DeSoto Airflow, 1937.** *The DeSoto name was given to the short-wheelbase versions of Chrysler's disastrous Airflow series, which lived only briefly (1934-7), yet was copied in Japan and Sweden because it was felt that America usually led the world in the popular marketing of new ideas.*

ABOVE **Cadillac V12, 1937.** *As traditional coachbuilding died out, GM used the Fisher and Fleetwood names to maintain the quality image of its prestige models.*

The beautiful Buehrig body

Difficulties also beset the mass market. Chrysler was not alone in trying to get away from the podgy look that was becoming the norm. Less drastic, yet very different from one another, were the looks of the Graham and the Hupmobile, both of them products of long-established Detroit companies. The Graham brothers were going for a performance image with their shark-nosed Supercharger Custom. The Hupmobile Aerodynamic, thanks to Raymond Loewy, had 'tunnel' headlamps and 'panoramic' three-piece windscreen in 1934. Both firms lived on borrowed time throughout the 1930s. All the right ingredients were in existence for the distinctive car these makers were seeking but, unhappily, no one had got the recipe.

The main ingredient was borrowed from Cord. With his Auburn–Cord–Duesenberg–Lycoming empire suffering, E. L. Cord had brought in Gordon Buehrig, who restyled the Auburn with simplicity and minimal chromium plate. The Cord car had already been dropped once,

and the Auburn and the Duesenberg were heading for oblivion, when Buehrig came up with the ultimate antidote to the heaviness of appearance that was besetting the average American car. The Cord marque name was restored and so revolutionary was its Buehrig bodywork with its retractable headlamps, that in May 1934 its shape actually was granted a patent. Front-wheel drive returned, and a V8 Lycoming engine was used. Later versions could be supercharged. The taut body curves (without running boards) contrasted with a clean, severe bonnet line, and the saloons and convertibles were equally distinctive to the eye.

Even the Cord could not be willed to survive, however. Like the Citroën's, its transmission would not look after itself and constant-velocity joints were often stationary ones. The electrically controlled, front-mounted gearbox was noisy and troublesome, and the body was inadequately tooled, which meant labour-intensive hand-finishing.

During a short lifespan, 1936–7, 2300 examples of the brilliant

Buehrig Cord were sold before the firm gave up. In recent times, the Auburn, the Duesenberg and the Cord have been brought back to life by enthusiastic tycoons; no one appears to have been given the same inspiration by the Airflow.

When Cord came to the end of the line, the Hupp Motor Car Corporation, which really should have been closing down, too, acquired what Buehrig saloon body dies existed and quickly designed an orthodox rear-wheel-drive car, calling it the Hupmobile Skylark. Thirty-five were made by hand before agreement was reached with near neighbour Joseph Graham, who had just injected a small fortune of his own into his Graham-Paige Motors to keep it in business. The agreement was that Graham would supply Hupp with Cord-shaped bodies for the Skylark, provided he, too, could make a car from the same dies! It would be called the Hollywood and use Graham's regular power plants – some supercharged – driving the rear wheels.

More time was lost but at last, in May 1940, nearly three years after

the Cord's demise, the beautiful new 'Buehrigs' began to appear; but it was all too late. Within six months, after only 319 had been completed, the Skylark disappeared. The war, however, enabled Hupp to survive in the accessory market. Graham, meanwhile, kept going well into 1941, making a total of 1859 Hollywoods. This firm also lived on, thanks to war contracts. The eminent historian Richard Langworth has pointed out that, after selling the remains of the car business to Kaiser-Frazer, Graham-Paige actually made more money from investment in professional athletics teams than motor car manufacture.

With the world at war once more, it was only a matter of time before the United States was involved. All the main belligerents adapted road vehicles for military use, or developed new ones – notably the Jeep.

First to come up with a lightweight four-wheel-drive field car was the Austin Seven licensee, the American Bantam Co; but Ford and Willys were the eventual producers of the Willys-designed General Purpose (GP) vehicle that gave the Jeep its name.

FAR LEFT *Cord 812 supercharged Phaeton, 1937. This example of the fabled 1935-7 series is in the Auburn-Cord-Duesenberg museum. Its Schwitzer-Cummins centrifugally supercharged Lycoming V8 engine put it in the rare 160+ km/h (100+ mph) category. There was a special magic in its unique styling by Gordon Buehrig and his team. The original plan had been to make a 'small' Duesenberg.*

ABOVE *Graham Hollywood, 1941. The superb shape of the four-door Cord sedan was not lost in this replacement for the 'shark-nosed' Graham of 1938-9.*

LEFT *Hupmobile Skylark, 1940. Hupp's general manager (former car maker Norman DeVaux) acquired the means to build Cord bodies. After the first few he enlisted Graham's cooperation, but only a few were made as Skylarks before the Hupmobile name disappeared.*

1945

The United States tried to introduce small cars, but discovered its national preference for big ones: the exceptions were the small sporting European types. The Big Three – the General Motors, Ford, and Chrysler groups – consolidated, leaving little scope for independents, for there was a price war, too. Nash rescued Hudson and they managed to soldier on together. Packard and Studebaker lived together even less happily, despite the latter company's pioneering 'European' style, which was such a refreshing break from the heavy, chromium-plated look that had spread to most American makes.

In the east, a new dawn was appearing over Japan, although few people noticed; Europe was too busy pulling itself together again. Although the Volkswagen had been readied for production before the war, it had so far been manufactured only for military purposes. In 1945 the 'Beetle' came to life under British supervision. Most German companies would continue to suffer the effects of war for a long time afterwards; a notable exception was Daimler-Benz.

Italy came to the fore in racing, with Alfa Romeo and a newcomer, Ferrari, leading the way initially, and Lancia and Maserati following; but when the Mercedes-Benz cars appeared they were always dominant. First there was the 300SL of 1952; then the W196 Grand Prix cars of 1954 and 1955, and the 300SLR of 1955.

The Jaguar was Britain's top race and rally car of the early 1950s with the fabulous C- and D-types and XK120s. Then came the brilliant years of Grand Prix racing, begun by Vanwall, and carried on by Cooper, who pioneered the modern Formula One concept. Lotus and BRM followed, and Britain was poised for a great motoring decade: the Swinging Sixties.

BEGINNING OF A NEW BOOM

1960

The immediate post-Depression years weeded out most of the American industry's born losers. Some of those skilful enough to hang on for war contracts were able to start out in business afterwards: but not necessarily in the motor industry, as we have seen.

There were still the adventurers. Failure of the Austin Seven to attract Americans did not put off Powel Crosley, who made neat miniature cars throughout the 1940s (apart from the obviously impossible years of 1943 and 1944). The Crosley was cheap and original; for a short period it had disc brakes but they had not been developed properly and were hastily deleted from the specification. The ensuing service problems helped the game little Crosley to its end in 1952.

Not quite so tiny was the 1947–51 Playboy, the brainchild of two former General Motors men who overreached themselves by anticipating a six-figure annual output for their economy car. In practice barely a hundred of these automatic transmission, three-seater roadsters left the Buffalo, New York, factory before it closed after three years: a production in no way comparable with Crosley, who built nearly 30,000 cars in 1948, his best year.

By contrast, the spectacular rear-engined Tucker and the three-wheeled, disc-braked Davis were bizarre enough to land their inventors in court, because they both pretended to have a production line going. It was a seller's market everywhere during the 1940s, but there were limits and, although their names were cleared, Gary Davis and Preston Tucker never succeeded in selling their products.

Willys-Overland, second only to Ford in the pioneering days of mass production, had spent most of the 1930s in the receiver's hands. Then came the contract for the Jeep which became the basis for a whole series of civilian vehicles for particular purposes.

Last of the big guns

Head of Willys (he dropped the Overland name) at the time of its immediate pre-war renaissance was Joseph Washington Frazer, whose former experience included periods with General Motors and Chrysler; for the latter he had thought up the best-selling Plymouth marque. As war work came to an end Frazer moved to Graham, who soon decided not to become involved in cars again. Financed by shipping magnate and aspiring car maker Henry J. Kaiser, Frazer initiated the last of the big American car corporations. Built in the Ford bomber factory at Willow Run, Michigan, the Frazer and the Kaiser were interesting cars, but never quite interesting enough: although one model, the Henry J, was even modified, renamed the Allstate and sold through the famous Sears Roebuck mail order catalogue! Kaiser-Frazer made nearly a quarter of a million cars in its finest year, 1951: better than the famous independents, Hudson, Nash and Packard, and close to style-setting Studebaker. In 1954, having ousted Frazer (the marque and the man), the Kaiser family also acquired Willys; but car buyers were still insufficiently interested and only transfers of manufacture to Argentina and Brazil was able to prevent collapse.

In 1948, Charles Nash died, George Mason took over as Nash company chief, and in 1950 revived an old marque name, Rambler, for a new 'compact'. It was Mason who enlisted the cooperation of Austin and Healey to create the Metropolitan and the Nash-Healey, and who orchestrated Nash's survival merger with Hudson. The latter company made some of America's fastest, sleekest saloons in the 1940s. They were so low that one slogan called them 'the cars you step down into'; but there was no money to retool when the time to do so was ripe. Mason was keen to increase the number of major producers from three to four and would have liked to include Packard and Studebaker in his plans, but when his American Motors Corporation was announced in January 1954, its constituents were just Hudson and Nash. Four years later AMC dropped those two famous names for good; but Rambler did well for several years.

Packard never regained its former glory despite some technical innovations, and production trickled to a halt in 1958, less than five years after it had purchased Studebaker.

Style returns to America

At Studebaker's South Bend, Indiana, works the influence of Raymond Loewy and the staff of his styling consultancy was strong. Studebaker had hit the headlines in May 1946 with the first full-width body and the panoramic rear window. Then, for 1953, came the brilliant new coupés. For sheer unadorned beauty, nothing had had such artistic appeal and individuality since the 1941 Buehrig-style Graham. This was a dream car come true. Indeed the design had started out as a 'concept only' project; its introduction took a long time and America's oldest vehicle-making company lost momentum that it would never regain. However, for the time being the 'Loewy' look encouraged Packard to join forces in 1954, and this kept Studebaker going.

The apparent coincidence of those two big 1954 mergers can probably be traced to the Detroit price war, which was particularly fierce that year and put Ford ahead of Chevrolet for the first time since its quick start of 1945–6: these two were the only brand names to have reached a regular million-plus annual sales figure, with Chrysler's Plymouth regularly in third place.

PRECEDING PAGES
Porsche 356A coupé and 356B cabriolet, 1958-60. Originally built at Gmünd in Austria in 1948, Porsche Project 356 went into production in West Germany in 1950, and such was the quality of design of this 'Super Volkswagen' that it seemed ageless when it came to the end of its road 15 years later. David Edelstein and Gordon Bond brought their cars to the once-famous Brooklands high-speed track near Weybridge, Surrey, to be photographed.

RIGHT *Chrysler convertible coupé, 1947.* This well-proportioned car shows how the revamping of pre-war styles would lead to over-decoration. Most mass-producers were culprits. (The aircraft is a Junkers Ju 52 of c. 1933, powered by three BMW engines.)

TOP **Nash 600 Airflyte, 1949.** Not quite as peculiar as the Chrysler Airflow of 15 years earlier, Nash's new Airflyte fastback styling for 1949 was also to prove a dead end. However, its curved one-piece windscreen and all-enclosed wheels were echoed a year later in the compact Rambler. Nash merged with Hudson to create American Motors in 1954.

ABOVE **Studebaker Commander Regal, 1954.** Designed by the famed Raymond Loewy studio, the 1953 and 1954 Studebaker coupés, long, low and highly individual, are considered by many to be the most beautiful cars of their day. Later models lost the clean lines. The Studebaker brothers had made their first wagons over a century earlier!

General Motors dominated the scene, with its carefully studied marque identities. Heavy styling was typified by the post-war Cadillac's twin tailfins; these had been advocated by William Mitchell, who got the idea from the Lockheed Lightning military aircraft.

More adventurous on the technical side, General Motors always held the lead in the practical research and development of transmission systems. After a brief period of semi-automatics, the Corporation had (in October 1939) announced its first fully automatic transmission; this had been available for Oldsmobile only in 1940, and Cadillac the following season. For 1949, Oldsmobile led again with the Rocket, the first of a breed of high-compression overhead-valve short-stroke V8 engines. Such was the divisional autonomy within GM that Cadillac was able to

bring out its own new V8, on similar lines, the same year.

Having recovered so well in the late 1930s, the Chrysler Corporation with its fast-selling Plymouth and Dodge ranges was well entrenched, even if its products were unexciting: except for the amusing 'Town & Country' models featuring estate car woodwork on saloons and coupés (a gimmick that Ford also took up).

The influence of ex-Studebaker stylist Virgil Exner and of Ghia in Italy helped to keep the Chrysler group up with the pace of the industry in the 1940s. From 1955, the name Imperial was given marque status, but it never approached the Cadillac for class; nor did Chrysler divisions ever achieve the consistent identity of those within General Motors, where apparent decentralization was almost a religion. On the other

ABOVE **Chevrolet Corvette, 1954.**
America's only true sports car to be made in volume was launched in 1953 with a glass-fibre body – a feature which it has retained to this day (see page 148). As a six its performance was nothing special. Soon it was given a V8, and special versions were developed by GM engineer-racer Zora Arkus-Duntov. The result was the 1963 Sting Ray.

RIGHT **Cadillac Eldorado, 1957.**
Quadruple headlamps and pillarless four-door construction were features. Costly, leaky air suspension was replaced by coil springs after four years of brave experiments. This photograph shows 1950s styling at its least appealing. Cadillac's fins were to get bigger before they got smaller. At over $13,000 this car was too expensive, even for a Cadillac.

RIGHT **Ford Thunderbird, 1957.**
Ford's response to the Corvette, first seen as an attractive two-seater for the period 1955 to 1957. The portholes at the rear *were offered for the hardtop at no extra cost. Later the Thunderbird's appearance 'went soft', and most models have been close-coupled four-seaters, for which,* *apparently, there was more demand. Ford achieved its competition results with other models.*

hand, Chrsyler was more prepared to go motor racing than GM. This is best illustrated in the assault on Le Mans by Briggs Cunningham, who did very well with two Cadillacs in 1950 but switched to Chrysler engines to power his own subsequent purpose-built cars. In 1953, a Chrysler-powered Cunningham won the first-ever World Championship sports car race at Sebring, Florida.

Ford was still essentially a family autocracy and old Henry did not give up the reins until just after VJ (Victory over Japan) day in autumn 1945 when he was 82. Then he handed over control to Henry Ford II, his grandson, who ran the business just as effectively for over 30 years.

Old Henry's son Edsel was responsible for much of the Ford development of the post-Model T era. In 1935 he had pushed through John Tjaarda's ideas for the Lincoln Zephyr, a splendid V12 which appealed in all the ways that the contemporary Chrysler and DeSoto Airflow did not. He had instigated the Continental (initially as a top Lincoln model), and in 1938 he had introduced a new market gap filler: the Mercury. Sadly, Edsel Ford died in 1943 at the age of 49, and his father took over again for a couple of years. (Ironically, one of Ford's rare marketing flops, between 1958 and 1960 was called the Edsel.)

The late pre-war Ford and Mercury V8s had Tjaarda's clean Lincoln lines and this carried over, so that early post-war Fords had a welcome simplicity about them. Thereafter the excesses of 1950s styling had to be indulged. Even Ford's Thunderbird – a real attempt at a sports car – was allowed to run to seed, leaving a clear road for the Chevrolet Corvette. On the sporting front, however, Ford ultimately taught everyone another lesson.

The sun rising

Ford and General Motors were already world names but did not always emphasize them abroad if a local title was more appealing to clients. GM created the famous Holden in 1948; this and later Australian cars have been largely for internal consumption.

Japan was always export-conscious and is today's miracle of car production. It was an American engine that powered Japan's first known car, built in 1902 by Komanosuke Uchijama and Shintaro Yoshida. These two engineers followed this with the Takuri, producing a few examples, but the indigenous *jinrikisha* – a two-wheeled carriage pulled by one man – remained Japan's regular type of personal vehicle. Many of these simple rickshaws were exported to China and elsewhere in southeast Asia by the enterprising Japanese, but the motor car itself was to be a long time in coming to Japan.

Slowly a fledgling industry emerged in which foreign influences were important. Den, Aoyama and Takeuchi (DAT) made a few cars from 1911 onwards. William Gorham, an American aero engineer, designed Gorham and Lila light cars for the Jitsuyo company of Osaka from 1920. Mitsubishi of Kobe dockyards based its earliest cars on FIAT designs, in 1917. Britain's first contribution to Japan's motor industry came in 1918 through an agreement with another shipbuilder, Ishikawajima, based at Tokyo docks, to assemble Wolseleys and distribute them in other parts of Asia.

Motoring, however, was still not integral to Japanese life when a catastrophic earthquake immobilized Tokyo in September 1923, destroying all railways and the tram and trolleybus systems. Ford, GM,

and Chrysler were on the scene quickly and, from 1923, 1925 and 1927 respectively, they sold cars and operated Japanese assembly plants. The main internal development was the merger of DAT and Jitsuyo in 1926; several years later they combined with Ishikawajima. The Datson (or 'son of D, A, and T') became the Datsun when the rising sun emblem was adopted as a symbol by Nihon Sangyo (Nissan), in whose Yokohama factory regular production of the Datsun (a copy of the Austin Seven) began in the early 1930s. From 1937, larger cars were built (on obsolete Graham-Paige tooling from Detroit) and given Nissan as a marque name, to compete with the Toyoda textile family's new Toyota car. By this time, too, Daihatsu and Mazda were making lightweight three-wheeled commercial vehicles and a young mechanic was building a racing car for himself around a discarded 8-litre Curtis-Wright aero engine. His name was Soichiro Honda.

With an industry of its own, Japan naturally placed increasing restrictions upon the American assemblers who closed down their Japanese operations in due course.

Starting from scratch again after World War 2, Japanese industry came under the Allied Occupation Authority, which allowed only 300 private cars to be made annually from 1947. This restriction was lifted in

TOP **Exports, 1948.** American Packard and British Rover make strange bedfellows somewhere in the Southern Hemisphere.

ABOVE **Datsun 15, four-cylinder, 722 cc.** This 1935 model was resurrected after the war. Later, Austins were built in Japan.

TOP RIGHT **Volvo PV444, 1944-58.** As a neutral country, Sweden was first to introduce a post-war car. This Volvo was tough and, from 1956, powerful. An estate car version was still in production in 1969.

RIGHT **Saab 92 two-stroke two-cylinder, 1947.** This prototype led to three-cylinder models of 750 and 850 cc. In its final form, 1967-79, this fast, front-wheel-drive model had a German Ford V4 engine.

October 1949 and for over a decade Japan struggled to rebuild, generally leaning on foreign technology. Hino and Isuzu emerged during the war, companies with their origins in the old DAT-Ishikawajima set-up; their first cars were licence-built Renault 4CVs and Hillman Minxes respectively. Nissan revamped the small pre-war Datsun and assembled the new Austin A40 Somerset and its successor, the A40/50 Cambridge.

The Prince (named after Crown Prince Akihito) was produced in the Tachikawa aircraft works from 1952. A new name, it would spearhead Japan's march into Europe before being absorbed into Nissan-Datsun.

Most distinctly Japanese was the Toyota Type SA (or Toyopet on its home market), built in small numbers during the restricted period. By 1952, however, Toyota was expanding and exporting at a rate that would have surprised Europe had it not been too busy putting its own business life together again to notice.

Emerging nations
Although most industrial nations assembled trucks, few had need of a full-scale motor industry. China fulfilled its needs by copying American cars. India's Hindusthans were Morrises and Studebakers.

Russia had dabbled in car making in Tsarist days, when a number of exotic western European makes had been imported. Modern manufacture had begun with the 1928–30 Nami. It was followed by the 1932 GAZ: essentially a Ford, built at the Molotov motor works in Gorky with technical help from Detroit. In 1946 Gorky introduced its Victory (or Pobieda) model; it was succeeded by the Volga in 1955. The Pobieda became Poland's Warszawa, while the 1947 Moskvich was pure Opel Kadett in appearance: this was not surprising, for the Russians had taken the dies home with them from Germany in 1945 as war reparations.

Of all the western European countries, Sweden was better placed than most to maintain research and development programmes during the war years (but in any case those at war were less ready to admit to civilian activities).

In 1944 Volvo held a motor show in Stockholm. Like most European countries, Sweden had stayed mobile with the help of producer gas units to replace petrol. Now it was ready to announce Europe's first definitive post-war car, and such was its combination of American and German features that it established a character all of its own. Modelled on the last pre-war Hanomag and looking like a scaled-down American fast-back Ford or Mercury, the PV444 was to take the name of Volvo – which few

people yet knew – to the markets of the world (see page 90).

The Volvo was a rear-wheel-drive, four-cylinder car of normal layout, but its local rival was a complete contrast. Rasmussen's DKW had always been a popular small car and two Swedish companies set out to copy it in the mid-1940s. One was the former Chrysler assembler Philipson, who announced a front-wheel-drive two-stroke saloon in 1946 but took matters no further. The other was the Svenska Aeroplan AB (Swedish Aeroplane Company) whose early three-cylinder Saab paved the way for international success.

Because of its thousands of kilometres of unmade oiled-gravel roads, Scandinavia was to originate the modern special-stage type of rally, which requires a particular breed of car and driver. Both Volvo and Saab proved themselves in these conditions and others learned from them.

Revival in Germany

Recovery of the countries at the heart of the battle zones was varied. Germany was split in two and the Volkswagen works at Wolfsburg, just west of the new artificial frontier near Helmstedt, thus came under British control from 1945 to 1949. The Volkswagen had been produced in various military forms under Hitler; now it provided civilian-type transport for the occupation forces. Its toughness and its unprepossessing looks were to make the 'Beetle' a hit, unparalleled in the history of motoring.

Its creator, Dr Ferdinand Porsche, was interned by the French. Soon

after his release, he was able to share with his son and namesake the pleasure of witnessing the completion of a small sports car at their new headquarters in Gmünd, Austria. It was the 356th design from the Porsche drawing board. Not before time, it was to bear the name of the man who had done so much creative engineering for other firms in his life. The Porsche 356 was developed for two more years in Austria before the younger Porsche returned to Stuttgart to put it into production. The 'Super Volkswagen' has come along way since then.

In starting up after the war Porsche was the exception rather than the rule. The number of car makers was dwindling and among those not to re-emerge from the war were Adler, who did make some more motorcycles, and Hanomag, whose 1951 front-wheel-drive Partner remained a prototype only.

There was a spate of shortlived bubblecars including three from German aircraft engineers: Heinkel, Messerschmitt and Dornier; the last-named was made by Zündapp and called Janus (after the two-faced Roman god) because it looked virtually symmetrical. NSU and BMW built motorcycles again before returning to cars; the latter firm was especially unlucky, for the Munich headquarters were now cut off from Eisenach by the new frontier. Eventually, Munich got under way with the 501 saloon and the beautiful and expensive 503 and 507 coupés; but even the licensed manufacture of Isetta bubblecars and BMW's own derivatives from them could not prevent BMW finishing the 1950s very shakily indeed. Meantime, after spending several years adapting the pre-war BMW 327 (as the EMW), Eisenach switched to DKW-type two-stroke miniatures: as did the famous Audi-Horch works in Zwickau, leaving the East Germans little choice in their personal transport. Geographical demarcation meant that all the Auto Union plants were nationalized: so Auto Union started up again in Düsseldorf, then moved to Ingolstadt, making a series of modernized DKWs.

With patrician certainty, it was Daimler-Benz who strode back with most confidence. The pre-war 170 had been sluggish on the road but solidly modern in design and very well made; and in 1947 it was being produced again.

The three-pointed star

Hans Nibel had died before the war but Fritz Nallinger and Rudolf Uhlenhaut continued the Daimler-Benz tradition admirably, and within five years had produced not only the larger 220 and 300 models, but also the unique 300SL 'gull-wing' coupé. It was runner-up in its first race, the 1952 Mille Miglia, and went on to win Le Mans and the Carrera Panamericana that year on good performance plus sheer reliability and

Ferdinand Porsche (1875–1951)

Born in Liberec (formerly Reichenberg), in what is now northwest Czechoslovakia, Ferdinand Porsche has gone down in history as the most inventive of Europe's great motor engineers. His father was a tinsmith, and he himself was clearly of an engineering turn of mind.

For many years he worked in and around Vienna, first as an electrical engineer and then as designer of Jacob Lohner's first petrol-electric vehicles. His first orthodox design work was with Austro-Daimler, where his attention to detail was to be seen in a variety of new models. These included the successful Sascha, with which Alfred Neubauer (later to run the Mercedes-Benz racing team) won his class in the 1922 Targa Florio. However, a cutback in its competition programme by Austro-Daimler soon contributed to Porsche's departure for Mercedes.

A later spell at Steyr ended his second 'Austrian

period' during the Depression, when he set up in business in Stuttgart as a freelance designer. He worked on many projects for Austrian, French, Italian and Swedish companies, but turned down

the invitation to settle in Russia designing cars. Instead he created for Germany two of the most celebrated of all machines: the first Grand Prix Auto Union and the Volkswagen. Inevitably the Porsche engineering studios became involved in the war effort. Late in the war, under increasing Allied attack, Porsche was able to move from Stuttgart to Gmünd, Austria, where his son, Ferdinand Porsche Junior, revived the racing car design work with the fascinating flat-12 Cisitalia project; all the while, there was the dream of a sports car bearing the name Porsche. Ferdinand Senior took considerable interest in it. The first of 50 early Porsche 356s ran in 1948, and in 1950 full-scale production began in Stuttgart. Soon afterwards Ferdinand Porsche died, aged 76; he had never recovered fully from the effect of his internment by the French after the war. The progress of the name Porsche has, however, remained a strong and continuous thread throughout the history of the 20th-century car.

FAR LEFT, CENTRE *Volkswagen 'Beetle', 1945.* Hitler announced the project as the KdF-Wagen or Strength-through-Joy car but the world called it the 'Beetle'. Still built in Central and South America, it is the only model of car to have passed the production milestone of 20 million. Although there had been other engineers with similar thoughts on a 'people's car' in the early 1930s, especially in Central Europe, Dr Porsche was the VW's undisputed creator.

ABOVE *BMW 503, 3.2-litre V8, 1956.* Because its car-building plant at Eisenach was in East Germany, BMW's post-war recovery in Munich was slow, and the 501 saloon was not produced in quantity until late 1952. The 1956-9 BMW 503 and 507 were styled by Albrecht Goertz. Beautiful coupés are still c BMW speciality today.

RIGHT *Citroën 2CV, 1959.* First seen in 1939, this remarkable car is still going strong. This one dates from the 1950s.

ABOVE **Targa Florio, 1955.** *Despite an excursion into a field, resulting in some extra work at this pit stop, Stirling Moss won the harsh, hot Sicilian road race for Mercedes-Benz. His co-driver in the 300SLR was Peter Collins. With help from Denis Jenkinson and John Fitch, Moss also scored victories in the Mille Miglia and the Tourist Trophy respectively, ensuring that the Mercedes-Benz 300SLR would be the champion sports car of that year.*

FAR RIGHT **Mercedes-Benz 300SL, 1955.** *First seen in 1952, when it scored several remarkable race wins (including Le Mans), the 300SL was later offered both in 'gull-wing' form (seen here in the Daimler-Benz museum) and as a convertible.*

GRAND PRIX DE PAU

ABOVE **Poster by 'Geo Ham'.** *Georges Hamel (1900-72) was one of the great motoring artists, influenced by Britain's F. Gordon Crosby.*

strength. Engineering excellence was matched by brilliant organization and tactics, and so the factory did not contest the 1953 season's big events. Instead, the 300SL was transformed into a superb road-going car, the first to have direct fuel injection as standard in place of the traditional carburettor.

In the same year, 1954, the Mercedes-Benz Formula One Grand Prix car was reborn. It was sensational in both its forms: fully enveloping for fast circuits, open-wheeled for tighter ones, not graceful, yet very impressive. The technical specification was the exciting part. The twin-overhead camshaft straight-8 engine had Bosch fuel injection and the valves were opened and closed mechanically. (Normally, valves are closed by the action of strong coil springs, which could cause the valves to 'bounce' at high revolutions.) The crankshaft and connecting rods ran in roller bearings. For a 2½-litre power unit to produce over 250 bhp in 1954 was a fine achievement. To keep the bonnet height down, the unit was tilted through more than 50 degrees from the vertical. Rear brakes were inboard and the five-speed gearbox was in unit with the final drive. As usual with Mercedes-Benz cars, suspension was independent all round; the swing axle rear meant that only the greatest drivers would be able to extract the full potential of the Type 196. Racing chief Alfred

Neubauer dealt with this problem by engaging the best driver of that time, Juan Manuel Fangio, who took the 1954 and 1955 World Championships.

In the second year, Britain's top driver Stirling Moss joined the team and was runner-up to Fangio. Also in 1955 Daimler-Benz took the remarkable step of contesting the World Sports Car Championship – and winning it. In this form of racing, Moss showed his mastery by winning the Mille Miglia, the Targa Florio and Ulster's Tourist Trophy race with the new Mercedes-Benz 300SLR, a 3-litre sports-racer closely related to the GP car. Its only 'un-Mercedes' feature was a huge airbrake, intended to assist the wheel brakes at the end of long straights; drum brakes were still almost universal, and they were prone to fade and wear quickly under extreme conditions.

There were several bad racing accidents in 1955, the worst of which occurred at Le Mans. Veteran driver Pierre Levegh's 300SLR hit a much slower car which had swerved; this launched the Mercedes into the air to land on the barriers and disintegrate in flames, killing many spectators, and Levegh. The repercussions reverberated around the world. Daimler-Benz pulled the remaining cars out of the event, and withdrew from racing at the end of that sad year, as had probably been

planned from the outset. The company went racing for business and did so on the very sound principle that when you are at the top there is only one direction to go. As a high-speed rally car, however, the 300SL continued to prove a winner with fine victories in the strenuous Acropolis and Liège–Rome–Liège events.

Fabulous Ferrari

Until the Mercedes-Benz return, post-war GP racing had been dominated by Italy. Alfa Romeo's 1½-litre supercharged 158 and 159, although designed over ten years before, had been revamped and were still invincible when, in 1950, the regular team drivers, Giuseppe Farina, Fangio and Luigi Fagioli, took the top three places in the first official World Drivers' Championship. In 1951 Fangio was a clear winner but Alberto Ascari and José Froilan Gonzalez, who came second and third, were driving very competitive cars by the end of the season: the badge, a prancing horse; the name, Ferrari!

It can be said with reason that motoring would not be the same without Ferrari; in the case of motor racing, it can be said with certainty.

There had been a similar feeling about Bugatti: an all-pervading sense that at the drop of Ettore Bugatti's famous bowler hat another magical masterpiece could be conjured up for the next race or motor show.

Few people had noticed the two unnamed sports cars that had led their class before retiring from the 1940 Mille Miglia. After all, Europe was at war by then. Those cars had no name, except the type number, 815, but they had been made by Auto Avio Costruzioni, a new machine-tool company formed by Enzo Ferrari. As soon as the war was over, Ferrari turned his attention to sports and racing car manufacture and success was immediate. With top engineers of the calibre of Gioacchino Colombo (the man behind the 158 Alfa Romeo) and former Isotta-Fraschini engineer Aurelio Lampredi, failure was unlikely. When Ferrari is not winning, it is regrouping for the next assault. Ferrari is a cult; Ferrari *is* Italy.

With such a bright star in the firmament it is easy to overlook the third great Italian competition car, the Maserati, which had been a serious contender since its birth in the 1920s. Its finest hour did not come until 1957, when Fangio took his fifth and final world title at the age of 46, driving the 250F model. This was just before Maserati began to cut back after overreaching itself in a way that Mercedes-Benz would never do. In sports car racing, the overall reputation of Maserati was fast, but fragile over long distances. Maserati never won at Le Mans; but then, neither did Lancia, which joined the fray briefly in the fabulous 1950s, gaining several sports car victories. The 1954 Lancia D50 Grand Prix car was designed by the veteran Jano to beat Mercedes-Benz, and was fast enough to do so. Before the project had really warmed up, however, Lancia was taken over by new management, which decided to cut costs by passing the competition cars to Ferrari. Rebuilt by Ferrari, these cars proved winners in 1956.

Jano's greatest practical design for Lancia was the 1950 Aurelia which, in B20 coupé form, is considered to be the original yardstick for the term *Gran Turismo*. The same year saw Alfa Romeo's first mass-production models arrive; four years later, the delightful 1.3-litre Giulietta from the drawing board of Orazio Satta would captivate enthusiasts worldwide.

ABOVE **Alfa Romeo 159, 1951.** *Two-stage supercharging gave the final version of the Alfetta well over 400 bhp and frightening fuel consumption. The swinging axles were replaced by a de Dion rear end. Juan Manuel Fangio's brilliance was the other major factor that made 1951 a great year. The five times champion is seen here in the British GP at Silverstone.*

TOP RIGHT **Ferrari 375, 1950-1.** *José Froilan Gonzalez of the Argentine gave the 4½-litre Ferrari its first victory when he beat his compatriot Fangio (see Alfa Romeo 159 picture above) at Silverstone in July 1951.*

RIGHT **Alfa Romeo 158, 1946-50.** *Designed by Gioacchino Colombo for the pre-war 'second division', the Alfetta became the premier GP car of the period immediately afterwards.*

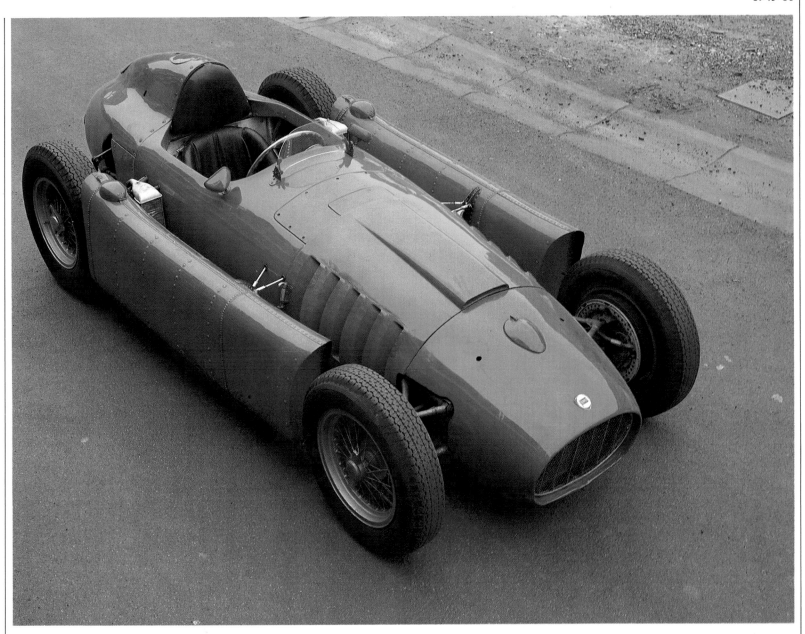

ABOVE **Maserati 250F, 1954-7.** A development rather than a new design, this was the most successful Maserati ever. It gave Fangio his fifth (and fourth successive) World Drivers' Championship in 1957 when his drive in the German GP alone proved him the undisputed king.

ABOVE **Lancia D50, 1954-5.** This was the first and only Lancia F1 GP car, and was designed by Jano for the new, 1954, formula. It had a four-overhead camshaft 2¹/₂-litre unsupercharged V8 engine, which proved as powerful as the all-conquering Mercedes-Benz W196's straight-8. Unfortunately its début was delayed until late 1954. Alberto Ascari scored two wins in non-Championship races in 1955, then crashed into the harbour while leading the Monaco GP. Shortly afterwards, while driving a different car, the popular champion was killed; so was the Lancia team's spirit. Gianni (son of Vincenzo) Lancia relinquished control and the Lancia GP car project was placed in Ferrari's care. With several modifications, including removal of the fuel-carrying sponsons, the 'Lancia-Ferrari' gave Fangio the 1956 World Championship.

FIAT recovered well to provide bread-and-butter motoring for post-war Italy, whereas the great Isotta-Fraschini went into liquidation in 1949, two years after announcing the big Monterosa, which had swing axles and a 3½-litre V8 engine at the rear: not quite like anything else except, perhaps, a super-Tatra.

FIAT maintained its ties abroad, although in France Simca (the Société Industrielle de Mécanique et Carosserie Automobile), which had assembled FIATs since 1935, was soon acquiring a character of its own with the 1951 Aronde. On the sporting side, Amédée Gordini's Simcas soon changed their name to his.

It was not a comfortable recovery for France. Louis Renault went to prison after the liberation of Paris in 1944 after being accused of collaborating with the occupying Germans. He died soon afterwards. The little Volkswagen-inspired Renault 4CV, which had been running in prototype form in January 1943, became the staple product as the great factories were brought to life as state property: the Régie Nationale des Usines Renault.

Peugeot's first new car was the fast-back 203 saloon, which stayed in production throughout the 1950s. Its excellence can be judged by the frequency with which it can still be seen in use in rural France.

The familiar four- and six-cylinder Citroëns were supplemented by the ultra-utility flat twin 2CV, also with front-wheel drive. Perhaps the most timeless of all cars, it poses the question: what is class? The *deux chevaux* seems as much at home today in London's West End as it does when trying to look like a corrugated French farm shed.

Of all the other once-great French marques, only Panhard was to survive into the 1960s. The Société des Anciens Etablissements Panhard et Levassor had kept its sleeve-valve six-cylinder engines and its weird styling right through to 1939. Meanwhile, J. A. Grégoire had been working on a number of new ideas, among them the secret 1942 Aluminium Français–Grégoire, a small front-wheel-drive saloon which Grégoire nearly sold to Australia and Britain. In the end, it was Panhard who decided to make this neat lightweight saloon, calling it the Dyna. Various sports versions were made and the Dyna changed the Panhard's image almost overnight. A fascinating scheme, which never saw the light of day, was the possible adoption of the Dyna by Daimler of Coventry: a company that had first copied Panhard cars in 1897.

Hotchkiss and Delahaye won several early post-war Monte Carlo Rallies but they, and Delage, all gave up manufacture by the mid-1950s, all under the Hotchkiss roof. The Hispano-Suiza never reappeared, although a corner of the former Barcelona works was used from 1951 to 1958 to make a magnificent V8 GT car, the Pegaso. That artistic oddity, the Voisin, disappeared too, but Gabriel Voisin did design the little Biscuter for Spain's Autonacional company. As for Bugatti, the marque did reappear briefly, but the master (who died in 1947) would not have been happy with the results. An equally unhappy newcomer was the Chrysler-powered Facel Vega hybrid. The smaller Facellia was pretty, but would not sell either.

Austerity Britain
For Britons, the return to peace from 1945 was slow and painful.

People in Britain had become used to a fairly heavy tax on cars, but commodity prices in the post-Depression 1930s had been low. Motoring became affordable for many. Petrol, although admittedly low octane by then, could be bought for 1s 6d (7.5p) a gallon in 1939. This was the fuel in the pumps at the beginning of the war when the oil companies pooled their supplies: hence the term Pool petrol. It had been even cheaper in the untaxed 1920s when a gallon of Russian fuel could be had for 9d, or less than 4p! Until 20 May 1950, fuel was rationed.

The old 'horsepower' tax remained a British anomaly until it was dropped (for new cars at least) in 1946, the year in which a 'Covenant' scheme was introduced to try and prevent a black market in new cars. Purchase tax had been introduced at one-third of cost in 1940, but jumped to its highest rate of two-thirds (66.7%) six years after the war in 1951. Purchase tax would fluctuate over the ensuing years until VAT ('value added' tax) was introduced in 1973, bringing Britain into line with the other countries in the Common Market.

Some British manufacturers survived through the 1930s only to reach crisis point in 1939. Two good examples were Triumph and SS Cars Ltd (soon to be renamed Jaguar, to avoid any possible confusion with the German significance of those initials).

William Lyons's company had had a difficult year in 1937–8, as it

ABOVE LEFT *Lancia Aurelia GT, from 1951.* *This great Italian race, rally, and road car – the two-door version of the Aprilia's successor – was called the Gran Turismo model and lived up to the name. The term 'GT' is used indiscriminately these days and has therefore become devalued. You have to look back at the Lancia in order to remember that the term was meant to describe the total design concept of the car.*

LEFT *Ferrari 250GT short-wheelbase Berlinetta, 1959.* 'GT' *with the accent on the competition side. It is difficult to imagine a more nearly perfect form – until you consider its 1962 development, the GTO! Such cars give the word 'classic' some value. This car was provided by Vic Norman.*

converted from coachbuilding to pressed-steel body making techniques, but 1938–9 had seen a record output of more than 5000 SS Jaguars. There was still no full-scale machine shop when war was declared, and for a few months it looked as if the whole factory might have to be shut down. Almost forgotten, in a small bay of Lyons's old shell-filling factory, Swallow Sidecars Ltd had continued in production throughout the 1930s and, at the crucial moment, the manager Howard Davies (once famous for his own make of motorcycle, the HRD) obtained a military order for 10,000 Swallow sidecars. Thus galvanized, the firm's doors stayed open; more contracts were soon obtained, mainly for aircraft components and, later, repair work. New workshops were built, machinery was acquired. Here was an example of war work ultimately helping a company recover some of its six 'lost' years.

Nearby Triumph was less lucky in the long run, although it had been part of the Coventry scene far longer than SS. In 1936 the car and motorcycle businesses had separated and the 1938–9 Dolomite with its 'waterfall' grille cut quite a dash in a land where the traditional radiator cowl still held sway. Nevertheless, Triumph had gone into receivership and was purchased in September 1939 by the Sheffield engineering firm of Thomas Ward who had kept it going with aero-engine work.

William Lyons had been offered Triumph but turned it down. Sir John Black of Standard (he had been knighted for his services to the industry, particularly in the 'shadow' factory scheme that made such a contribution to war production) still wanted to have a share in the Jaguar enterprise which his cooperation had made possible; the answer remained negative and the furious Black told Lyons he would put him out of business. In late 1944, Black bought the Triumph Motor Company, thus creating the first of the post-war groups, Standard-Triumph.

The first of the new

It was another Coventry firm, Armstrong Siddeley, that was first to announce its post-war programme with its elegant but underpowered Hurricane and Lancaster: names recalling the famous aircraft its related companies had been making. Later came the excellent Sapphire, but the marque's life ended in 1960.

Only three completely new major makers got started, each the product of an arch-enthusiast. Sydney Allard had put his name to a number of pre-war 'specials'; the Allard car with its choice of big American engines and divided front axle was to provide spectacular entertainment for enthusiasts. Allard himself proved his car's worth by taking a third place at Le Mans in 1950 and winning the 1952 Monte Carlo Rally. Former Monte Carlo Rally winner Donald Healey had been engineer-in-charge at Triumph, then he moved to Rootes; but it was a Riley engine he chose for his shapely Warwick-built Healey car of 1946. Later, some Alvis and Nash engines were used. Manufacture at Warwick ended in 1954, soon after conclusion of a deal between Healey and Austin chief Leonard Lord to make sports cars at Longbridge. The Austin-Healey would become a classic of its kind.

The third of the newcomers was the Bristol, originally called the Frazer Nash–Bristol, which began as a British reincarnation of Fritz Fiedler's sporting six-cylinder BMW 327. Fiedler himself was released from captivity to help get the project under way, but was in fact based at Frazer Nash. The old chain-drive Frazer Nash sports car was produced throughout the 1930s and sold alongside 'anglicized' BMWs by the Aldington brothers. They managed to obtain a streamlined 1940 Mille Miglia BMW 328 when with the Allied forces in Germany. This car became the basis for a post-war Frazer Nash.

In Coventry and elsewhere some specialists did not modernize quickly enough to expand and survive. Alvis produced nice cars to the end; but Lea-Francis, which had always made good-looking cars, sang its swansong in 1960 with an artless Ford-powered open car called

ABOVE *Armstrong Siddeley Hurricane, 1951. Introduced as a 2-litre, the attractive post-war range was still very underpowered when enlarged to 2.3 litres. Its successor, the Sapphire (1953 to 1960), was fast and good-looking, but could not save this great Coventry marque.*

William Morris, Lord Nuffield
(1877–1963)

Britain's first motor magnate to be created a baron, William Richard Morris began his career by mending bicycles in the 1890s. Construction of bicycles and motorcycles followed, and in 1911 he opened his redeveloped premises in Oxford as The Morris Garage. A second site led to creation of Morris Garages and W.R.M. Motors; the latter was to become Morris Motors, famed for the first Morris car, the distinctive 'Bullnose'.

Made largely from proprietary parts, the Morris was Britain's biggest-selling car of the 1920s, often with well over one-third of the total market.

The Morris Garages business was turned into the M.G. sports car company, under Cecil Kimber;

Wolseley was acquired in 1927, Riley in 1938. Lord Nuffield, as Morris became in 1934, also bought up suppliers' businesses to ensure long-term control. One of his most far-sighted moves was to work with the patentee of pressed-steel bodywork in America, Edward Budd; the result was the Pressed Steel Company, with a factory alongside his own at Oxford.

Lord Nuffield, with no family of his own, was famous for his huge gifts to charity. Like many successful men he was also known for being difficult to work with. One of his most unfortunate losses was of Leonard Lord, the colleague who in 1938 went to Austin. When the British Motor Corporation was formed, Lord was the top man. Lord Nuffield retired quietly and sadly.

Leaf-Lynx. The spares and the name were bought by engineer-enthusiast Barrie Price who as recently as 1980 made an eye-catching Jaguar-engined Lea-Francis sports car, in the hope that it would be a prototype rather than a 'one-off'.

Daimler was still the Royal marque, producing staid yet splendid straight-8s and -6s, but reaching the headlines at motor show time through the spectacular creations of Sir Bernard and Lady Docker, who went in for the unashamed luxury of gold and silver plate. Attempts to produce new Daimler cars with Panhard or General Motors cooperation came to nothing. The post-war Lanchester was a limousine in miniature but there was not a big enough market to sustain it. After an abortive attempt to introduce the intriguing Hobbs Mechamatic (positively controlled automatic) transmission, the revered name of Lanchester disappeared from all car badges in 1956. Daimler struggled on, spurred by the performance potential of two new V8 engines. Perhaps these (and a new rear-engined double-decker bus chassis) would encourage someone to buy the famous old firm as a going concern?

To many, the prettiest of all the new cars was the 1946 Riley saloon. It seemed to enthusiasts to indicate that the Nuffield Group really did want to maintain the idea of the slogan: 'As old as the industry, as modern as

TOP **Morris Minor, from 1948.** *Like most important post-war designs, the Morris Minor (instigated by Miles Thomas, engineered by Alec Issigonis) began to take shape during the early days of the war. Instead of the flat-four engine Issigonis wanted, the old 918 cc side-valve power unit (copied by Morris from that of the* Ford Y-type) was substituted. In its final form, the much-loved Minor had an 1100 cc overhead valve unit. Although production ceased in the early 1970s, people still go to specialists and trade in for, effectively, brand-new cars; such is the cult of the Minor.

ABOVE **Standard Vanguard, 1951.** *Unashamedly American in style, the 2.1-litre overhead valve four-cylinder Standard Vanguard represented a positive one-model policy for the long-established Coventry firm run by Sir John Black.*

ABOVE **Bentley Continental by H. J. Mulliner, 1954.** *Following the winding-up of Bentley Motors in 1931, Rolls-Royce technology and craftsmanship went into a new style of Bentley, from 1933, dubbed the 'Silent Sports Car'. The theme was continued from 1951, with the high-geared 190 km/h (120 mph) R-type Continental. This example is from the Nigel Dawes collection and dates from 1954.*

LEFT **Bristol 400, 1950.** *The Aldingtons intervened as members of the British forces to secure BMW designs (including the famous 2-litre cross-pushrod engine) and top designer Fritz Fiedler for Britain – as a form of war reparations. Introduced in 1946 as the Frazer Nash-Bristol, this beautifully built and expensive car developed by the Bristol Aeroplane Co started a highly specialized marque which lives today. It makes interesting comparison with the BMW 327 on page 72.*

the hour'. They should have known better. Already masters of badge engineering, Nuffield soon entangled its marques once more, Riley and Wolseley being the first major sufferers. M.G. sports cars were, however, permitted to develop along traditional lines and made a long-term hit on the North American market. The other Nuffield sensation was the Morris Minor, designed by Alec Issigonis. Although not produced exactly as he wanted, the Minor would become the most-loved of post-war small cars, defying all attempts to oust it from the catalogues.

Leonard Lord, who had transferred his allegiance from Nuffield to Austin in 1938, was very much in charge at Longbridge and trying hard to match Nuffield's variety. Austin was certainly ahead in limousines, producing not only the Sheerline but the Princess, a product of the British Vanden Plas coachbuilding firm in which it took a controlling interest.

Not all small coachbuilders were as fortunate, but well-founded ones had other irons in the fire. For example, Patrick Motors, who had provided special bodies for Austin, Triumph, Wolseley and others, had seen the warnings in the 1930s. More and more popular makes were going over to all-steel construction and there would not be room for everyone indefinitely. Patrick diversified into aviation and, as motoring returned, expanded its garage network. For Patrick Motors, still a family business, diversity has paid off.

Longbridge's first fully integral model, the Austin A30 (called the Seven initially), immediately preceded the surprise announcement in 1952 that Austin would merge with the Nuffield Group. The British Motor Corporation would change the face of motoring in Britain.

In Coventry, the Rootes Group updated the Hillman and the Humber ranges. In the mid-1950s the name Talbot was dropped from Sunbeam-Talbot; soon afterwards the Singer Company, following the failure of its post-war range, was taken over.

Standard-Triumph established clearer identities. The American-looking Vanguard was, for five years, the only new Standard; smaller models came along in 1953. The post-war Triumphs were unusual in style – the whims of Sir John Black. Two of them, the razor-edged Renown and the rounded Roadster, attracted favourable comment and sales; the Mayflower's mixture of curves and straight lines did not. The TR sports cars that followed these oddities were, by contrast, international image builders. The autocratic Sir John Black had been forced to retire by then and from 1954 Standard-Triumph was led by Alick Dick.

Rover, another of the Coventry firms, continued to be thoroughly

independent. It transferred production to its wartime Solihull factory in 1945; and the company that had started with bicycles now added gas turbine research to its many accomplishments.

Rolls-Royce and Bentley cars remained similar to one another until 1951, when the magnificent R-type Continental was introduced as a Bentley only, as a reminder of that marque's sporting heritage.

The early post-war Vauxhalls were disappointing, giving no promise of the great cars that were one day to come from General Motors' British offshoot. Ford of Dagenham led the economy car field with the Anglia (later the Popular), which was really the old Ford Eight dressed up a little. It cost £293 including tax in 1948, when an Austin A40 Devon was listed at £416, a Slough-built Citroën Light 15 at £729, and the lovely 2½-litre Riley at £1125: halfway between the 2½- and 3½-litre Jaguars.

Jowett continued to produce its traditional two-cylinder utilities as Bradfords, and came out with the promising Javelin and Jupiter flat-4s; but they never gained sufficient public confidence, and the marque died. Industrialist David Brown purchased Aston Martin's few assets; then he bought Lagonda as well. W. O. Bentley and a small team had already established the design for a 2½-litre six-cylinder luxury Lagonda with all-independent suspension. Brown provided the cash for it to proceed, and made use of the engine for a new generation of Aston Martins. A prototype four-cylinder sports car won the 1948 Spa 24-hour race in Belgium, and soon afterwards the glorious DB2 coupé was proving its

RIGHT **Riley 1½-litre, 1954.** Rileys were good-looking and sporting until the Nuffield takeover of 1938, which led to a characterless 1939 model. However, there must have been ructions behind the scenes during the war, for September 1945 saw the arrival of a highly individual new model with torsion-bar independent front suspension. This 1½-litre model was supplemented by a 2½-litre a year later. This mid-1950s example, from the Patrick Collection, has the later front wing-line (running boards deleted) but was still lovely to look at, and refined to drive. The Riley name continued, but this was the last car to have traditional Riley character.

speed and reliability in the toughest events. Styled by Frank Feeley, who had done much for Lagonda before the war, the DB2 scored at Le Mans, in the Mille Miglia, the TT, the Alpine Trial and many other classics, including the RAC Rally which it won outright in 1956. Success breeds success, and David Brown launched into a full racing programme, the main object being to win the Le Mans 24-hour race; but bad luck plagued the team there, until 1959. Then the 3-litre DBR1 of Roy Salvadori and Carroll Shelby not only won Le Mans but, thanks to Stirling Moss's brilliance, took the World Sports Car Championship as well. Apart from the Mercedes year, it was the only time Ferrari ever forfeited that title.

Britain's sporting lead

It was the Jaguar that assumed the mantle of Le Mans victor in the 1950s, taking five wins in all, with the famous C-type and D-type. Jaguar introduced its new twin-overhead camshaft six-cylinder sports car, the XK120, as a virtual mock-up for the first post-war London show, in 1948; within a year, however, its speed capabilities had been demonstrated on the Belgian motorway (long before Britain had one) and won its first race at Silverstone, a carefully chosen former airfield, now one of the fastest Grand Prix circuits anywhere.

Jaguar shone not only in racing but in rallying, outperforming the field in the Monte Carlo, Alpine, Tulip, Acropolis, Liège–Rome–Liège and RAC rallies. Outstanding performer was Ian Appleyard, who won five Alpine Cups in Jaguars, an unequalled tally on one of the toughest events on the calendar.

Meanwhile, Jaguar sales rocketed. Stirling Moss and Mike Hawthorn both drove for the Jaguar team. If Moss was Britain's uncrowned king of racing in the 1950s, Hawthorn was the man who achieved the title. In 1958 – the year of Fangio's retirement – driving for Vanwall and Ferrari respectively, Moss and Hawthorn made it a needle match for the drivers' crown; Hawthorn took it by one point. It was not just that British drivers had 'arrived'. A British car, Tony Vandervell's Vanwall, had become the winner of the manufacturers' championship.

Britain's rise to Grand Prix supremacy

The Vanwall's success marked the end of an era and the beginning of a new one for Britain in motor racing.

While Italy was dominating the scene in Grands Prix, followed by Germany in 1954 and 1955, Jaguar's Le Mans performances remained the outstanding British victories. Formula Two did, however, provide smaller companies with the opportunity of becoming competitive; three

makes showed potential here: Connaught, Cooper and HWM. Yet it was another make, Vanwall, that came virtually from nowhere to lead the British assault on Grand Prix racing. In 1957, the high-tailed flyer took three championship races; in 1958 six of eleven title events were won (three each by Stirling Moss and the quiet, underrated Tony Brooks) and the newly instituted Championship of Makes was Vanwall's.

Although the new champion, Mike Hawthorn (assisted by Phil Hill of the United States), made sure that his team was second among the manufacturers, it was a sad year for Ferrari, for the great drivers Peter Collins and Luigi Musso lost their lives. It was another British make, Cooper, that came third and shared the British limelight with the triumphant Vanwall.

Charles Cooper and his son John had led the early post-war movement to provide cheap motor racing, with their rear-engined 500 cc single-seaters; this was 'Formula Three', which proved so successful that it became an official international category. The Coopers made front-engined sports and Formula Two cars, then reverted to a rear engine for their 1955 central-seat sports-racer. Its Coventry Climax

ABOVE **Aston Martin DB2, 1950.** This famous car began with the Claude Hill-designed four-cylinder 2-litre engine before being fitted with one of the first 'W. O. Bentley' (ex-Lagonda) 2.6-litre twin-cam sixes for development purposes. The car was crashed by Godsal in the 1952 Alpine Trial, but its Frank Feeley-designed body looks as purposeful today (in the Nigel Dawes collection) as ever.
LEFT **Vanwall at Monza.** The 1957 and 1958 Italian Grands Prix were dominated by the Vanwall. Stirling Moss won in 1957, and Tony Brooks in 1958. Here Brooks leads Moss and Stuart Lewis-Evans in the 1957 event. The manufacturers' championship was inaugurated in 1958, and Vanwall won it.
RIGHT **Jaguar XK120, 1951.** First seen (with dummy engine) at the 1948 London show, this 3.4-litre twin-cam sports car launched William Lyons's company on the export trail. The owner is Joss Davenport.

ABOVE *Jaguar D-type, 1955.* This ex-works long-nose car, rebuilt in Coventry from the components of several dismembered cars, was sold to former Le Mans winner Duncan Hamilton. Twenty-five years and several owners later he bought it for the second time. The Jaguar D-type is held in such regard that even hardened businessmen crave ownership. Hamilton is not the only ancien pilote to be willing to pay for nostalgia with bags of gold.

RIGHT *Jaguar at Le Mans.* After winning in 1951 and 1953 with the XK120C, Jaguar scored a further three victories in 1955, '56 and '57 with the purpose-built D-type. With Ivor Bueb, Mike Hawthorn (here) was the 1955 winner in a race marred by a tragic accident which led to many changes in race administration. The (recently revived) Edinburgh-based Ecurie Ecosse team gave the D-type its last two victories in the most famous marathon motor race of them all.

engine was based on those used in fire pumps and was an instant winner. Soon this power unit was developed for a new Cooper single-seater, first for Formula Two, but almost immediately for Formula One. The Cooper-Coventry Climax took two Grand Prix victories in 1958, five in 1959, and six in 1960: clearly it was the top make in the latter two years. The Australian Jack Brabham was individual champion both times.

That the future lay in the rear engine was emphasized in 1960 when Ferrari was pushed down to third place in the manufacturers' table by another 'upstart' British car, the Lotus, brainchild of Colin Chapman. In a sense, the Lotus has become Britain's synonym for 'Ferrari', its brilliant designs sometimes being pursued until they are outdated, only to be replaced by new ones that leave the opposition floundering. Chapman know-how had gone into the Vanwall, and the first Lotus for Formula One looked like a scaled-down version of it. All the early Lotus cars had front engines, including the beautiful little glass-fibre construction Elite GT car: the star of the Earls Court show in 1957. Lotus was quickest to follow Cooper's lead, however, and in 1960 the diminutive rear-engined Lotus 18-Coventry Climax snatched two surprise Championship Grand Prix victories, just as Cooper did in 1958.

HWM and Connaught never had the financial resources to stay in the game, but one other British car, after a decade of varying fortunes, was now starting to come into its own. The industry's first national effort to make a top-notch racing car, the V16 BRM of 1949–50, had been a flop. It had been succeeded by a simpler model which scored its only (yet still historic) championship race win in Holland in 1959; but already BRM was on the verge of introducing its own rear-engined Grand Prix machine.

With two wins in 1959 and one in 1960, Ferrari was to be the last of the competitive front-engined Grand Prix winners at World Championship level; but, as ever, Modena was looking ahead. Ferrari's prancing horse would soon lead the pack once again.

ABOVE **Lotus Elite (Mark 14), 1962.** *Seen at the 1957 London show, this glass-fibre GT car had a 1.2-litre Coventry Climax engine. Its many achievements included five Le Mans class wins. This former Team Elite car is in the Nigel Dawes collection.*

LEFT **Britain's best drivers of the 1950s.** *The contrasting Stirling Moss and Mike Hawthorn. Moss was the more dedicated, but Hawthorn became World Champion. They tended to overshadow the excellence of Tony Brooks and Peter Collins, both of whom were also fine sportsmen of star quality.*

ABOVE **Cooper-Coventry Climax GP car.** *In 1959 and 1960 Jack Brabham and the works Cooper took the world crown. The front-engined GP machine was obsolete thereafter. Stirling Moss scored a number of wins in this Rob Walker-owned car seen here at Monaco in 1959. This rear-engined car was developed from the 500 cc car.*

1960

The 1960s began with Britain establishing itself, at last, as a leading force in Grand Prix racing. After the Cooper, the Lotus became the standard setter. Great drivers emerged, with two Scots, Jim Clark and Jackie Stewart, breaking Juan Manuel Fangio's racing record.

The world's motor industries struggled for supremacy. In Britain, despite the success of the Mini and other great designs, fears of further American takeovers (the latest was Chrysler's acquisition of Rootes) led eventually to the forming of British Leyland. Government intervention later also resulted in the separation of Rolls-Royce Motors from its aviation interests. Safety and emission controls became matters of legislation, with the United States leading the other nations, and the big manufacturers investing heavily in new fields of research to stay in business.

Japan became a leading exporter, proving itself capable of producing not only mundane saloons but genuine European-style sports cars for the American market. German industry closed ranks. Apart from Ford and GM, the loss of Borgward left just three main groups: Daimler-Benz, Volkswagen, and BMW, the last of these being saved from the brink of takeover to become a leader in sports-saloon car manufacture. Italy introduced new super-cars and helped France make one: the Citroën SM. Through Citroën, the world's oldest makes (Panhard and Peugeot) came together; Panhard was never revived.

THROUGH FREEDOM TO RESTRICTION

1975

After so long in the doldrums, Britain's Grand Prix teams were achieving results, with a new race winner every year for four years since 1957: Vanwall, Cooper, BRM and Lotus in that order.

In 1961, however, the new formula caught the British flat-footed. From 1958 it had been known that a change was proposed, reducing the permitted engine capacity of Grand Prix cars from 2.5 to 1.5 litres unsupercharged; fuel had to be of a type that could be bought commercially and self-starters had to be fitted. The United Kingdom contingent fought for a reprieve, but motor racing had seen more than its fair share of tragedy in the late 1950s and the authorities were determined to try and reduce speeds: a problem that has to be dealt with every so often.

Ferrari and his top racing technicians, Carlo Chiti and Romolo Tavoni, had read the signs and decided that the new formula was inevitable; their Tipo 156 V6 cars reigned supreme simply because they were ready on time. Vanwall had pulled out, and BRM, Cooper and Lotus ran with four-cylinder Coventry Climax engines designed for the old Formula Two. Stirling Moss took Rob Walker's Lotus 18 to a couple of superb victories over the Ferraris, attributable largely to his superiority as a driver.

British cars, British drivers

The British *were* ready in 1962. BRM and Coventry Climax produced new V8 engines. BRM had been around for fully 12 years and now at last it was its turn. Graham Hill won the World Championship at the last race, snatching victory from Lotus star Jim Clark, who would have been champion if a crankcase bolt had not dropped out. But 'if' is the story of racing, and BRM deserved its break after so many years of trying. Clark, however, turned the tables in 1963; the young Scottish farmer won seven of the year's ten title races, a record yet to be equalled in Formula One.

The Lotus 25, the first of the monocoque Formula One cars, was supreme. John Cooper was unable to pull his team together (he had been injured in a road accident), and so Cooper cars were out of the Grand Prix limelight. Former champion Jack Brabham was making his own cars now, but BRM and Ferrari constituted the greatest opposition to Lotus as Clark prepared to defend his title. As in 1962, the 1964 champion could not be declared until the end of the last race, the South African GP. Clark led until an oil pipe split and the engine seized on the last lap. Racing is a 'swings and roundabouts' affair and Ferrari was now making a comeback with its own V8; team leader John Surtees snatched the title for his delighted Italian master to become the only World Champion in the top classes of both car and motorcycle racing.

PRECEDING PAGES *The coming of the Cosworth. After the Coventry Climax and Repco, it was the Ford-financed V8 Cosworth (Costin and Duckworth) DFV 3-litre engine that took over as the dominant GP racing power unit. Lotus was first to race and win with it, when Jim Clark beat Jack Brabham in the 1967 Dutch GP. This picture shows Jackie Oliver practising with the Lotus 49 at Monaco in 1968.*

Only six years had passed since Mike Hawthorn had won the championship for Britain. Now it was becoming a regular occurrence. In 1964 Britons took the top three places. In 1965 it happened again!

Coventry Climax, by now part of the Jaguar group, developed a spectacular flat-16, but this engine's public début coincided with the announcement that the company would supply racing engines for only one more season before withdrawing to concentrate upon the fire pumps and fork trucks that were its bread and butter. Instead, the overworked V8 was given a new lease of life with four valves per cylinder, and once again Jim Clark ran away with the Championship. Second and third for BRM were Graham Hill and Jackie Stewart, the latter achieving the rare distinction of winning a race in his first Grand Prix season. The biggest surprise was, however, left to the very end of the season when Graham Hill's former team mate Richie Ginther gave Japan a major victory, driving a Honda with V12 engine mounted crosswise.

Another sign of the times was that the winner ran on Goodyear tyres; for many years previously, Dunlop had held a virtual monopoly in this field of development. For five years the new form of Grand Prix car, with its engine behind the driver, had proved itself the most compact and efficient racing machine yet devised. From 1966, with another new formula and ever-increasing tyre sizes, the cars began to get bigger once again – as we shall see later in this chapter.

Sports car racing also changed radically in the 1960s. From 1953 to 1961 there was a World Sports Car Championship, but following the 1955 Le Mans catastrophe fear of high-speed accidents had led to some late and ill-planned changes in the regulations. The early days of the Championship saw works participation by Britain's Aston Martin and Jaguar; Mercedes-Benz and Porsche from Germany; Gordini and Talbot-Lago from France; Cunningham of the United States; and the Italian Alfa Romeo, Ferrari, Lancia and Maserati, all seeking honours. Apart from Mercedes-Benz (1955) and Aston Martin (1959), Ferrari

LEFT **Lola GT, 1963.**
Other mid-engined GT
cars (such as the Tojeiro-
Buick) had been made
before this magnificent
machine appeared at the
racing car show in
London in January 1963,
but Eric Broadley's Lola
was the design that caught
Ford's imagination.
Ford, having failed to
take over Ferrari,
'borrowed' Broadley's
engineering knowledge
and facilities with the
result shown on pages 122
and 123. Here, that
original Lola-Ford V8 is
seen at Le Mans in 1963,
when it was driven by

former Jaguar trainees
Richard Attwood and
David Hobbs. Later,
their old firm hired them
to assess the Jaguar XJ13
mid-engined car – but it
never raced.

ABOVE **Jim Clark and
Lotus.** This association of
driver and marque lasted
nearly a decade. Clark
first raced a Lotus Elite in
1958; he died in a Lotus
Type 48 F2 car at
Hockenheim in 1968. In
those years, the personable
Scottish farmer (inset)
won more Grands Prix
than anyone had ever
done before, and was
twice declared World
Champion. From 1962,

he was the driver to beat.
Here he is winning at
Reims in 1963 with the
Lotus-Coventry Climax
Type 25.

always won the title. In 1957, Alfonso de Portago, his passenger and several spectators lost their lives in the Mille Miglia. This high-speed Italian road race had always claimed lives, but this accident was at least as bad as any previous one, and the event was banned for good. Hoping to get speeds down, the authorities imposed an upper limit of 3 litres from 1958 to 1961, by which time Ferrari's only challengers were Porsche (advancing quickly) and Maserati (making a brief revival). All the other big names had gone, and from 1962 the Championship acquired a complex format of classes and categories, which Ferrari continued to dominate (in both sports and GT guises) until the mid-1960s, while Porsche was supreme in the 2-litre categories.

Like Grands Prix, sports, GT and touring car racing were to see big changes for 1966 with the arrival of Ford.

Motor rallies come of age

In rallying, the 1960s opened with the toughest of all the 'controlled road-races' still going strong: the Marathon de la Route from Liège to deepest Bulgaria and Yugoslavia and back without rest. Stirling Moss's sister Pat and Tom Wisdom's daughter Ann made a great partnership, and their outright victory in 1960 was the undisputed pinnacle of women's motoring achievement. They drove the beefy, relatively crude and very tiring Austin-Healey 3000. More sophisticated if less quick were the Citroën of Lucien Bianchi, the 1961 winner, and the Mercedes-Benz of Eugen Böhringer who charged to victory in 1962 and 1963. In the Marathon's final year, 1964, an Austin-Healey took the honours once again, driven by Finland's Rauno Aaltonen. (Thereafter, the event became an 84-hour circuit race at the Nürburgring.) The days of the other great open-road event, the Alpine Rally or Coupe des Alpes, were numbered too. The age of the stage had arrived.

The 'special stage' is simply a timed section on closed roads or tracks, and rally results are calculated on the time taken for a given number of these sections. Except to keep overall rally administration under control, the time taken between stages does not affect the results.

Scandinavian organizers, manufacturers and drivers had a head start when the stage rally began to take over internationally, for they already had the events and the terrain.

In Britain the Royal Automobile Club first worked with the Forestry Commission and other landowners in 1960, and the RAC Rally has become the best and toughest of its type. For three years, to 1962, Erik Carlsson's little Saab put its opponents in the shade. Another Swedish combination – Tom Trana and Volvo – was impressively victorious in 1963 and 1964.

ABOVE **Rallying in the 1960s.** *Compact, agile, controllable, the transverse-engined Mini proved ideal for rallying, scoring many victories including three in the Monte Carlo Rally: by Paddy Hopkirk and the original 'flying Finns', Timo Makinen and Rauno Aaltonen. Here the Mini-Cooper S of Makinen leads the 1967 Monte. Later a rock landed on his car, and Aaltonen went on to win.*

Sir Alec Issigonis *born 1906*

Born in Turkey of a Bavarian mother, Alexander Arnold Issigonis was educated in London. After three years as a draughtsman with Humber, Issigonis joined Morris as a suspensions engineer in 1936. He worked closely with Sir Miles Thomas (who would, in due course, resign his vice-chairmanship, unwilling to work for Lord Nuffield any longer) on the 'Mosquito' project which led to the Morris Minor of 1948.

Although it was not produced exactly as Issigonis had envisaged, the Minor's popularity was, and is, unbounded. Issigonis built his own Lightweight Special, a highly professional single-seater with all-independent suspension, alloy-and-wood monocoque construction, and a supercharged Austin Seven engine; he used this in sprints.

The Minor took him to the top of the Morris engineering tree, but the pre- and post-BMC politics left him disenchanted, and he went to Alvis. There he improved the existing range, and planned a new V8 model with Hydrolastic suspension devised by his friend Alex Moulton. This car came to nothing; but Sir Leonard Lord invited Issigonis to join BMC, to bring its forward planning in line with that prevailing in continental Europe. The outcome was the Mini-Minor, or 'Mini'.

His own Morris Minor had been a classic miniature of orthodox layout, but Ferdinand Porsche's Volkswagen had become the world car, despite its rear engine. It was Alec Issigonis who started the trend of today (by no means confined to small cars) of placing the engine transversely under the bonnet. The space-saving, rubber-suspended Mini, launched in 1959, was still being produced in the mid-1980s. Both his Minor and Mini showed his clear thinking at its brilliant best.

BMC was still Britain's leading rally team and its manager, Stuart Turner, started a trend by hiring the first of the 'flying Finns', Rauno Aaltonen and Timo Makinen, to supplement top-class British drivers such as Paddy Hopkirk and Donald Morley. At last, in 1965, a British car won the new-style RAC Rally – but the Mini-Cooper S was driven by Aaltonen. In 1966 a Swede, Bengt Söderström, took a Ford Lotus-Cortina to victory, one of the first indications that Ford would soon be taking rallying very seriously indeed. A fascinating feature of rallying was that, unlike racing, it was a sport in which no specific type of car was yet emerging as the ideal. The Citroëns, DKWs, Minis and Saabs had front-wheel drive; the Austin-Healeys, Fords, Mercedes-Benzes and Volvos were front-engined and rear-wheel driven, yet all were winners in the early 1960s. The Porsche was the only regular rear-engined winner; the Alpine-Renault would succeed later. Rallying was, indeed, one area in which many manufacturers were finding they could prove their products to the public and to themselves; and, if it turned out costly in terms of bent metal, there was consolation in the sport's very reasonable safety record in terms of personal injury.

The coming of the Mini
The 1960s brought change to the British small-car scene. For a start, 1959 was the last year of the 'early perpendicular' Ford Popular. Basically this was the car that had been taking the '£100' market by storm a quarter of a century earlier; its final price was nearer £400, yet it

had still been the cheapest of British cars. It had no true successor, although the more modern-looking New Popular (a *very* basic Anglia) made Ford the last mass producer of side-valve engines in Britain as late as 1962.

Vauxhall stayed with orthodox family cars. The Viva of 1963 was GM's first under-1200 cc saloon for Britain and had dimensions similar to Ford's new 105E series. Ford and Vauxhall both expanded on Merseyside, as part of the plan to spread employment opportunities. Also in 1963 a much-needed new model was added to the Rootes range: the Hillman Imp, a very attractive little saloon with its 875 cc alloy engine (based upon a Coventry Climax design) mounted in the tail. Unfortunately it did not come soon enough to prevent the financial position at Rootes from becoming critical. The main reason for the Imp's consistent failure to achieve the market share it needed can be summed up in that one word: Mini.

If it did nothing else, the merger of Austin with Nuffield had given the British Motor Corporation a real hold on the small car market. The Morris Minor and the baby Austins A35 and A40 gave BMC a wide range which, before being outdated altogether, kept it in the public mind as *the* small car maker. (The very attractive and practical Farina-styled A40 uncannily anticipated today's popular small hatchback size and layout, yet it was never followed up.) Although rendered obsolete in theory, the Morris Minor lived on into the early 1970s. However, the Mini was the car that created overnight obsolescence for so many others, and marked the high point of Alec Issigonis's career as a designer.

Introduced in late 1959 as the Morris Mini-Minor (and soon afterwards as the Austin Seven to protect marque dealerships), the front-wheel-drive Mini was to set the pattern for the modern popular car. It had an 850 cc engine mounted transversely, and the gearbox was in the sump: this layout emphasized the 'big inside, small outside' effect that so impressed the world's motorists.

Not only was everyday motoring changing. With a tuned engine, it was soon realized that the Mini was a wonderfully nimble competition car for racing and rallying, as mentioned earlier.

Although it did sound a warning, the Mini did not spell the end of the traditional sports car. BMC's M.G. had always been the world's favourite small sports car and it remained so despite losing its traditional looks, and being supplemented by the splendid Austin-Healey.

It did not take long for BMC to start bringing in bigger models with the new saloon format: the pretty 1100, the impressive 1800 and, towards the end of the decade, the Maxi.

ABOVE *RAC Rally, 1962.* From 1960, Britain's premier rally featured 'special stages' on private ground and became, in many respects, the best rally in the world, thanks to good organization and the variety of terrain to be found in the parkland and the forests. Here Olle Dahl's tough little Saab leaps a Scottish bridge. Erik Carlsson won the event three times (1960, '61 and '62) in such a car.

LEFT *Austin-Healey 3000: the other extreme.* Healeys came second in the RAC Rally six times, but never quite won the event. The Austin-Healey 3000 was tiring and crude by comparison with BMC's other serious rally car, the Mini-Cooper S (opposite), but it was very effective when properly protected underneath. This model won the Liège–Sofia–Liège marathon twice; Pat Moss's 1960 victory was a landmark. Here she and Ann Wisdom storm to third place in the 1962 RAC.

The Jaguar phoenix

Meanwhile, Jaguar had recovered from a massive fire in 1957, and developed a new compact range. First seen in 1955 as the 2.4, the 'small' Jaguar became the Mark 2 in October 1959. It was available with three engine sizes. The 3.8-litre version was not only a high-speed touring car; it was, for four years, the leading long-distance contender in saloon car racing. The Coventry factory prepared cars for dealers and customers, and it was Peter Nöcker of Germany, driving a 3.8-litre Jaguar, who was declared European Touring Car Champion of 1963, the inaugural year of yet another annual contest.

Jaguar had grown rapidly since moving into its present Browns Lane headquarters in 1952, and annual production had more than doubled to over 20,000 units. In 1960, Sir William Lyons was able to buy Daimler from BSA, thus acquiring not only the space he needed for further expansion (without having to move away from Coventry as had once seemed inevitable), but also the production facilities for what would become the biggest-selling double-decker bus chassis. Anxious to capitalize on the opportunity, he created a Daimler truck design office; this, however, was transferred to Wolverhampton in 1961, when he bought the famous truck and bus company Guy Motors from the receiver. That spring, Lyons launched his stunning E-type at Geneva and followed it with the Mark X saloon at the autumn shows. Those who might have wondered what Jaguar's engineers had been doing since giving up racing wondered no more.

In 1963 Coventry Climax Engines was bought, a purchase that brought Walter Hassan back to the Jaguar fold. This gave added strength to Bill Heynes's engineering team, already well on its way to conceiving the famous XJ6 and XJ12.

With all these successes it was no wonder that, over the years, Jaguar had been courted with a view to marriage. Among the unsuccessful bidders was the Leyland commercial vehicle company, with which Lyons had chosen to compete instead. (Jaguar had gone as far as arranging to sell Leyland trucks in North America in 1959.)

Leyland makes a move

Leyland Motors had once made Britain's costliest motor car, but that had been a brief gambit in the early 1920s; as was the same company's sponsorship of the Trojan economy car. Leyland was best known for its trucks and buses. In 1960, however, Leyland's Sir Henry Spurrier and Standard-Triumph's Alick Dick started talking about their mutual interest in selling abroad.

Standard-Triumph had not been having an easy time. Despite replacing the unimaginative Standard 8 and 10 with the Michelotti-influenced Triumph Herald in 1959, the company was in trouble. The Vanguard was never updated satisfactorily. (The name Standard was dropped in 1963, except in Madras where a locally produced Triumph Herald was current as recently as 1980; but then, so was the even older Indian version of Morris Oxford!) Only the Triumph sports cars

provided continuous cheer for the Coventry combine which had lower priority on body supply since BMC had acquired the Fisher & Ludlow works in the early 1950s; it had also wasted much time in resolving its relationships with Ferguson (for whom it had been making tractors), and with possible partners including Chrysler, the still separate Rootes Group and Rover. The eventual merger with Leyland was a laborious affair. When it finally went through in 1961, Alick Dick left and Leyland men moved in. This was, in a sense, the true beginning of the British Leyland company.

Jaguar and Rover remained independent for a while. Rover engineering was highly respected and the pioneering work by Spencer King and Peter Wilks on gas turbines culminated in two successful demonstrations of reliability with the Rover-BRM completing the Le Mans 24-hour races of 1963 and 1965, driven by Richie Ginther, Graham Hill and Jackie Stewart. The Land-Rover gave Britain an all-purpose 'super jeep' and was an effective and profit-making workhorse; a light alloy ex-GM V8 engine was on its way and, in the meantime, the Rover 2000 was proving itself to be a fine concept. Alvis was acquired in 1965. Rover, one of the grand old 19th-century cycle companies, had a lot to offer in the 1960s.

Then, in the summer of 1966, the final, fateful moves were made. The Jaguar group merged with BMC to form British Motor Holdings (BMH). Soon afterwards, and as a direct response, Leyland absorbed Rover: a move that brought the name of Donald (later Lord) Stokes into great prominence as effective successor to Spurrier as head of Leyland.

Stokes and Sir George Harriman (who took over from Lord at BMC in 1961) had talked before. In late 1966 they were talking again, in the company of the Minister of Technology, Anthony Wedgwood Benn. The subject was the Rootes Group, which had needed rescuing since the death of William, the first Lord Rootes, in 1964 shortly after he had visited Detroit and obtained £12 million and the promise of overseas cooperation from Chrysler. This had left the Rootes family in control and Benn now wanted to see the group stay in British hands. By the spring of 1967, however, Sir Reginald Rootes was retiring and Chrysler was taking charge, bringing in Massey-Ferguson's Gilbert Hunt as chief executive of what would be renamed Chrysler United Kingdom Ltd a few years later.

Meanwhile, having turned down all ideas of becoming involved with the Rootes Group, and spurred on by an evening as Harold Wilson's guests at Chequers, the Prime Ministerial country residence, Harriman and Stokes began serious talks about bringing *their* corporations together. These discussions became more and more acrimonious,

ABOVE LEFT *M.G. MGB roadster, from 1962. Practical, pretty and popular both at home and abroad, the MGB maintained the quality of the M.G. breed most admirably. The styling of the later fixed-head coupé version was equally outstanding. The MGB was produced for 18 years. It was to be Abingdon's last product, for despite great efforts to save it, the factory closed at the end of 1980. This 1967 model was provided by E. F. Williams.*

LEFT *Jaguar E-type, from 1961. Its shape owed much to Jaguar's Le Mans experience. The sensation this car created when it was introduced was on a par with that occasioned by the XK120 12 years earlier. This example was provided by Derek and Graham Bovet-White.*
ABOVE *Lotus Elan Sprint. Entry into serious GP racing did not prevent Colin Chapman and his team from coming up with this delightful and practical sports car in the early 1960s.*

Sir William Lyons *born 1901*

The man who was to become the elder statesman of Britain's motor industry was once seen by its 'establishment' as an upstart. In the immediate post-Depression period he expanded his business while others were pausing to think about it.

The son of an Irish musician, William Lyons joined the retail motor trade in his home town of Blackpool, Lancashire, after a short and unsatisfactory apprenticeship with Crossley in Manchester; his aim was always to run his own business. This became a reality when he and a neighbour (guaranteed by their parents) began making motorcycle sidecars. Their Swallow company was formed on the day Lyons was 21, in September 1922. Soon coachbuilding supplemented sidecar making; but Lyons found it difficult to achieve the line and style he wanted on the high chassis of the day. Soon after moving to Coventry, he made an agreement whereby the

Standard company would produce engines and specially lowered chassis for him; the result was the long, low SS of 1931. From it came the first of the SS Jaguars, in 1935. Soon the transition from coachbuilder to manufacturer was complete.

From 1935, Lyons had run the business single-handed and in 1956 he received his knighthood. He acquired the Daimler Company from BSA in 1960, Guy Motors in 1961 and Coventry Climax Engines in 1963, re-establishing each of them as profitable businesses as subsidiaries of Jaguar Cars Ltd.

In 1966, Sir William accepted the opportunity to continue to run the Jaguar Group in his way, while joining forces with BMC, a merger which led quickly to the formation of British Leyland. Although Sir William retired in 1972, his influence undoubtedly helped Jaguar's return to autonomy, and frequent consultancy visits by him to the company's styling studios have ensured that a Jaguar will remain a Jaguar for many years to come.

particularly after BMH's accounts, which showed a loss, were published in late 1967.

When in January 1968 the announcement was made, it was clear that this was, in effect, a takeover by Leyland. Even the name of the new company – the British Leyland Motor Corporation – made skilful use of words and, sure enough, it was often shortened to Leyland. ('BL' was to be coined later, when there was less to shout about.)

BLMC suddenly, but briefly, became the largest of all the world's vehicle makers apart from VW and the three American giants. It began operations in May 1968, with Stokes as the top man. Later that year Harriman resigned, an ill and unhappy, but not rancorous man.

For five years, the monster lumbered onwards, down a steepening decline; in late 1973 this would become a precipice, with the coming of the Arab oil embargo, the consequent fear of shortages, and the fact of soaring fuel prices.

Specialist survival
Even before this, Britain's smaller manufacturers had been having solvency difficulties.

Sir David Brown's Aston Martin seemed to enter the 1960s strongly, having just won Le Mans and the World Sports Car Championship, and introduced a fine new GT car, the DB4, built on the Italian *superleggera* ('extra lightweight') principle. The car was much admired, and there were some even lighter versions including the brutal, blunt-nosed, brilliant DB4GT Zagato. It may be that if Brown had left racing alone while he was on top, instead of unsuccessfully trying to produce a Grand Prix car *and* another Le Mans winner; if he had not tried to reintroduce the Lagonda; and if he had gone into partnership with Alvis, which had seemed likely for a while, then perhaps the company would not have started another of its downward trends. As it was, John Wyer, the man in charge of operations, decided to leave and only the exciting new DBS of 1967 kept serious trouble at bay. However, the pressure upon Sir David Brown was ultimately to become too strong. His companies had been subsidizing Aston Martin more and more (in return for the prestige), and in 1972 he sold his absorbing hobby.

In 1971 Rolls-Royce appeared to be in trouble. During the main company's bankruptcy proceedings it was made clear that the car division was solvent and it was permitted to continue separately from the aero engine side, almost immediately announcing the splendid Corniche version of its successful Silver Shadow, which had been on the market since 1965.

Bristol, which had begun as an anglicized BMW, kept going by switching to American engines and 'acting small', which has proved a sufficiently effective policy for maintaining high customer loyalty and low overheads. Frazer Nash (the other British BMW connection) had stopped making cars in the late 1950s, but the family association with German quality makes was maintained through the importation of Porsche cars to the United Kingdom.

Like Bristol, Jensen of West Bromwich was now using a big American Chrysler V8 engine, but the company's most sensational announcement was the FF version of the Vignale-styled Interceptor in 1966. The first modern private car to have four-wheel drive, the FF featured Ferguson-type transmission. Racing drivers Fred Dixon and Tony Rolt had worked with four-wheel drive in the 1940s, and this had led to the formation of a company sponsored by Harry Ferguson, the tractor designer and advocate of motoring safety.

Several experimental cars were built and these can be seen today in Coventry's Museum of British Road Transport. Despite its unfashionable front engine, the Ferguson Project-99 Formula One racing car was driven by Stirling Moss to a fine win in the 1961 Oulton Park Gold Cup race. This car again proved its ability to get all its Coventry Climax power down on to the road in 1964, when Peter Westbury won the hotly contested RAC Hill Climb Championship. The 1966 Jensen FF featured not only the Ferguson's transmission but also the Dunlop Maxaret anti-lock braking system, making it (in theory) one of the safest and most expensive cars on the market. The division of labour between the four wheels was handled by a central self-locking differential unit.

This fine machine was hampered by the need for further development after its announcement; there was not enough cash for that and, despite *Car* magazine's summing up of it as the 'supreme compromise', the Jensen FF had only a brief production life. Alan and Richard Jensen retired and, in the series of management changes that followed, the lead role was taken by the American economist Carl Duerr, and then by the California-based Norwegian Kjell Qvale, who already knew as much as anyone about selling unusual motor cars in the United States. Once the cars bearing their name ceased to be produced by Austin (now part of British Leyland), Donald Healey and his sons were free to introduce a new car. This was made by Jensen from 1972; the Jensen-Healey sports car helped keep Jensen's doors open, but only for a few more years.

Lotus, who later supplied the Jensen-Healey's engine, continued to advance throughout the 1960s, supplementing the Coventry Climax-powered Elite with a new sports car, the Elan, powered by a twin-cam Ford-based engine. This unit was adapted by Harry Mundy shortly

RIGHT **Aston Martin Volante, 1968.** *In other words, a DB6 convertible powered by the Marek-designed 4-litre six-cylinder engine. Despite several changes of ownership, and even factory closure, the exotic Aston Martin and Lagonda have survived, and today's V8-engined beauties retain the almost animal grace and power that once made them Le Mans winners.*

RIGHT **Ogle SX250, 1962.** David Ogle's last styling exercise was this well-balanced GT body on Daimler's high-performance SP250 2½-litre V8 chassis. It was later fitted to the Ford-powered Reliant chassis which became the Scimitar – the car that changed Reliant's image overnight.

ABOVE **Jensen Interceptor Convertible, 1974.** A rare late model, based on the Chrysler V8-powered Interceptor saloon which had been designed in Italy by Touring (shortly before that company went out of business), then taken to Vignale to produce from 1966. Despite such innovations as disc brakes (from 1956) and four-wheel drive (from 1965), the Jensen company and its splendid cars could not survive the 1970s.

A revival, however, was suggested for the mid-1980s. This car was provided by Newton E. Deiter, Ph.D, and was photographed in Hollywood, California.

before leaving *Autocar* magazine (where he was technical editor) to join Jaguar. The work was carried out at the request of Colin Chapman who had had to price the Elite higher than he had wanted. In 1968 came the first of a new wave of Lotus road cars, the Europa, a compact and very low-built coupé with its overhead-valve 1.5-litre Renault engine behind the driver. Here it should be mentioned that the term 'mid-engined' was now being used increasingly, and this car certainly justified it. Nowadays any car with its power unit ahead of the rear axle and behind the driver tends to be described as mid-engined, whereas early machines of this layout – such as the Auto Union Grand Prix cars – were once automatically termed rear-engined. The Europa was later available with the twin-cam power unit.

A complete contrast was provided by Morgan, a company that has been making sporting machines at Malvern, near Worcester, since 1910. Three-wheelers overlapped with, and were succeeded by, four-wheelers, always (with one exception) designed and built in the traditional way; and in the late 1960s the 3.5-litre GM-Rover light alloy V8 gave Morgan's top model a remarkable power-to-weight ratio.

In 1962 another Midland firm added four-wheelers to its programme. Reliant of Tamworth had been making light vans based on the single-front-wheeled Raleigh since the 1930s, and these could now be had as simple family transport, with glass-fibre bodywork. The first Reliant sports model, the Ford-powered Sabre, looked like a 'special' and was a failure as a rally car; but the firm persevered, with help from Ogle. In fact, this was an unusual company for Britain although familiar enough in Italy.

The Hertfordshire firm of David Ogle Ltd earned its bread and butter from the design of everyday packaging: record sleeves, labels, perfume bottles, radio and television cabinets. Ogle himself was an industrial designer with a passion for cars and, after testing the market with six Riley 1.5-based prototypes, went into limited production with the Ogle SX 1000, a crisp little GT car with Mini mechanical components. In 1962 Ogle was killed in a road accident, having completed most of the work on another prototype, one of six commissioned by the head of Helena Rubenstein cosmetics. The company pulled itself together under Tom Karen, who completed the exercise, which was exhibited at that year's Motor Show as the Ogle SX 250.

A sleek and highly individual coupé in glass-fibre reinforced plastics, the new Ogle was built on the Daimler SP 250 sports car chassis. Jaguar had already tried restyling this unusual but very powerful sports car which the company had inherited, and had decided to drop it. (It could not be made very much cheaper than Jaguar's own E-type, so its

potential was strictly limited.) Ogle now had a design for sale; Reliant needed one, and so it was that the Scimitar was born, giving Reliant a new image and a new lease of life. In 1966, the Scimitar acquired Ford's V6 engine. Reliant made further strides in 1968 with its Scimitar GTE, a sporting estate car, and shortly afterwards bought out Bond Cars Ltd of Preston, which had been following a similar course to Reliant, but not quite so fruitfully. At the start of the decade, Reliant was hardly considered as a manufacturer. After the formation of British Leyland, however, it became a standing joke – but a startling fact – that Reliant was, suddenly, the second-largest all-British car maker.

Legislation looms large

There was one important reason for the closure of many small firms and the termination of certain famous models in the late 1960s and early 1970s: Federal legislation.

Suddenly safety and emission controls became news in the 1960s. They became political issues, leading to legislation that affected all North American manufacturers and importers. Early over-reaction led to a number of unreasonable measures that, for a time, seriously affected the very 'driveability' of some cars. Engines that had breathed freely became rough and unresponsive as makers set up extra laboratories to find ways of reducing the carbon monoxide, unburned hydrocarbons and other polluting emissions from their cars, in order to meet the new requirements in the United States: particularly in California, famed for

RIGHT *Rolls-Royce Corniche, from 1971. Unashamed luxury is still a Rolls-Royce feature. The combined H. J. Mulliner and Park Ward companies – traditional London coachbuilders – continue to produce specialized work for Rolls-Royce, including Queen Elizabeth's latest Phantom VI state car. This Corniche (actually a 1979 car) was photographed in the United States by courtesy of Kenneth Smith.*

its localized smog, where legislation was toughest, yet where imported cars sold best. The removal of lead from fuel was also to become a big social and political issue.

In the matter of safety, many makers had demonstrated their sense of responsibility over the years. Starting virtually from scratch as a car builder and exporter, the Volvo company had used American techniques and the Swedish tendency to build into its products extra tolerance in both materials and structures, and had pioneered the use of seat belts; but it was not alone in safety-consciousness. To stay in business, any firm had to make its cars do more than just go. The power to stop a car had increased immeasurably with the arrival of the disc brake. 'Handling' had now become part of the motoring vocabulary, covering all the nuances of modern car control where once the simplicities of 'springing' and 'roadholding' had sufficed. Tyre development also moved forward into a new era.

It seems a long time ago, now, since the first big pressures on car design were exerted from outside the industry. Certainly, sufficient time has passed for the worst of the bitterness to have departed. The main victim was General Motors; more specifically, it was a new 1960 Chevrolet called the Corvair.

This good-looking car had an air-cooled flat-six engine mounted at the rear. It was one of several vehicles that followed closely behind the 1959 Studebaker Lark in heralding a new breed of American 'compact', aimed at stemming an increasing tide of popular cars from Europe. Its

all-independent suspension incorporated semi-trailing swing axles at the rear, and early models were open to criticism for their handling. Few cars with this type of rear axle arrangement have ever been regarded as perfect, but with properly designed controlling devices the varying angles of the rear wheels in relation to the road can be minimized and many constructors (including Volkswagen, Mercedes-Benz and other descendants of the Ledwinka–Porsche–Rumpler design school) continued to feature the system into modern times. In Czechoslovakia, where ride quality and winter grip take precedence over high speeds on the generally poor roads, the system actually predominates.

The Corvair, however, was the first American volume-production car to have swing-axle rear suspension and, although the oversteering tendencies of early cars were soon rectified, the car's reputation suffered at the hands of author Ralph Nader whose book *Unsafe at Any Speed* contributed to the ultimate failure of the model which, by the late 1960s, had become a delightful and sporting machine.

American responses
The American motor industry was having to react to marketing attacks from all sides, yet the 1960s saw relatively few new designs as bold as the Corvair. General Motors' effective replacement for it was a beautiful close-coupled coupé called the Camaro. This had all the best features of American orthodoxy: simple, reliable mechanical units, including a straight-6 or a V8 under the bonnet, plus classic and relatively

unadorned lines. As a Firebird, with its Pontiac grille, the new car looked sportier still. Earlier, Harley Earl and his successor William Mitchell had given the United States their first and only full-blooded sports car, the Chevrolet Corvette, which has sold steadily ever since: more on its style than on any particular mechanical properties. The 1967 Chevrolet Camaro and Pontiac Firebird from the Mitchell design team brought the sporting element to a much wider public, and both models are classics of their kind.

Another mid-1960s classic was the big Oldsmobile Toronado which, together with its Cadillac cousin, the Eldorado, brought front-wheel drive to modern America and paved the way for GM's broad engineering policy of today. Yet again, General Motors had taken styling a step further away from the befinned and befuddled shapes that much of Detroit had allowed itself to produce for so long.

Ford of America had tried to follow GM's Corvette in the 1950s with the Thunderbird, but it was blown off course, remaining uncertain of its market and letting the Corvette establish all the territorial rights in the sports car field. Enthusiasts cried out for a sporting Ford; Ford obliged by making a rear-engined show car and watching the reaction to it. Front-engined prototypes followed and in 1965 the button was pressed. Ford's styling studio may not have employed such famous or public figures as GM, but from time to time it came up trumps. The 1964 Ford Mustang was one of the best-looking and most timeless of automotive exercises; well over a million of these neat two-door four-seaters were made within the first two production years.

The Ford Mustang was the first of the 'Ponycars' as listed by *Car Life*, which claimed responsibility for the new terminology without being able to define it precisely. Yet the Ponycars were undoubtedly in a new class of their own. In 1967, the category included the Camaro and the Firebird from General Motors (together with the later 'misunderstood, maligned and finally martyred' Corvair); the Javelin from American Motors; and, with rather less certainty, the Mercury Cougar (an 'upmarket Mustang') and the longer Plymouth Barracuda, a somewhat hasty response to the sporting coupés of Ford and GM. Chrysler was still very much in the big-car field. Lee Iacocca, the man behind the Mustang, was to join Chrysler many years later, luring some of the Ford

customers he had once wooed. Chrysler would be back in the fray.

From 1966 to 1969, the Anglo-American Lola-inspired Ford GT40 had impressive victories at Le Mans. Ford of America led a new wave of Ford competition activity which was also to spread to Grand Prix racing.

In 1965, the Ponycars were working up to about one-eighth of the American market and that year turned out to be a US production record at over 9,300,000 cars: a figure exceeded only once in the 20 intervening years and some five times as many as Britain, which had also reached a watershed, whereas in Germany output was still accelerating to new production records, followed by France. Behind them all, at under 700,000, lay Japan.

The incorporation of Ford of Europe Inc. in 1967 was as significant a move as any in Europe, where General Motors was strong. Chrysler, however, was still weak abroad, despite the setting up of several subsidiaries back in the 1920s, the purchase of Ford's shareholding in Simca in 1958 and, in the early 1960s, the acquisition of 40 per cent of the Spanish Barreiros firm. The previously mentioned stake in the Rootes Group would become total ownership in the early 1970s: but, ironically, the most powerful Rootes car of all (the 1964–7 Sunbeam Tiger) used a Ford V8 engine. As Chrysler had no suitable alternative power unit, it put a stop to this and Rootes returned to mundane motoring.

The offensives and counter-offensives of the Big Three left little room for anyone else and even Studebaker, the oldest name in American road transportation, survived only until 1966, for all the styling efforts of Brooks Stevens and Raymond Loewy. Loewy's design for the Studebaker Avanti was a minor classic, but it took too long to get the glass-fibre body tooled up and customers were lost. Two dealers took

ABOVE **Oldsmobile Toronado, from 1966.** *Seeking to improve the poor reputation of big American cars in terms of road behaviour, GM introduced this stylish 7-litre front-wheel-drive coupé. The recipe continued into the 1980s.*

RIGHT **Ford Mustang hardtop coupé, 1966 model.** *Created by Lee Iacocca (later of Chrysler), the compact Mustang gave birth to the term 'Ponycar'. It was a brilliant yet simple concept and it is noteworthy from the photographs on this page and page 121 that the American motor car was now becoming extremely attractive to the eye once again.*

over the design and put in a Corvette engine; the Avanti II tootled on into the 1980s, a neat coupé for connoisseurs and not all that much more costly than a Corvette.

American Motors (formerly Hudson and Nash) kept its foot in the door with the Rambler, which lived on as a marque until 1970. Before that, however, AMC had become a marque in its own right, with the Mustang-challenging Javelin. From then on, American Motors got down to specializing in the sort of vehicle which other manufacturers did not produce – notably four-wheel-drives and compacts.

Oriental sunrise

Japan was on the move by the 1960s in no uncertain way. It increased its annual car output from less than 200,000 in 1960 to more than two million in 1968 (overtaking both Britain and France that year) and three million in 1970. The Western world may have shaken its head in wonder for it seemed like only yesterday that Japanese transport had been either cheap and nasty, or of European origin and built under licence.

By this time, Japan was producing its own cars and at every motor show something new was to be seen. Now-familiar names like Daihatsu, Datsun, Isuzu, Mazda, Mitsubishi, Subaru, Suzuki and Toyota became part of motoring vocabulary. One of the most significant arrivals on the scene was Honda. Soichiro Honda's personal enthusiasm has been mentioned earlier. In 1962, already the world's leading motorcycle manufacturer, he introduced his first miniature sports car; in 1966 Honda's interpretation of the Mini theme (front-wheel drive, transverse engine) marked the beginning of a determined assault on small-car markets abroad.

In the meantime, the early makers Hino and Prince had been absorbed into Toyota and Datsun-Nissan respectively; these became the holders of the lion's share of world markets. Daihatsu, whose Compagno was, in 1966, the first Japanese car to be sold in Britain, came under Toyota control in 1968.

A sports car from Japan

An idea of just how quickly the Japanese interpreted the ideas of others, and improved upon them, may be gained by looking at the history of any of their top-selling cars – and not just the popular saloons. Japan also made the world's top-selling sports car!

Honda's early sports car was just too small to become a success internationally, but the Datsun Fairlady, an MGB-sized two-seater, began to get the Japanese message into United States sports car circles by the mid-1960s. Datsun-Nissan's first small coupé, first seen at the 1964

ABOVE LEFT *Chevrolet Corvair 500 hardtop coupé, 1969 model.* Delightful but doomed, the Corvair was much improved in all respects; but it was too late, even for this good-looking model. This was its last year of production.

ABOVE *Pontiac Firebird Formula 350, 1971.* When it was decided that the Corvair would have to go, GM's Chevrolet Camaro 'Ponycar' project came to the fore, meeting the Mustang head-on from 1967. Pontiac had a sporting image and a distinctive front-end style, so the Firebird was introduced to extend the appeal of this simple, satisfying and muscular design. Provided by John Poole.

OVERLEAF *Ford GT40, 1966.* In 1963 Eric Broadley, designer of the Lola GT (see page 110), was retained to set up Ford Advanced Vehicles with Roy Lunn and former Aston Martin chief John Wyer. After two poor seasons, the resultant car – the GT40, and the related 7-litre Mk 2 – won the 24-hour Le Mans race four years in a row, from 1966 to 1969. By that time, Wyer was running his own Gulf-sponsored team and it won the International Championship of Makes for Ford. These fabulous cars spearheaded Ford's determined assault on all the main sectors of competition motoring in the 1960s. This road-equipped car, formerly used by Shell, was provided by Dr Michael Dawes.

Tokyo Show, was styled by Albrecht Goertz, a former colleague of Raymond Loewy.

A delightful example of Japan's ability to examine a Western idea and interpret it in its own way was the 1966 Toyota 2000GT. Strictly a two-seated hatchback, its skilful blending of lines was reminiscent of the Jaguar E-type. It had pop-up headlamps like the Lotus Elan and fine detail design work, particularly in the glass area: a hint of Ferrari there perhaps? Or Porsche? Or Corvette? Or BMW? A bit of each, more likely, for there is a common denominator.

A decade earlier, Goertz had been the unsung creator of the beautiful BMW 503 and 507, more delicately wrought than their Mercedes-Benz counterparts. They had brought a breath of fresh air to Germany where styling was generally on the heavy side, but only a few hundred of each were made, for BMW had been in deep financial trouble. Later he helped Porsche with the 911.

Goertz is not considered one of *the* great car designers; in the manner of Ogle, he is a designer for many other industries. In the early 1960s, however, this German-born American was retained by Nissan, then working with Yamaha on a joint project: a six-cylinder, twin-overhead camshaft, GT car. After two or three years, Nissan dropped the idea

because of doubts over the Yamaha-designed engine and Goertz's contract came to an end. It is unlikely that the remarkable technical and visual similarity of the 1966 Toyota 2000GT to the Nissan-Yamaha prototype was pure coincidence. There has never been a full explanation of Toyota's failure to capitalize on its position as the producer of Japan's first true grand touring car; less than a thousand 2000GTs were produced.

Meanwhile Nissan, still anxious to update the Fairlady, returned to its own GT project. The Datsun Z series, announced in 1969, had a slightly blander shape than the three-year-old Toyota and the 'Yamaha' prototype. The Z was the car that would outsell all other sporting machines. More than any other Oriental vehicle it would meet a demand the West had, somehow, failed to do. Over half a million Zs were made within a decade. The car gained a reputation as successor to the Austin-Healey 3000 in the world of rallying. Twice it won the toughest of today's rallies, the East African Safari.

It was not until the 1980s (as *Autocar* editor Ray Hutton has revealed) that Nissan actually acknowledged, publicly, the 'fine work' of Albrecht Goertz, which had influenced the Z's designers so strongly.

One of the Z's features, not shared with many other Japanese cars of

ABOVE **Datsun Z in the East African Safari.**
The Z series, which could be described as the world's most successful sports car, won this gruelling event twice in the early 1970s. Known in Japan as a Nissan, this has replaced Datsun as its international marque name. Still a fine car in its latest guise, the Z was ousted by the sophisticated rotary-engined Mazda RX7 as the most individual Japanese sporting car.

RIGHT **Toyota 2000GT, 1966.** *It seems strange that such a good design should have been withdrawn so soon. Three years later the Datsun 240Z, which was not at all unlike the Toyota, took the North American popular GT market by storm.*

the day, was a cockpit designed to accommodate Westerners. On the whole, the small build of its people had led Japan to build small cars. Some of these were adapted to suit export markets.

There was one other Japanese sporting car in the 1960s. It did not have the universal appeal of the Datsun but it did start something that makes the marque, Mazda, unique today. In 1967, the first Mazda coupé with a twin rotary piston engine went into limited production.

Europe advances

In 1960, Japan's progress was still not being seen, generally, as a great threat to the future of Western industry. Recovery from World War 2 was far from complete, and Europe's factories were in widely differing condition. Progress in West Germany had been prodigious.

One of Germany's older companies was NSU, its initials derived from the name of its home town, Neckarsulm. In the 19th century it had made knitting machines and precision products: among them the steel-spoked wheels for one of Gottlieb Daimler's first experimental cars in 1889. By the 1960s NSU was well advanced in its development of the rotary-piston engine designed by Felix Wankel, a completely new departure that dispensed with the normal reciprocating components, reducing the size and weight of the power unit. In 1964, the NSU Sport Prinz Spider became the world's first Wankel-engined production car, to be followed by the unusual front-wheel-drive Ro80 with a twin-rotor version of the new unit. This fine saloon had many new and attractive features, and good road behaviour; however, many Ro80s were converted to orthodox engines when the Wankel unit began to cause trouble. There have been other Wankel experiments but Mazda is the only patent holder to have persevered and got its money's worth from this smooth if somewhat thirsty engine.

The K70, a less revolutionary car than the Ro80, was put into cold storage; but it came in useful when VW was finding it difficult to broaden its range. This Ro80 derivative was to be the basis for a completely different kind of Volkswagen.

VW was going from strength to strength with the 'Beetle', but attempts to supplement it with larger rear-engined models were not meeting with public approval. Ownership of Auto Union came to the rescue here. As mentioned earlier, Auto Union, with its old factories now in East Germany, had been re-formed in the West, largely under the aegis of Daimler-Benz. The Horch and Wanderer marques were not revived, only the DKW (a few versions of which were called Auto Union). In 1964, seeking investment elsewhere, Daimler-Benz disposed of its controlling interest in Auto Union to Volkswagen. In 1965 the

Audi name was brought back for a new range of front-wheel-drive cars and, soon afterwards, the small two-stroke Ingolstadt-built DKW was dropped for good. This convoluted story continues with the merging of Audi with NSU in 1969. With both makes under its banner, VW adopted NSU's orthodox front-wheel-drive K70 as a stopgap saloon until the Audi 80/VW Passat established Volkswagen's new direction properly in the early 1970s. Despite the popularity of the 'Beetle' (production of which passed the 15 million mark in the winter of 1971–2), all future VW cars were to have their power trains in the front.

German progress

Apart from the Wankel-engined C111 of 1969, Daimler-Benz (like Jaguar) was eschewing super sports and racing cars, but it did support touring car events. Jaguar had the upper hand on the circuits; but four victories in the Argentine cross-country race, three each in the East African Safari and the Acropolis Rally, plus individual wins in the Monte Carlo, Liège–Sofia–Liège, Thousand Lakes and other rallies proved that (given drivers of the calibre of Walter Schock, Eugen Böhringer and the sensational young Finn Rauno Aaltonen) the big Mercedes-Benz SE saloons could take on any opposition when the going was at its most arduous.

Under its Anglo-German development chief, Rudolf Uhlenhaut, Mercedes-Benz engineering made particular progress in the safety field at this time. The idea of the passenger 'safety cell' between progressively crumpling front and rear zones was pursued with diligence; thus Stuttgart was readier than most motor towns to deal with safety regulations as they began to come into force internationally. Throughout these years Dr Joachim Zahn presided over the company with great

ABOVE RIGHT *NSU Ro80, 1968. This unique front-wheel-drive saloon had many advanced features, the bravest being the fitting of a twin-rotor Wankel engine as standard. Although catalogued for nearly a decade, the Ro80 had to go, sadly, after less than 40,000 had been made.*

RIGHT *BMW 1500, 1962. A formula for revival. Until this* Neue Klasse *appeared, BMW had been on the brink of despair; since then, the marque has consistently strengthened its grip on the expanding 'executive' market through quality, style, and sports car performance. Not only was BMW the leading make of touring car racing in Europe in the 1970s, but by 1983 its power units were becoming F1 GP winners. Such activity emphasizes BMW's high technical standards.*

wisdom and his leadership through the energy crises meant that his company came out of those dark days making and selling more cars than before.

Porsche, Stuttgart's other great motor manufacturer, had also gone from strength to strength. In 1964 the Type 911, styled by Ferdinand 'Butzi' Porsche (the eldest grandson from that great motoring dynasty), began another long line of spectacular coupés for road, rally and racetrack. Vic Elford of Britain, Pauli Toivonen of Finland (father of the 1980s rally star) and Sweden's Björn Waldegård won one Acropolis, three Monte Carlo, and three Swedish rallies between them in the 1967–9 period. Bigger and more powerful sports and GT prototypes were introduced to suit each new set of race regulations, culminating in

the magnificent flat-12 Type 917, which brought Porsche two long-awaited outright victories at Le Mans in 1970 and 1971, following the Ford monopoly, and countless other successes. The Porsche 917 took advantage of a new regulation which permitted a minimum number of 25 (instead of 50) 5-litre sports-racing cars to be built. Porsche had managed to find sufficient funds to build that number for 1969; Ferrari followed suit with the V12 512 in 1970 but those 12 months made all the difference. Porsche had the best drivers and two regular teams (including one run by former Aston Martin race director John Wyer), and the 917 was rarely beaten. These cars were so fast that, once again, the regulations had to be changed and sports-car racing reverted to confusion. At last this would give other makes a look in.

BMW's return to fame and fortune was laborious. The company had ended the 1950s with its splendid but expensive and ageing V8 500 series at the top end of the range, and a variety of baby cars – but nothing in between and less in the bank. In the winter of 1959–60, a form of takeover by Daimler-Benz was being recommended by the Deutsche Bank. Fortunately, those who believed in BMW formed an action group and a new car was created quickly to fill the 'middle ground'. This *Neue Klasse* BMW, as it was called, was launched at the 1961 Frankfurt motor show. Designed by Alexander von Falkenhausen and his small team, its 1.5-litre overhead camshaft high-compression four-cylinder engine gave the new saloon a special place in the market, not filled by any other car. The engine, the car, and their derivatives, have turned BMW into one of the most sophisticated and successful marques the world has seen. As the commercial situation improved, so involvement in racing increased, and the rate of recovery in Munich, at least up until the fuel crisis, was little short of miraculous.

By the early 1970s, the German Ford and GM (Opel) companies were in their stride and producing image-building cars for the modern age of business motoring. The little Opel GT of 1969 was a pretty variation on the Kadett theme. The performance of Cologne's Capris and Escorts did much to help Ford of Europe cut a new dash, taking the famous name a further step away from its austere, homely style of old, through 'international' design and clever marketing.

West Germany's other surviving group, Carl Borgward's former

LEFT *Porsche 917K, Le Mans, 1971. The* spectacular 917 was the absolute last word in sports-racing cars, and gave Porsche its first two outright Le Mans victories, in 1970 and 1971. Twenty-five were made to meet the regulations and they were rarely beaten. Britain's Richard Attwood was the most successful 917 Le Mans driver. With Victor Elford he led in 1969 from the 4th hour to the 22nd when the clutch failed; with Hans Herrmann he won in 1970; and in 1971, with Herbert Müller, he came second (to Helmut Marko and Gijs van Lennep in a similar car). John Wyer's Aston Martin and Ford experience made him the ideal chief for the Gulf-Porsche team. Here the 4.9-litre flat-12 monster's thirst is quenched while Attwood and Müller change places. A year later, under new regulations, the magnificent beast would be eligible no more.

ABOVE *Porsche air-cooled 3-litre Carrera. The* Carrera's excellent road manners and its mechanical layout have led to its being called 'a triumph of development over design'; and in that sense its inspiration can be traced from the 1921 Rumpler through the 1934 Auto Union of Dr Porsche to his KdF-Wagen. The 911 and its many derivatives thrive: whether winning races or rushing across the Sahara as (surely) the ultimate four-wheel-drive rally car.

Hansa-Lloyd-Goliath empire, did not live on for long. Its twin-cam engines took Cooper cars to a number of Formula Two victories in 1959–60, and the British-based tuner Bill Blydenstein showed that the Borgward Isabella could be a race winner. His best victory was in the Spa–Francorchamps touring car race of 1961, the year in which the Borgward company folded. Fussy styling had always tended to deflect attention away from the Borgward's fine technical specification, the appeal of which enabled Isabella spare parts to be built up into new cars for a further five years. Meanwhile, a manufacturing licence for the even more typically German *Grosse* Borgward – a biggish saloon intended to compete with the Mercedes-Benz 220 SE – was taken out in Mexico, keeping the Borgward alive until 1970.

The smaller manufacturing countries

The Low Countries had become places of car assembly rather than origination: with one exception. Well established in the commercial vehicle field, the Van Doorne brothers decided to put the Netherlands back on the car-making map and in 1958 their unique DAF (Van Doornes Automobielfabriek) surprised the motoring world because of its infinitely variable belt-drive Variomatic transmission. It was a pretty little car, almost too easy to drive; but not quite enough people took Europe's first economical 'automatic' seriously enough, and the dreams of Hubert and Wim van Doorne were only partly realized. Acquisition by Volvo was to end the days of the DAF car in the mid-1970s, but it is

fascinating to see how many car makers are taking the Van Doornes' transmission seriously nowadays.

The Swedish company Volvo, and its compatriot Saab, moved ahead with the times in the 1960s, continuing to do well in long-distance rallies and races. Volvo's PV544 stayed in production as a saloon until 1965 (even until 1969 in P210 estate car form), and the equally popular Amazon series kept going until 1970. Overlapping both from 1966, the140 series began a new generation of unexciting but essentially honest saloons and estate cars. The rally wins were, suddenly, a thing of the past but the important workhorse characteristics remained. The 1960s and early '70s, however, did see a somewhat tentative look by Volvo at the GT market. The resultant P1800, in the high-waisted Frua-Ghia idiom of the day, did not set the world alight and became a cult car rather than a competition model. Its short-lived successor, the 1800ES two-plus-two hatchback, was more attractive and practical: the sort of car enthusiasts do not notice when it is there, but miss sorely when it has gone. (Britain's last Morris Minor is in that category.)

Saab kept its sporting traits for longer and, as the three-cylinder two-stroke went out of fashion, Ford's Cologne V4 was brought in to power the Saab 96, enabling it to win the RAC Rally for a fourth time in 1968 and again even as late as 1971. The Saab 99 had a straight-four overhead camshaft engine designed by Standard-Triumph. Even Stig Blomqvist was hard put to win rallies with this model: probably the first car to show that the combination of high power and front-wheel drive

ABOVE AND RIGHT
Pininfarina + Ferrari = pure automotive art.
Almost simultaneously, in 1968-9, came two classic Ferraris, arguably unmatched before or since as true GT cars. Both were shaped by Pininfarina, Italy's most famous coachbuilder. The 365 GTB4 (ABOVE) had a 4.4-litre 60° V12 engine that developed some 350 bhp, and its five-speed gearbox was mounted at the rear. It had coil-spring independent suspension all round, and was the last of the truly great front-engined Ferraris. By
contrast, the production 246 GT Dino (RIGHT), with a 2.4-litre 65° V6, shows just how Ferrari could challenge the contemporary Porsche road-car market to good effect.

(only) was not ideal for high-speed stage rallying.

By the 1960s, Spain had become an 'assembly' nation, with the demise of Wilfredo Ricart's four-overhead camshaft Pegaso dream car after several years of production at the rate of less than one vehicle a week, although Pegaso commercial vehicles kept the name in circulation.

Italian dash

Italy lived up to its reputation as *the* sports car nation. Alfa Romeo's Giulietta and Giulia led to a succession of fine touring car race and Alpine Rally winners, and in 1964 Carlo Chiti set up a sort of latter-day Scuderia Ferrari when he founded Autodelta to specialize in competition work for Alfa Romeo. In fact, Chiti had left Ferrari in 1961 to join a consortium intent on giving Italy a new racing and sports car marque: the abortive ATS (Automobili Turismo e Sport). The Grand Prix car was a failure, but the handsome GT models might have got somewhere if the partnership had not broken up. Chiti had trained as an aeronautical engineer and had worked for Alfa Romeo before. Autodelta's efforts to put the marque back in the winner's circle in prototype sports car racing did bear some fruit in the end. Chiti's technicians produced the Tipo 33 Alfa Romeo in 1967, and by 1970 and 1971 it had become a race winner in the 3-litre Group 6 category. At this time, however, the V12 Ferrari 312P and flat-8 Porsche were more consistent than Chiti's V8 machine. Alfa Romeo's Montreal front-engined coupé of 1970 used a derivative of that unit, but a more popular model was the Alfasud (so-called because the state-assisted company built it in a new factory to relieve unemployment in southern Italy), a 1.2-litre flat-4 front-wheel-drive saloon of great character.

Exotic GT cars from new companies replaced some of Italy's long-extinguished stars. Examples were the Iso Rivolta and Grifo; the Maserati Mistrale and Ghibli; the Lamborghini 400GT and the exciting Miura; and the de Tomaso Longchamp and Pantera. None of these cars was a serious competition machine. All were responses to the demand for an Italian super-car: a demand that Ferrari still fulfilled supremely well, from the 250 GT/GTO and 275 GTB4 to the ultimate front-engined model, the 365 GTB4 or Daytona. Porsche progress also made Ferrari decide, in the late 1960s, to produce a smaller road car with the engine behind the driver. The V6 Dino was the first of the new line of 'bargain' Ferraris.

Lancia kept up its reputation for innovation with the 1961 Flavia, which *Topolino* man Fessia had adapted from his 14-year-old design for the Caproni Electromeccanica Saronno (CEMSA) company, better known for aircraft. This low-slung, front-wheel-drive machine featured a flat-4 engine ahead of the front wheels, and gave Lancia another modern car after lying dormant for so long. The Flavia was followed by the Fulvia, which had Lancia's traditional V4 type of engine. Both inspired GT versions which proved to be very fine rally cars. Sweden's Harry Kallström won the RAC Rally twice with the Fulvia and was European champion in 1969, the year in which FIAT took control of the famous old company.

FIAT continued to spread its wings with models being made under licence, or copied with permission, in more than 20 countries. A company in which FIAT took a 15 per cent interest was Citroën, always a producer of intriguing motor cars.

A French super-car

The Citroën DS/ID, the 2CV and their derivatives were the Paris company's staple products throughout the 1960s; then came the SM and the GS of the early 1970s. The GS was a practical family car with the typical and endearing Citroën features of soft suspension and smooth ride qualities. The SM was something completely different. For many years, for fiscal reasons, none of France's major producers had made a super-car of the type Italy was so adept at. Gone were the last of the Talbots, formerly Darracqs, which Antonio Lago had produced after the break with Britain in 1935, when Rootes had been marshalling itself. Gone were the great Delages, Delahayes, Hotchkisses and Salmsons. Presidential and VIP transport generally took the form of lengthened and heightened luxury Citroën DS cars. They looked splendid, but these were neither personal nor super-cars.

It was from another of Citroën's Italian links – Maserati – that the new French dream car emerged as the star of the 1970 Geneva Show. The Citroën SM *looked* a dream and its mechanical specification implied that it could fulfil the promise of its appearance. To the full power assistance and complex suspension to which DS owners were accustomed was

ABOVE **Lamborghini Miura, 1966-73.** *No car is perfect, and it was the imperfection of his own Ferrari that made tractor magnate Ferruccio* *Lamborghini go in for car production himself. Every car bearing his name has been spectacular, but an all-time pinnacle was reached with the beautiful* *3.9-litre V12 (transversely mounted) mid-engined Miura, engineered by Gianpaolo Dallara, styled by Bertone and, in this case, provided for* *photography by Michael Gertner. Perhaps wisely, Lamborghini has eschewed motor racing and concentrated on road cars.*

added the power of a four-overhead camshaft Maserati V6 engine. This unit, despite its modest 2.7 litres, propelled this veritable mechanical goddess faster and more comfortably over France's expanding *autoroute* network than any other road car produced in motoring's mother nation. The Ligier factory was acquired in order to build the SM, which was given fuel injection in 1973. Sadly, problems even of the kind that can be remedied at the prototype stage cannot always be held at bay in a production car of the SM's complexity, and this expensive toy could not hope to be an exception. After being taken over by Peugeot, Citroën could count the days to the axing of its mighty Maserati-engined SM.

Panhard's end

It will be recalled that the first Peugeots had been powered by Panhard's engines and that both marques had gone into production in 1891: the motor industry's real start in France, and in the world. When Peugeot acquired Citroën in 1974 it also acquired its old ally and supplier: for between 1955 and 1965 the Société des Anciens Etablissements Panhard et Levassor had been drawn closer and closer to Citroën, who wanted space rather than the product. The last Panhard was a worthy little coupé called the 24CT. It was entirely French in character, which is what most Panhards had become since showing the world the format of the motor car all those years before. Citroën dropped the marque name in 1967; Peugeot has never reintroduced it. Perhaps this is not surprising since Panhard is even less pronounceable than Peugeot for most non-French speakers, and marketing is a more verbal activity than it used to be.

The later Panhards had owed much to J. A. Grégoire who, from 1962, actually manufactured a few Chapron-bodied cars bearing his own name. These were based on his earlier Hotchkiss-Grégoire project upon which Hotchkiss had burned its fingers.

Peugeot prosperity and Renault success

Peugeot itself had maintained its impressive form. In 1960 Pininfarina's styling made the 404 somewhat anonymous but four victories in the East African Safari removed any possible doubts as to its competence. Its effective successor, the 504 of 1969, was another fine car, in which an element of French charm was restored to its appearance. In estate car form it rivalled the big Volvo as a family workhorse for Europe.

Renault's first winner of the 1960s was the diminutive 1962 R4 which had a sealed cooling system and the unusual feature of a fractionally longer wheelbase on one side, due to the geometry of the rear suspension. This long-lived utility was a challenger to Citroën's 2CV and

the beginning of a universal swapping of ends (from rear to front) of all Renault's power packages. Other important newcomers were the 16 in 1965 and the 5 in 1972. Renault's main sporting associations at this time were through *Le Sorcier*, the nickname given to their contracted tuning wizard, Amédée Gordini, who made the rear-engined Dauphine and R8 occasional rally winners. Jean Redélé's little Alpine sports car used Renault and Gordini experience extensively. In the late 1960s, the beautiful Alpine Berlinette became a force in rallying. Jean-Claude Andruet was the clear 1970 European champion, and Alpine took the manufacturers' title in equally convincing style in 1971 and 1973 with many wins, including the Monte Carlo and Acropolis in both years.

France returns to Grand Prix racing

France had not had a competitive Grand Prix car since the days of the Talbot-Lago and the Simca-Gordini. The Gordinis were fast and fragile; the Talbots were capable of winning only in the absence of the faster Italian entries: their finest hour was when they were given mudguards and lamps and came in first and second at Le Mans in 1950. Stardom had eluded the post-war Grand Prix efforts of the Bugatti, CTA-Arsenal, Sacha-Gordine.

It was a new make, Matra, that was to bring success to France. Matra-Sports was formed as an offshoot of the Engins Matra aerospace company in 1964 from the remnants of René Bonnet's sports car business. (Bonnet's former partner, Charles Deutsch, had gone his own way several years earlier. Until then they had been making DB competition specials since 1939.)

Matra's aim was Grand Prix racing and among the first top-line drivers to try one was Jackie Stewart. Earlier in this chapter, the story of Grand Prix racing has been taken as far as 1965. In 1966 a new Grand Prix formula was introduced. It allowed 1.5-litre supercharged engines, or 3 litres unsupercharged. Everyone chose the latter.

LEFT *Citroën SM 2.7-litre four-overhead camshaft V6, 1970-5.* Strangely beautiful and no less novel than other Citroëns, this shortlived sports-saloon had a Maserati engine, a five-speed gearbox and, of course, front-wheel drive. This example is from the Patrick Collection, which is housed on the site of a former papermill in King's Norton, Birmingham. The frontage of the mill is retained as a feature of this new motor museum, open in 1985.

RIGHT *Alpine-Renault Berlinette, 1974 Tour du Maroc.* The Alpine A110 was a pretty little coupé when not dressed for battle. In its later years it became a champion rally car, taking the top title in 1971 and 1973. Among its notable individual wins were the Moroccan rallies of 1973 and 1974. (The Citroën SM caused an even bigger surprise in 1971 when it won this crippling event.)

The 1966 GP formula

By far the quickest into the arena was Jack Brabham, who did not waste time arguing against the change of formula, but went home to Australia to speed the development of a GM-based V8 power unit by his friends at Repco engineering. Since leaving Cooper at the end of 1961, Brabham had been producing and driving his own cars. The 1966 formula and the new engine worked for him straight away, and he took the World Championship for a third time. In 1967 his team mate, New Zealander Dennis Hulme, was victorious with Brabham runner-up. In these early seasons, however, BRM, Cooper, Ferrari, Honda, Lotus, McLaren and others were resolving their problems with varying degrees of success. The new Ford-financed Cosworth DFV engine gave Jim Clark's Lotus 49 a début victory in the 1967 Dutch GP, and then three more wins to show that Clark and Lotus would be the combination to beat. His death in a minor race at Hockenheim early in 1968 shocked the whole motor racing fraternity, for he had been liked and admired universally. He had been the first Briton to win the famous Indianapolis 500-mile race and had taken more championship Grands Prix than anyone else in history.

Clark's friend, Graham Hill, already something of an elder statesman, pulled himself and the Lotus team together and became 1968 World Champion. Hill had returned to Lotus, his first team, in 1967 after seven seasons with BRM. His former team mate, Jackie Stewart, had stayed on for 1967 but switched to Matra when his Formula Two and Three entrant Ken Tyrrell, the man who had given Stewart his big chance in the first place, came to an arrangement with that French company to use the new British DFV engine, proved by Clark. In 1968, Stewart finished the season runner-up to Hill.

Aerofoils and other controversies

One feature of 1968 Formula One racing (inspired by Texan Jim Hall's 1967 Chaparral GT prototype) was the adjustable aerofoil and, by the end of the season, several GP cars had acquired ludicrously high suspension-mounted wings front and rear, to increase downforce and therefore grip. Early in 1969, on the Montjuich street circuit in Barcelona, Graham Hill and Jochen Rindt crashed out of the Spanish Grand Prix with wing collapse. Soon these devices were banned; but they had marked the start of an era of controversy in which technology versus safety became just one of a series of arguments caused, basically, by rapidly increasing tyre sizes. Stewart, who had promoted safety from the outset (he pioneered the use of safety harness in Formula One soon after joining the Grand Prix circus), went on to become World Champion in 1969 ahead of another Tyrrell protégé, Jacky Ickx.

Change and crisis

Also in 1969 Matra came under the wing of Simca. Simca was newly involved with Chrysler, and it was easy to see why Tyrrell was under pressure to use Matra's new V12 engine rather than the Ford-sponsored DFV. In 1970, therefore, Ken Tyrrell (after a brief attempt to race March cars) introduced his own Grand Prix machine, while Lotus returned to power – although it was another tragic year in that Jochen Rindt became champion posthumously.

During the next three seasons, Jackie Stewart won two more world crowns and surpassed Jim Clark's record as the most successful Grand Prix driver of all time. The new Scottish ace promoted the sport as being technical rather than gladiatorial, and he tackled his racing in a totally serious and professional manner, as indeed Stirling Moss had done before him. When Stewart withdrew permanently from racing at the end of 1973, it was becoming a thoroughly commercial sport at international level, with ever-increasing media coverage.

It was a time when all car manufacturers needed every possible sale, for the very idea of motoring was, for a brief period, almost anti-social. The oil embargo made fuel costs soar, and rationing seemed likely. The motor car represented only a small percentage of fuel oil consumption but it was hit hardest. This was the beginning of true inflation, as costs, wages and prices went up and consumer demand went down.

Britain's record output of nearly two million cars in 1972 has never been approached again. The USA's slide began a little later, its production peak of almost ten million cars being achieved in 1973. The smaller dips in production of Germany, France and, above all, Japan, were the keys to the next decade of the motor car.

LEFT **Dennis Hulme (Brabham-Repco), Zandvoort, 1967.** *Following Jack Brabham's 1966 world GP title (his third) in a car of his own make, he and his team mate Dennis Hulme shared the honours for 1967. Hulme was champion driver, with his boss runner-up and, once again, winner of the manufacturers' championship. On this day in Holland, however, Brabham and Hulme were beaten by Jim Clark, whose success gave the DFV-powered Lotus its first win.*

ABOVE RIGHT **Graham Hill (Lotus-Ford DFV), Monaco, 1968.** *After a racing career spanning more than 20 years it is a sad irony that Graham Hill (INSET) was killed – as Mike Hawthorn had been – after he had retired from the sport. He was World Champion twice, in 1962 and 1968. His speciality was the tight, tricky, unforgiving Monaco GP, which he won no fewer than five times (in 1963, '64, '65, '68 and '69).*

Colin Chapman (1928–1982)

Anthony Colin Bruce Chapman gave up secondhand car sales and a career in the Royal Air Force to take advantage of his BSc and become an engineer. In his spare time he built and drove specials, to which he gave the name Lotus; the first of these were Austin Seven-based.

Soon this meant full-time work as Lotus became a business. Sports, single-seater and production GT cars followed one another thick and fast from Colin Chapman's drawing board. Always slim and smooth and very light, Lotus cars of the 1960s had a reputation for superb handling. Although Chapman switched to rear-engine configuration after Cooper, likewise using the Coventry Climax series of four- and eight-cylinder power units, his cars were soon Britain's leading GP contenders: and innovation has kept Lotus in front. Chapman's Lotus 18, 25, and 33 dominated the 1961 to 1965 Formula One period. (The Lotus 25 was the first F1 car of monocoque construction, i.e. with integral body and chassis.) In this, Chapman's success was also due to the natural brilliance of Scottish farmer Jim Clark, who won 19 of the 47 World Championship races held during the 1.5-litre (u/s) formula.

For many years, Lotus held the greatest number of makes' World Championships: a total of seven by the end of the 1978 season. (This record was beaten by Ferrari, whose eighth title came in 1983.)

Born in Richmond, Surrey, Colin Chapman became as famous for his business skills as for his engineering ability. Lotus and Ford began a long association with the introduction of the Ford Lotus-Cortina in 1963. Chapman worked closely with other manufacturers, as well as developing Lotus production models to a consistently high level. But Grand Prix racing remained the great aspiration. Lotus had just scored its first victory for several seasons when Chapman died suddenly in late 1982.

1975

Was the crisis over? Even the European Economic Community was in grievous financial trouble, yet business and life in general seemed to become more and more automated and efficient. As ever, the motor car was at the centre of industrial activity. The acceleration of Japan just had to slow: there was simply a limit to demand. In cutting back, however, the Japanese proved as adaptable and skilful as ever, and their cooperative arrangements in other nations led to cars as diverse as British Triumphs, Australian Fords, and Italian demi-Alfas.

Technologically, Grand Prix racing was British-based (although James Hunt was the only British champion of the decade), and the Ford Cosworth DFV V8 power unit proved itself the most successful racing engine in history. As a maker of racing cars and engines, Ferrari held its lead, but in sports, GT, and prototype racing the name of Porsche dominated. Renault led the move away from 3-litre racers to 1.5-litre turbocharged GP cars, which had become virtually universal by the mid-1980s. Alpine-Renault, Ford, Lancia, FIAT, Opel, and others shone in rallying, but the focal point of the 1980s was the extremely powerful Audi Quattro. This led to a whole new breed of four-wheel-drive rally cars from rival manufacturers.

American manufacturers suffered because of their long tradition of producing large cars, but responded to the new social and economic pressures with some brave new designs, quite unlike anything they had built before; however, the big car did not die out entirely. The state of flux continued in Europe, but one thing was certain: the standards of design and manufacture everywhere in the world had never been better. As well as being a necessity, the motor car could still give pleasure after a hundred years.

THE FITTEST SURVIVE

1985

This is not a book of statistics. It is a book about a century of the motor car and the people involved with it. It has been an exciting and entertaining century. Even so, happenings of the 1970s and 1980s cannot be put into perspective without a few hard facts.

In terms of millions of cars, world production for 1973 was 9.7 in the United States, 4.5 in Japan, 3.6 in West Germany, 2.9 in France, 1.8 in Italy and 1.7 in Britain. In 1974, the first full fuel crisis year, the same top six produced, respectively, 7.4, 3.9, 2.8, 2.6, 1.6 and 1.5 million motor cars. The following year saw Japan rally to 4.6 million and Germany to 2.9 million, whereas the others continued to fall away. The best recovery year was 1977 when the United States was back to 9.2 millions, with Japan now up to 5.4, West Germany at 3.8, France 3.1, Italy 1.4 and Britain 1.3.

The year 1980 showed that the inexorable march of the East really was beginning to hit hard in the West, for Japan (7.0 millions) had overtaken America (down to 6.4 millions). West Germany, France and Italy were relatively steady at 3.5, 2.9, and 1.4 millions, but Britain's output – for the first time since 1957 – was down below a million, its 900,000 putting it behind Russia and Spain.

What the statistics do not show is just how international the whole industry had become, nor the proportion of overseas components built into so many home-produced cars. By the 1980s considerable research was needed in some cases to establish the actual nationalities involved in a single model.

Customers determined to buy British stood a chance of getting within 10 per cent of their aim if they bought one of the products of BL (formerly called British Leyland): but not the Triumph Acclaim, basically a Honda Ballade – built (and very well, too) at Oxford – which was Britain's first truly incognito offering. It was a very good car for one introduced as a stopgap at a time of desperation.

Despair had never left BL. A particularly low point was reached in spring 1975 when Sir Don Ryder's team of investigators produced its report. The team had been appointed by the Government following the discovery that BL's net liabilities had already reached £43 million.

Lord Stokes and his right-hand man John Barber left, and British Leyland became a completely nationalized concern. When Jaguar lost its own London Motor Show stand it seemed as if the last bastion of marque identity within the organization was under threat. In 1974 the E-type, always a great crowd-puller, even though chiefly for export, had been put on show for continuity's sake as part of a subversive, long-term 'keep Jaguar Jaguar' campaign generally thought doomed to ultimate failure. In fact E-type production was virtually at an end. That E-type won a

gold medal: the last of its many accolades for, early in 1975, news of its demise was made public. When the completely different XJ-S was announced that autumn, customers used to personal service had to hunt around to find a car, let alone find anyone who knew anything about it, on the 'car park', as some wag described the Leyland Cars Earls Court show stand.

It was not until 1977 that action was taken to halt BL's slide to oblivion. It would take time to repair the damage, but there is little doubt that the sometimes controversial leadership of Michael Edwardes marked the start of an effective salvage operation. The 1980 Triumph Acclaim was simply part of the open-heart surgery he performed.

In 1978 there was a new development in the story of Chrysler UK, formerly the Rootes Group, when Peugeot, who already owned Citroën, took over all Chrysler's European activities. A new man was appointed to lead the British company into the future. Back in 1973, after a row with Stokes and Barber, he had left the Austin Morris part of BL by 'mutual consent' and added to his public reputation within a year by creating a new car with Italian styling and Japanese engineering – for Korea. The car was the Hyundai Pony and the man was George Turnbull. Under his command, Chrysler UK soon became the Talbot Motor Company Ltd.

Talbot was in fact the family name of the Earl of Shrewsbury who in 1903 decided to go into car manufacture by financing a British version of the French Clément-Bayard. The Talbot name disappeared from British cars in 1954, and from French ones in 1960. It seemed an unusual move, 20 years on, to bring back the dead marque and rename Hillmans and Sunbeams as Talbots. But the name Chrysler had been a marketing failure in Europe and was taken back across the Atlantic. The rescuers, Peugeot, had already decided to replace the French Simca and Chrysler marques with Talbot: pronounced the French way, of course.

The most successful of the new Anglo-French Talbot cars were the small ones. Associating the Talbot name with the Ligier GP team was an attempt to gain a sporting image quickly. This was achieved much more effectively, and on a shoestring budget, when Talbot won the 1981 World Rally Championship for Makes despite the arrival of the Audi Quattro on the scene. The great moment of glory, however, was in 1980, when young Henry (son of Pauli) Toivonen won the RAC Rally in the weirdly named Talbot Sunbeam-Lotus. This was the first really big result for the competition department at Ryton, Coventry, since Andrew Cowan, Brian Coyle and Colin Malkin had scored their laudable long-odds victory in the London-to-Sydney marathon 12 years before in a Hillman Hunter.

PRECEDING PAGES
Bentley Mulsanne Turbo, 6.7-litre V8, from 1982. Since the Continental was dropped in the 1960s, Rolls-Royces and Bentleys have been similar in all but name and cosmetics. The Rolls-Royce for the 1980s, the Silver Spirit, was offered as a Bentley Mulsanne, its name a reminder of the marque's pre-war exploits at Le Mans. The Mulsanne Turbo option helped to separate these two top British makes slightly.

LEFT *Ford Escort, San Remo Rally, 1981.* Consistently successful since its introduction in 1968, the rear-wheel-drive Escort remained competitive into the 1980s, providing Finland's Ari Vatanen with the world rally drivers' crown in 1981. In 1983 Ford took a break from participating in motor sports, but this intermission was not to be for long. Ford had worked on its sporting image for over 20 years, and was not going to let it fade away.

LEFT *MG Metro Turbo, from 1982*. Britain's new super-Mini was launched in 1980 as the Austin Metro. BL's final throes as a corporation saw most cars come under the Austin Rover banner. The MG name was revived in 1982, however, and in 1984 came a mid-engined V6 four-wheel-drive rally prototype, the MG Metro 6R4. Meanwhile, Rover had become a symbol of the new aggressive marketing, and the Maestro and Montego saloons made Austin a strong name once again.

ABOVE *Jaguar XJ12 HE, from 1981*. Having resisted the BL corporate machine for so long in the late 1970s, Jaguar and its award-winning XJ6 and XJ12 are going it alone. The most refined road cars in the world have kept their individuality, and Jaguar has become Britain's proudest marque of the 1980s. There has also been a successful return to motor racing. A completely new XJ range was to be launched in 1985.

Whereas the Talbot success was something of a surprise, Ford was now so involved in competition programmes that results were expected. The arrival there of Stuart Turner (the man whose strategies had brought fame to BMC in rallying) ensured Ford's consistently good performances in rallies from the late 1960s. The Ford Escort TC had won the 1970 World Cup Rally, from London to Mexico City, driven by Hannu Mikkola and Gunnar Palm. (The London–Sydney and London–Mexico were the two most remarkable transcontinental events since the early days of the motor car. Citroëns crashed in both events while leading; BLMC cars were second both times.) The Ford Escort went on to win no fewer than eight successive RAC Rallies (1972–9), Roger Clark proving twice that at least one Briton could beat the Scandinavians and Finns (but they won the other six!). In 1979, for the third time, Ford took the world makes title. Ari Vatanen of Finland was the individual champion in 1981, driving the obsolete Escort RS. However, plans for a rally version of the new Escort were cancelled by Stuart Turner's announcement in early 1983 that Ford would pull out of competitions – although the implication was that this was a strategic withdrawal, not a permanent retreat.

The most popular Ford
Before the Escort, the Cortina had filled a big gap in the market and had proved itself a fine family or competition car, with that special brand of Ford imagery that enabled it to be the ultimate saloon for all kinds of people in every walk of life. The conventional Cortina, in its various forms, had lived for nearly 20 years, always a top seller, when it was finally phased out at the end of the 1982 season. It was such a classic that it was given a farewell television programme all to itself.

The Cortina's successor, the Sierra, was based (in shape) on an experimental car, but it managed to sell well in spite of its unusual lines. Far from controversial were the lines of the front-wheel-drive Fiesta

ABOVE *Ford Sierra XR4i, from 1983. A complete change from the Cortina it replaced, the Sierra emphasized the aerodynamics that are essential to modern motoring, what with costly fuel and declared consumption figures. (As in most popular ranges, however, a diesel-powered version was included – although running costs* *were not actually much better.) However, Ford never lets the grass grow long, and more new models, including an XR5, were expected in the centenary year of the motor car.*

(1976) and new Escort (1980), which were particularly crisp. If they left room for a smallish 'booted' Ford, then the Orion filled the niche well, towards the end of 1983. With all the activity surrounding the smaller Fords on the European market, the make cannot be left without mentioning the competent manner in which the large Granada saloon and the Capri coupé (Europe's answer to the Mustang idea) spread the Ford name across the motoring spectrum very effectively during the period. A Grenada replacement was expected for 1985.

General Motors gets moving
For years, Vauxhall had failed to match Ford's panache in Britain, even though the Victor and Viva had beaten the Cortina and Escort in adopting the curvaceous 'Coke-bottle' look. The tide began to turn for the Luton marque when it adopted international GM shapes with the Chevette hatchback (a rally winner in the making) and the totally gimmick-free three-box Cavalier (also marketed with some differences as the Opel Ascona). This renaissance for a once-great marque moved a stage further in the 1980s with a switch to front-wheel drive and transversely mounted engines, all duplicating Opel policy. The Astra came late in 1979, the new Cavalier (GM's universal J car) in 1981, well ahead of the Cortina replacements, and the smaller Nova in 1983; the last-named, like some Fiestas, was assembled in Spain. Their generally undistinguished looks belied their worth and did not prevent GM becoming a bigger force in Britain than ever before.

A super-critical public and a self-critical industry had turned the workaday car into a precision instrument in a relatively short time; new models cannot now be described with any conviction simply as facelifts. Already considered dated, Ford's Fiesta was awaiting a replacement quite urgently by the mid-1980s.

The Issigonis legacy
By this time Austin-Rover, BL's new-look volume-car group, was pitching strongly with its Austin Metro (1980) and Maestro (1983), truly modern successors to the great Issigonis Mini, founder of this particular movement. (The Mini itself was still in production, well past its 25th birthday!) The last MGBs were made in 1980 and it looked as if the marque would die when the Abingdon factory was closed down amid strenuous protest, and several schemes failed to materialize. The M.G. name was brought to life again, however, for high-performance versions of the Metro, Maestro and Montego. Initial doubts gave way to acceptance of the idea; after all, enthusiasts knew that the first M.G.s had been sporting Morrises, so why not sporting Super-Minis now?

Morris was one name that did disappear from car catalogues shortly before the motor car's centenary: a pity in a way, for the 'Bullnose' had been Britain's first mass-produced car, and the marque had existed for more than 70 years. The Triumph car, as a British design, was axed (even while the TR6 and Stag were still being mourned by some) when the TR7 and TR8 succumbed to a contracting market for open-top sports cars. People wanting such cars were still catered for by such diverse specialist designs as the Super Seven (once a Lotus), the Morgan (still very much a Morgan) and TVR's sleek Tasmin, another of today's unhappily concocted type names, but otherwise a worthy and truculent survivor. (Survival has never been guaranteed for anyone in the century of the motor car.) The 1980s also saw the continued presence of the 'revivalist' firms, of which Panther was typical, that bring out new cars in the spirit of those of an earlier era.

Triumph's saloon range had included the last car to be made in the tradition of the old-style fast, luxurious British compacts, epitomized by the 2½-litre Riley and Daimler's Conquest Century of the 1950s: the revived Triumph Dolomite, in overhead camshaft 1850 and Sprint forms. It had many attractive features without the built-in potential for updating. If tooling did not present such technical and financial

problems, many British designs could have lived much longer than they did. Strangely enough, it was the interesting yet unpopular front-wheel-drive Triumph 1300 of 1965 that had provided the structure for the sporty Dolomite of the 1970s; the Honda Ballade, known as the Acclaim, was a reversion to front-wheel drive and 1.3 litres, but it kept the Triumph name going on life-support only.

The Rover, which had once overlapped with Triumph in the larger saloon field, was another endangered British species. The regular early-1980s Rover type was the David Bache-styled SD1, born as a large and aggressive-looking saloon – with distinct Ferrari Daytona overtones! – in 1976. The largely discredited Ryder Report had been no more helpful to Rover's prospects as an entity than to Jaguar's. Michael Edwardes had not yet arrived and the Rover management – once a real team on a par with Jaguar's – was now split up, so it was too late for a Rover car company to re-emerge. The only way that could happen would be to combine it with the special-purpose Land-Rover and Range-Rover operation at Solihull; but that became highly improbable, once Rover SD1 production was transferred to Cowley.

With its choice of four-, six- and eight-cylinder petrol or four-cylinder turbo-diesel engines, and a racing programme, Rover had taken on a

LEFT **Morgan, the ageless enigma.** There have been few variations on this theme from a very British little factory, nestling beneath those Malvern Hills that inspired the composer Edward Elgar and, surely, the Morgan family. On the other hand, the 1984 4/4 for California met the emission control laws with a not-quite-so-British 2-litre FIAT engine running on propane. The Morgan is still loved as a sports car made in the old way, with true craftsmanship.

ABOVE **Vauxhall Cavalier SRi, from 1981.** GM European policy for the 1980s meant front-wheel drive for the family cars: Cavalier, Astra, and Nova in Britain; Opel names in most other places. This top model may not turn heads like the Ford opposite; but the Cavalier did bring Vauxhall from also-ran to front-runner with amazing speed in what had always been Ford Cortina market territory.

OVERLEAF **DeLorean DMC-2, 1981-2.** A Giugiaro-formed stainless steel-clad futuristic coupé in the Patrick Collection – a modern collector's piece if ever there was one. Hindsight is so easy, yet this project (which saw the light of day in 1976) was given the go-ahead at a time when specialist car makers were treading as gingerly as they had ever done. Strength and long life through the use of new materials – these were the claims of former GM man John Zachary DeLorean who brought only brief joy and shortlived prospects to

Northern Ireland when he built a car factory there. The notoriety he achieved after the factory had been put into the receiver's hands in February 1982 was soon the subject of several books. Here we can only contemplate the neat V6 engine installation, the fully equipped interior and the gull-wing doors and continue to ponder the improbability of the whole surrealistic episode.

completely new image: but could it be sustained? The marque was expected to acquire an Oriental character as the SD1 came up for replacement. Whither the British Rover? That was the new question.

It might also be asked what direction Lotus would take, were it not for the fact that the famous company's road-going cars, like the Esprit and Excel, continued to be the most exotic practical GT machines made in Britain, bearing comparison with the best Italy could offer. Lotus in the mid-1980s was establishing close ties with Japan. More traditionally styled by Ogle, the Reliant Scimitar, like so many other models, brought open-air motoring to the 1980s after it seemed that it might be gone for ever.

The DeLorean remains an enigma. Forgetting the notoriety of its founder, it is hard to imagine anyone financing a high-volume GT car in the 1980s, yet John Zachary DeLorean persuaded a whole government! Built in the UK, this ill-fated car – with its gull-winged doors reminiscent of the Mercedes-Benz 300SL and its odd stainless-steel finish – was chiefly aimed at the United States. However, the demand simply was not there, and the company went out of business in 1982.

Turbocharging became an essential part of motoring in the 1980s, and was even adopted for the esoteric Bentley Mulsanne and Bristol Brigand and Beaufighter. Diesel engines continued to make progress in terms of smoothness and performance.

Still incorporating Bentley, Rolls-Royce maintained its standards into motoring's second century. It retained all the essential ingredients to substantiate its 'Best Car in the World' claim, including a price that was approaching £90,000 in the case of the Pininfarina-designed two-door Camargue. The saloons were made in Crewe, Cheshire, but the Corniche convertible and Phantom VI state limousine were built at the London premises of the firm's traditional coachbuilders H. J. Mulliner and Park Ward, also under the banner of the Vickers engineering group which took control of Rolls-Royce Motors in 1980. In 1984 a new management team was working hard to modernize the marque, to ensure its long-term future.

Aston Martin, like Rolls-Royce, had been in financial difficulties and actually folded up at the end of 1974. However, private and industrial (as opposed to state) aid rescued it and kept it afloat at the Tickford Street, Newport Pagnell, factory (formerly Salmons' coachworks). The name Tickford was revived for the making of extra-exclusive versions of anything from Metros and Capris to a Camargue-priced Lagonda revealed in 1983.

Sir David Brown had always wanted a Lagonda in the range but his two attempts had been abortive. It was the futuristic styling by William

Towns of the 1976 Lagonda, rather than its highly automated controls (later deleted), that brought back the Lagonda as the world's most unusual four-door luxury car – built only to order, like its stable mate, the Aston Martin super GT car.

There was a tendency among many enthusiasts in the 1980s to dream of times past, and in 1983 a brand-new Jensen Interceptor was announced: the first to be seen since 1976 and not, apparently, the last. The Jensen parts and service operation was planning, tentatively, to make up to one car a month. At the same time, another company obtained the right to build the classic Cobra as an AC: not that the AC had disappeared, for the mid-engined AC 3000 ME coupé had at last come through its long gestation period.

Amid all the fascinating 1984 cars, one new British model stood out from the rest, for October 1983 marked the return of a Jaguar stand at the London motor show for the first time in nine years. It had been that long since an open-topped Jaguar had been seen there. For many enthusiasts, the Jaguar XJS-C Cabriolet provided the freshest breath of air at the show. This, however, was a relative breeze compared to the gale of anticipation that awaited Jaguar's new saloon for centenary year, codenamed the XJ40.

This symbol of Jaguar's independent spirit was the culmination of more than four years of teamwork. Sir Michael Edwardes (as he had now become) was responsible for restoring a Jaguar directorate. The appointment of John Egan to re-establish Jaguar Cars Ltd in April 1980

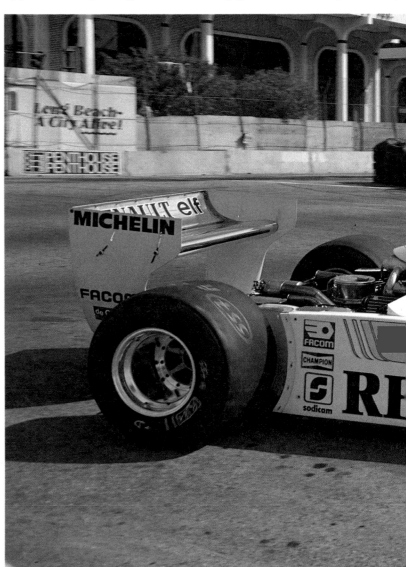

RIGHT **The Renault's return.** *As we have already seen, Renault was the world's first Grand Prix winner, in 1906. In 1979, a Renault became the first of the new breed of turbocharged cars to win a GP. Alain Prost (seen here at Long Beach in 1983) could have been World Champion in 1982 and '83 if the car had been more reliable. There was a lot Renault had to learn the hard way. Now the turbos rule and are virtually universal in Grand Prix racing. In a sense, the rally-winning mid-engined Renault 5* Turbo* (INSET RIGHT) of 1979 anticipated the MG Metro 6R4 by five years. This Renault started out like the Metro as a fashionable front-wheel-drive 'super-Mini'. Renault's many worldwide enterprises have included cooperation with American Motors in manufacturing the 1982 Car of the Year, the Renault 9. The 25 was a leading new contender for 1984.*

resulted in an unprecedented recovery in terms of quality, output and morale. Technical and manufacturing chiefs James Randle and Michael Beasley worked together to achieve these goals and at the same time look to the future. The danger of falling into the trap of complacency was avoided and, in its 50th year (the marque name was first used in 1935), the new Jaguar was born. Jaguar had always relied upon maintaining its North American market; the progress of Egan and the Jaguar team made them the toast of America. A limited programme of motor racing was started. The experienced Robert Tullius (who had raced the E-type and the XJ-S to several national championships) won four races and was runner-up for the 1983 GT prototype title of the United States, driving a Jaguar-sponsored V12-powered car called the XJR5; Britain's Brian Redman was to join the team for 1984. In Europe, Tom Walkinshaw began racing an XJ-S in the 1982 European Touring Car Championship and came third; in 1983, running as Jaguar's representative, he came second, and won more races than anyone else in the series. The champion, for the fourth time, was Dieter Quester (BMW).

Before passing on from the revitalized British scene, the recovery of the World's Land Speed Record by Britain should be noted. Britain's two previous record holders, John Cobb and Sir Malcolm Campbell's son Donald, had gone on to attempt the water speed record, only to lose their lives in doing so.

In October 1983, after nine years of planning and promoting, Londoner Richard Noble established a new Land Speed Record averaging 633.468 mph (1019.465 km/h) for a mile (in each direction) on Nevada's Black Rock desert with his Rolls-Royce Avon jet-engined car *Thrust II*, a record held by America since 1964. This unusual project was backed by some 200 British companies.

Development and innovation in Grand Prix racing

The general success of Formula One was confirmed by excellent media coverage around the world – a measure of the acceptance of product advertising. With every season, one team or another would find some technical advantage and then, sometimes literally, have its wings clipped. Engineering advances are always magnified when they occur in racing. After being first with the use of wings, the American Chaparral originated active 'ground effect' as a means of improving a car's adhesion to the track. It involved 'skirts' to seal the area under the car. This technique became progressively more significant as GP car designers developed it, until it was banned at the end of 1982. Another feature of race strategy which appeared briefly, and became vital to success in 1983, was the pit stop. This led to fascinating racing, because of the varying effects of running on low or full fuel tanks, worn or new tyres. Pit stops – sometimes under ten seconds in duration – became part of the spectacle of racing; yet the added dangers, caused by possible fuel spillage and pit-road haste, could not be denied and, for 1984, such planned stops were banned.

Throughout the 1970s, the Ford Cosworth DFV engine was the

engine to beat. Brabham, Matra and McLaren followed Lotus in its early use; then March and Tyrrell. As times and teams changed, so Hesketh, Wolf, Ligier and Williams joined in, all of them winners. Soon the majority of cars would be powered by the DFV.

The Brabham team, which had been run briefly by Ron Tauranac, to whom Sir Jack Brabham had sold out, next became the property of Bernard Ecclestone. Like Ken Tyrrell and Frank Williams, he was a former F3 driver. His role was also to be that of spokesman and promoter for the racing 'circus'.

In its 16 full competitive seasons, from 1968 to 1983, the DFV engine won ten manufacturers' titles (five for Lotus, two for Williams and one each for McLaren, Matra and Tyrrell); the other six went to Ferrari. In the same period, 12 drivers' championships went to DFV users, the exceptions being Ferrari's Niki Lauda (1975 and 1977) and Jody Scheckter (1979), and Brabham's Nelson Piquet in 1983. This was Piquet's second world title and the first for the driver of a modern turbocharged car, the new Brabham-BMW. One by one, the teams were turning to turbos: Lotus, McLaren, Williams; everyone, it seemed, except Tyrrell. Ferrari had already made the move, and the combined talents of Didier Pironi, Gilles Villeneuve, Patrick Tambay and René Arnoux, plus the reliability of the engine, gave the famous Italian company the honour of being first to be champion with a turbocharged car, in 1982 and then again in 1983.

Least rewarded at the end of those two seasons was Renault, who could have produced a champion in Alain Prost both times, but parted company with him at the end of 1983 instead. Renault had shown the way by being the first to take advantage of the rule permitting 1.5-litre cars to have turbochargers: that is to say, devices that use exhaust gas pressure to drive a turbine and 'force feed' the induction tract, to improve combustion and give more power. The idea was not new, but its application to the ultimate form of motor racing was very experimental, and Renault was gambling on finding enough power and reliability to beat the well-tried 3-litre cars. The new Renault GP car first raced in 1977, and Jean-Pierre Jabouille won the French GP at Dijon with it in 1979. It was a great day for the French for their very first Grand Prix, in 1906, had been a Renault victory. The DFV unit continued to win, but its days were numbered. Its last victory in 1983 was its 155th World Championship race win. (Ferrari has yet to win its 100th. Third in this league table of Grand Prix engines is still Britain's Coventry Climax.) In December 1983, Ford made its expected announcement: a new engine was to be developed by Cosworth, and so Ford would be back in GP racing in the late 1980s.

RIGHT *Lancia Rally (Acropolis, 1982). Epitome of the extremes of design which changed the face of rallying in the 1980s, the mid-engined Rally coupé gave Lancia its fifth World Rally Championship for Makes in 1983. Its top drivers were Walter Röhrl and Markku Alen. This model's predecessor, the Stratos (see pages 146-7), was an even more significant trendsetter in the 1970s.*

The rallying scene: a professional affair

The big technical change in rallying came at the end of 1980, when Audi declared its intention to enter a team of its newly announced four-wheel-drive Quattro sports coupés.

In its own way, rallying had become as big a business as racing. It had had its own makers' championships for over a decade and in 1978 a world drivers' championship was introduced, in addition to the existing European one. With the loss of the 'Liège' and the 'Alpine', the East African Safari became the top rally for severity but other, newer, cross-country rallies now replaced them.

As a stage rally, the Monte Carlo became less of a lottery than it had been; but more than any other event, it showed how the days of the enthusiastic amateur, taking his private car on a January jaunt, were long gone, never to return. The 1970s scene had been set by Lancia when it launched the fiery little Stratos to oust the Alpine-Renault as the leading lightweight rally car. Lancia's new masters, FIAT, took to rallying with great success, winning the world title three times. Ford made a mid-engined car, the GT70, but reverted to developing the Escort, which had become such a superb rally car.

The fascination of rallying continued to be in the variety of types that

stood a chance of winning and, although the presence of four-wheel drive was controversial, the Audi Quattro added a new dimension. Its arrival coincided with the cancellation by Daimler-Benz of its plans to field a world rally team, which reigning champion Walter Röhrl would have led. The Audi's first season was fraught with misfortune but its top driver, Hannu Mikkola, won the Swedish and RAC Rallies, and Michèle Mouton won the San Remo event, proving what many people already believed: that she was the first truly great lady driver in rallying since the days of Pat Moss. Matters improved for Audi in 1982, largely due to Michèle Mouton's brilliant handling of the ferocious and complicated machine. The French girl won no fewer than three big rallies outright, just missing the opportunity of becoming the first woman to win a major motoring title. Hannu Mikkola won two events, but the complex Quattro did not finish in enough of the others to prevent Walter Röhrl regaining his personal crown – ahead of Mouton – through the good offices of Opel. That company's Ascona and Manta 400 came into their own to show that powerful, well-prepared, front-engined, rear-wheel-drive cars could still shine. However, the combined efforts of the talented Quattro drivers did give Audi the 1982 makers' title.

Fortunes fluctuated in 1983, too, when the Stratos replacement, the mid-engined Rally coupé, showed sufficient domination of tarmacadam events to give Lancia its fifth world rally title. Audi's consolation was to provide the most consistently successful rally driver of modern times, Hannu Mikkola, with his first personal world championship.

With four-wheel drive and super- or turbocharging being taken up by more and more makers of everyday cars, the future of professional rallying looked promising, once the advantages and disadvantages of the revolutionary Quattro were realized. There remained a lurking feeling that a spate of new limited production, high-speed rally cars could highlight the shortage of top drivers to handle them.

Restriction and cooperation

The Japanese makers had been on the verge of greatness in the world of motor sport, ever since the start of their rise to power. (In motorcycling, of course, they had a walkover.) A feature of the 1970s and '80s was the manner in which other nations combined their restriction of imports from Japan with manufacturing and marketing cooperation with that country's car industry.

Chrysler's withdrawal from Europe preceded a recovery plan that made Lee Iacocca an American hero as he repaid his corporation's vast debts to the US government: for, put plainly, Chrysler had been broke until then. Mitsubishi, long-term associates of Chrysler, took over the Australian plant as the company changed direction. Previously the firmest adherent to the big V8-powered car, Chrysler made rapid strides, due in no small part to Iacocca's marketing skills. The transversely mounted front-engined Chrysler, Dodge and Plymouth 'European-sized' saloons and coupés were a most important factor here. Legislation had settled down to known sets of rules and the customer was, once again, the priority. It was Chrysler who brought fully open-air motoring back to a public that had sorely missed it in the late 1970s.

Ford adopted the European Escort in America but modernized and downscaled famous models such as Mustang (with four, six or eight cylinders), Fairlane and LTD to meet the new demand for fuel efficiency. For the mid-1980s the Ford Tempo and Mercury Topaz fell into line, with their four-cylinder 2.3-litre fuel-injected overhead camshaft engines, manual and automatic transmission options, front-wheel drive and unadorned low-drag bodywork. An interesting pointer was the introduction of the front-drive Australian Ford Telstar and Laser, which were actually Mazdas at heart.

Different emission-control requirements in different parts of the world meant a variety of engine power outputs for the internationals. The General Motors front-wheel-drive series (Opel Ascona and Vauxhall Cavalier in Europe; permutations of Buick, Chevrolet and even Cadillac in the United States) was representative of the way ahead. America had a wider variety of styles but the European versions, with their overhead camshafts, were the more attractive from a driver's point of view: not that the twain were expected to meet for comparison. GM kept its classic Toronado and Eldorado in production as smaller models than before; likewise the Camaro and Firebird. The Corvette's 30th birthday was celebrated with a new and futuristic coupé; but a more modern sports model, announced soon afterwards, showed GM's intention of holding its position as the premier sports car maker of America. The two-seated Pontiac Fiero marked America's first production venture to have a

ABOVE **Audi Quattro four-wheel-drive, from 1980.** *This amazing car was the star of a whole series of new, inventive production models from the revived Audi company. Only after it was well established did Audi announce a rally programme. In its first full season (1981) it won three big events; in the next year* six – three of those victories being taken by the French girl, Michèle Mouton. Hannu Mikkola became World Champion in 1983, and 1984 began with great victories for Walter Röhrl, Stig Blomqvist and Mikkola. The Quattro was the car to beat.

OVERLEAF **Lancia Stratos, V6 rally car, 1972-5.** *After rallying successfully with front-wheel-drive coupés, Lancia used its connection with Ferrari (through FIAT who owned both companies) to obtain the Dino V6 power unit and place it crosswise behind the seats of the specially designed, Bertone-bodied Lancia Stratos – an aggressive-looking yet strangely beautiful machine. This car was outstanding in mixed conditions, as it proved in the Monte Carlo, San Remo, Corsican and other* rallies on many occasions. Several hundred were made, to meet competition regulations, and soon the model became a collector's item. Ian Fraser of Car magazine provided one of the cars photographed and Nick Mason/Morntane Engineering the other.

transversely mounted engine just behind the cockpit.

More indicative of world cooperation, perhaps, was the Japanese Isuzu Piazza. Isuzu was one-third General Motors-owned, and here it utilized a European GM project, by Opel out of Ital Design. The result was a thoroughly international twin-cam 2-litre sports coupé of pleasant proportions. Another pretty Isuzu was the Gemini, which adopted the style of Opel's old Kadett coupé. Opel's fastest Kadett of the 1980s was the front-wheel-drive GT/E; as the Vauxhall Astra GTE it competed with VW's GTi in Britain from 1983.

It was an independent German company, Bitter, which provided Opel with its most exotic relative. The Bitter SC coupé and cabriolet had simple, Italianate lines and were based upon the Opel Senator. Long-term cooperation between Opel and FF Developments (formerly Ferguson) in Coventry had also led to the offering of a four-wheel-drive Bitter coupé – a most desirable combination of beauty and safety.

Vive l'Américain!

There were many other external influences at work on the American industry by the mid-1980s. Perhaps the most striking example was afforded by the American Motors Corporation which, in the 1970s, was maintaining individuality but insufficient market share with its Gremlin, Pacer and other compact cars. Renault and AMC had begun talking in 1978. In 1980 the American automotive industry suffered its most abrupt decline. Later that year, Renault became 46.4 per cent equity owners in American Motors, probably saving the company and its unusual model programme of Eagle and Jeep four-wheel-drive vehicles. Soon the award-winning Renault 9 became the US-built Alliance, the Renault 11 the Encore: two particularly well-chosen names, it seemed. AMC's Eagle was the tenth marque to bear that name since the birth of the motor car. As it is the national emblem, it is hardly surprising that seven of the others were also American.

Most distinctive of Japan's cars of the mid-1980s was the unique Mazda RX7, the smooth, race-proved exponent of the Wankel rotary engine, which was at last beginning to achieve an improvement in fuel economy. Subaru was the first company to market a reasonably priced range of family cars whose looks did not give away the fact that four-wheel-drive was part of the specification. Daihatsu, Suzuki and Honda maintained their progress in advanced baby car technology; and the Nissan Cherry Europa (the name Datsun was dropped) represented the arrival of Japanese body production techniques in the country that was about to lose the Alfasud. The new car was actually labelled Alfa Romeo in Italy, for it was largely Alfa beneath the surface. Toyota's best-selling Corolla was one of a host of popular models to switch to front-wheel drive and transverse engine mounting. In doing so it disqualified itself from ever overtaking the VW 'Beetle' as the world's top model in production terms. Honda, Nissan and Toyota were leaders in showing the world how many new forms the station wagon could take. Japan showed particular imagination in this field.

Moving West, for a final look at the industry there, it is worth noting, *en route*, that Communist bloc countries were advancing. Russia's most significant development was a plan to make a modern front-wheel-drive people's car; the technology contract was won by state-owned Renault at the expense of FIAT, whose older designs were still the most familiar ones in many undeveloped territories.

Last of the Ledwinka line?

Among the Comecon countries, Czechoslovakia remained the most significant, with reminders of some of the great engineers who worked there, notably Ledwinka. Plans for a new front-wheel-drive Skoda seemed imminent and the make with the longest history in that country,

the Tatra, was still being produced in a very interesting form in the mid-1980s. (See the Vignale-styled T613 illustrated below.)

Ledwinka's big, streamlined Tatras had been novel and comfortable to drive, but only at speeds well below those of which they were capable. The 1970s saw the rear engine moved forward over the final drive, to improve the weight distribution. The Italian stylist Vignale's submission for a completely new body style was accepted (after the rejection of one that looked like an outsize Allegro), and the Tatra 613 became the first genuine 160 km/h (100 mph) state official's cruiser, well-suited to the combination of new motorways and indifferent old roads for which it was designed. In 1983 it was noted that low-volume production was proceeding in a small factory in Příbor, a short distance from the main commercial vehicle works in Koprivnice. Whether there would be a policy to produce another big new car at either plant in the future remained a matter for conjecture.

Swedish, Dutch and French connections

In 1975, Sweden's Volvo completed its acquisition of DAF, whose infinitely variable transmission was now being refined by others. The Dutch-built cars became Volvos: compact but, according to the advertising, still tough enough to carry a caravan on the roof.

Saab became the leader in turbocharging everyday road cars and continued to develop that theme, which Volvo and so many others were to pursue later.

LEFT **Chevrolet Corvette, 1984.** There had been a Chevrolet Corvette sports car from GM for 30 years (see page 88) when this clean-cut yet traditional version was introduced.
ABOVE **Pontiac Fiero, 1984.** GM's new American sports model for the late 1980s also has clean lines; but its mid-engined layout and compact dimensions are clearly designed to attract first-time buyers, not to entice established sports car customers.

ABOVE **Subaru four-wheel-drive.** Subaru, with one of the most distinctive ranges of cars to come from Japan, has been offering 'on demand' four-wheel-drive saloons and estate cars since the 1970s.
ABOVE LEFT **Tatra air-cooled V8.** Still being made in the mid-1980s in Příbor, Czechoslovakia, the 3½-litre Vignale-styled T613 owes its uniqueness to Hans Ledwinka. It rides well over rough roads and can cruise at 160 km/h (100 mph) on motorways.

A new area of cooperation for Volvo came in the mid-1970s when it got together with Peugeot and Renault on engine development. (This V6 was to power the ill-starred DeLorean.)

Renault was enjoying considerable success in the mid-1980s. At the bottom of the range, the Renault 4 was still popular after its intended replacement, the 6, had virtually vanished. The Renault 5 had been the darling of many motorists in many lands, and a replacement was on the way; a mid-engined version of the R5 with turbocharger was a nimble rally car. Most outstanding of the new breed of Renaults for Europe and America were the 9 and the 11. A thoroughly international marque, the Renault seemed unaffected by the anonymity of its medium-sized saloons and coupés. The bigger 20 and 30 models were highly practical

hatchbacks in their day, but were due to be succeeded by something more sophisticated for the later 1980s. The aerodynamic Renault 25 was the first of the new breed.

Peugeot, too, seemed to have lost some of its essentially French character, which Italian styling influence had never totally eliminated. (For example, the 504 cabriolet and coupé were ageing, but engaging.) Then came the neat little 205, a further advance in the world of the super-Mini. Acquiring Citroën had undoubtedly sapped Peugeot's resources, as did its formation of Talbot from Chrysler Simca.

Under Peugeot's wing, Citroëns continued to have a character of their own, the splendid GS and CX being supplemented in 1983 by the award-winning family model, the BX. The Peugeot ancestry was well

Enzo Ferrari
born 1898

The combination of Enzo Ferrari's talents makes him the complete man of motor racing. He might have been an opera singer or a racing driver, and he became the latter through his work in the immediate post-war years as a part-time tester with CMN (Costruzione Mecchaniche Nazionali). In 1920 he joined Alfa Romeo, coming second in the Targa Florio. He followed this with a second place in the 1921 Circuito del Mugello, and victory in the 1923 Circuito di Ravenna. For the latter event he won a shield with a prancing horse on it, the emblem of a fighter pilot killed in battle, which was presented by the airman's parents. The emblem would become one of the most celebrated in the world of motoring.

Ferrari had several more wins, but indifferent

health prevented him racing full time. He turned more to the management side, and one of his great services for Alfa Romeo was to woo Vittorio Jano to that company from FIAT; later, when Alfa cut down on its own racing programme, he ran its cars under contract from his own Modena premises. He called his racing stable the Scuderia Ferrari. His first move as a manufacturer coincided with the outbreak of World War 2, but his first cars did race once (in the modified 1940 Mille Miglia) under the name of his own company Auto Avio Costruzione. They were designed by Alberto Massimino, later of Maserati.

The first car to bear Ferrari's name was the 1947 Tipo 125 Sport designed by Gioacchino Colombo (formerly a Jano trainee, later a colleague of Massimino at Maserati), who had been responsible for the 158 Alfa Romeo, a car with which the first 1.5-litre supercharged Ferrari could not compete on level terms. Ferrari therefore appointed Aurelio Lampredi to produce a 4.5-litre unsupercharged car and this enabled Ferrari to vanquish Alfa Romeo several times in 1951.

Since those days, Ferrari has been built up into the world's most famous producer of road-going sports and GT cars, and all types of competition machines. In almost every field of racing, the name of Ferrari heads the record books. When Ford of America wanted to go motor racing it tried to buy Ferrari. FIAT now has the major holding, but the policy and the image of Ferrari the car have always been dictated solely by Ferrari the man, whose marque won the GP manufacturers' title under his command in 1983, for a record eighth time.

hidden by the familiar eccentricities of Citroën style, smooth, soft ride, originality, comfort and character – above all, character!

Character was a feature of every Citroën, right down to the 2CV which was still going strong. The 2CV, like VW's 'Beetle', had been seen in prototype form before World War 2; yet it was still quaintly fashionable as it approached its half century of existence.

Choice Italians

Italy remained a land of infinite variety. Not all FIATs had been a great success in the 1970s; the Panda was a good utility family car, but the Uno was even better and gave Italy a new line in economy cars. The Topolino's successor, the 126, had been popular enough in Italy but had proved that, ultimately, the preference for small hatchbacks was putting engines in the front, where they had started.

Alfa Romeo undoubtedly lost a classic design in 1983 when the Alfasud was phased out, for its road behaviour had set new standards for the small sports saloons of the 1970s. The famous little machine was hardly recognizable in either the Alfa Romeo 33 or the Nissan Cherry Europa (or Arna), which sustained the southern Italian industry in conjunction with Japan. Alfa Romeo's GTV6, however, continued to excel in its class in European touring car racing, and the Pininfarina-bodied Spider survived as one of the last of the old-fashioned two-seaters.

Lancia's return to its traditional form in both sports car racing and rallying helped bring the famous Italian make back into the enthusiast's market, especially with the Volumex supercharged alternative models.

Maserati had felt the pain when Peugeot killed the Citroën SM, but de Tomaso (who had severed connections with Ford of America) acquired both Maserati and the former British Leyland company Innocenti in late 1975. Exotic front- and rear-engined Maseratis continued to appear but the emphasis for the 1980s was upon the Biturbo, a much smaller and more modern concept for the famous marque, lacking only in that it took a long time to become established in world markets. A famous model, the Quattroporte, was by now Italy's top prestige four-door model.

Ferrari's Pininfarina-styled range continued to be the enthusiast's dream, led by the 512 BBi, the 5-litre flat-12 Berlinetta Boxer with Bosch fuel injection. This sleek beauty scored over its mid/rear-engined rival, the space age Bertone-bodied four overhead camshaft V12 Countach, both in appearance and in the practical matter of visibility from within. The Countach was made by Lamborghini, and was undoubtedly the most dramatic-looking car in series production in the

mid-1980s – but a very small series! Realistic thinking resulted in the introduction of the Jalpa, a V8 to compete with Ferrari's V8. For a company without Ferrari's background of competition work, Lamborghini had achieved classic status to a remarkable degree.

Germany digs in

West Germany still set standards that the world tried to match. The Volkswagen Golf was so good as leader of the high-performance hatchbacks that its mid-1980s styling changes seemed almost unnecessary. Technically several other cars rivalled the Golf, yet it remained the car to beat.

The VW Polo was a class leader too; and the Audi and VW ranges were beginning to dovetail more clearly. The Audi Quattro never lost its impact as the first production four-wheel-drive car of really high performance, despite its heavy styling. A Quattro version of the Audi 80 did, however, seem much nearer to the everyday motoring of the future. The 100 and 200 models were sleek and slippery saloons with, at the time, the lowest drag factor of all. Audi had had a good name in Germany in the 1930s with its early front-wheel-drive models; now the reborn marque was a world name, and deservedly so.

A longer sporting pedigree was the property of BMW, which was providing power for GP winners by the mid-1980s. The Bavarian marque dominated many spheres of racing: mainly production-related categories (in the manner of its great forebear, the 328).

The BMW's flared nostrils and Bertone-originated styling did not make it the most aerodynamic of cars by comparison with (say) Audi, but the company's ability to come up with exciting vehicles such as the exotic M1 showed that BMW was back from the brink, and a cult marque of the most acceptable kind. The middle range of front-engined rear-wheel-drive saloons, the 5 series, got better and better over the years; one model was in the running for the 'fastest diesel saloon' title by

ABOVE LEFT *Ferrari 512 Berlinetta Boxer, 1976.* *The first BB appeared in 1971. This 5-litre version came on the scene in 1976 to challenge the Lamborghini Countach (opposite) as the fastest road car on the market. The flat-12 engine had two overhead camshafts each side, and four Weber carburettors. Styling, as expected, was by Pininfarina. Few would dispute the notion that the Ferrari is the world's most evocative dream car for the enthusiast, as was the Bugatti in the 1920s and 1930s. This must be*

because of the continuity of influence of the marque's founding father (see below), as well as motor-racing activity that has never flagged. In 1984 Ferrari still had more Grand Prix and World Sports Car championships to its credit than any other make. In that year, too, the firm brought back the legendary GTO name. This BB was provided by L. Page.

RIGHT *Lamborghini Countach. After the lovely Miura (page 129) Bertone's styling of its successor rather went 'over the top' for a pure road car – in which role this machine is hardly practical. The Countach – its name derives from local slang meaning (roughly) 'Phew!' – has turned heads since the early 1970s. Its immensely powerful 4-litre engine is a four-overhead camshaft V12. Despite the use of proprietary engines in its less exotic models, Lamborghini continues to fulfil fantasies.*

OVERLEAF *Maserati Merak SS. Unlike Alfa Romeo, Maserati went on making its own special brand of super-car in modern times, including the mid-engined Bora and Merak. The latter model was updated in 1975 as the Merak SS. From 1968 Citroën and Maserati worked closely – until Citroën's masters*

dropped the SM (see page 130). Its V6 engine went in the Merak, shaped by Ital Design. Left high and dry following Citroën's difficulties, Maserati found its salvation through Alessandro de Tomaso. This fine Merak is from the Patrick Collection.

SUGGESTIVE MOTION

TOP **Front-engined Porsche 928S.** First with the 924, then with the 928, Porsche supplemented its famous air-cooled rear-engined range with GT models of orthodox configuration, while retaining the marque's famous qualities of performance and handling. The 928S is powered by a 4.7-litre V8 engine.

LEFT **Volkswagen Golf 1.8-litre GTI, 1983.** After several unsuccessful models, VW switched to the front-wheel-drive transverse engine formula in the 1970s as a replacement for the 'Beetle'. This sporting version was emulated in due course by other leading manufacturers. The popular sports car has either disappeared or got fat. Cars like the Golf are the true successors.

ABOVE **Bitter coupé, 1982.** Since 1973, Erich Bitter has been making attractive and exotic Opel-based GT cars. Styled with the aid of Michelotti's and Opel's own studios, trimmed by Carrozzeria Ocra of Turin, and assembled by Bitter at Schwelm, West Germany. This example from the Patrick Collection has the optional FF (Ferguson Formula) four-wheel-drive system.

1984. Opel did tend to outshine BMW for style, and offered similar performance for less money; but Opel was more international in its make-up. BMW remained essentially German.

Porsche continued to plough what had become a traditional furrow as the producer of Germany's best out-and-out sports cars for road and track. The Type 956 racing coupé followed a long line of Le Mans winners, while the evergreen 911 and its derivatives were supplemented by a new family of front-engined coupés.

The 'popular Porsche' idea had begun with the short-lived mid-engined VW-Porsche. It had been overpriced (because it could not be made as cheaply as anticipated, despite being manufactured at a VW, rather than Porsche, plant). The VW-Porsche (or 914) was clean but unexciting to look at, and never caught the public imagination sufficiently. It never made the grade as a competition model; nor did it possess the luggage space of a true grand tourer. Its effective replacement was the front-engined 924, a practical if mundane coupé. The other front-engined Porsche was the 928.

The 928 was very clean of line, and very lithe, too, with its 4.5-litre water-cooled V8 engine under the bonnet. Indeed it might have replaced the air-cooled 911, had not the older car built up a reputation and a character all its own. As it was, front- and rear-engined Porsches appealed, generally, to enthusiasts of totally differing tastes – so there was room for both types, and a bigger market overall for Porsche cars.

Daimler and Benz: 100 years on

It is not mere chance that the last individual marque to be mentioned in this chapter is the Mercedes-Benz, Germany's most famous marque of all. From the 1970s, the S-class saloons kept the Daimler-Benz company on course as a world leader in the design and manufacture of motor cars.

No new model of Mercedes-Benz ever seems to receive the kind of rave notices that come its way when it has been around for a few years. The faint praise that greeted the 190 series in some quarters at first soon gave way to accolades, as Stuttgart was seen to have entered the compact saloon car world with a vengeance. Slightly ironic, at a time when some American cars were beginning to look almost plain, was a tendency for specialists to add skirts and spoilers, dams and wings to well-designed saloon cars to make them 'different'. Mercedes-Benz cars were among the greatest sufferers during this phase of over-personalization for, when spared these adornments, the modern Mercedes could be seen to have lost much of the heavy styling of its forebears.

On the other hand, for sustained speeds of over 240 km/h (150 mph), even the works fitted drag-reducing extras. Yes, 240 km/h! – for that

speed was exceeded (including stops) by three special versions of the 190 in the autumn of 1983: not just momentarily, but for over a week. The high speed test track at Nardo in Italy has seen some amazing demonstrations in its relatively short existence. The remarkable achievement of these three ordinary-looking saloons was to maintain that average for 50,000 km (31,000 miles). This meant 'cruising' at 257 km/h (160 mph) for more than eight days. It is true that these cars had the new 2.3-litre 16-valve power unit (developed in conjunction with Keith Duckworth, the man behind Cosworth engineering), but it is also true that they gave virtually no trouble, which is why the average speed was so high. Having rescinded its plans for competition work in 1980, Daimler-Benz had used its absence to good effect, and looked ready for a genuine return. What a celebration that could be for Stuttgart!

With its combination of the names of the makers of the world's first two cars – Benz and Daimler – the famous company had much to celebrate on the occasion of the motor car's centenary; but then, so did the other stalwarts who survived military, political, and industrial conflicts to stay in business in the toughest industry of them all.

A happy anniversary

The motor industry goes into its second century on an optimistic note. The crisis may be permanent, but development does not stop.

The restraints of conforming to stringent worldwide safety and emission laws, and the genuine need to reduce fuel consumption, have led to a new set of engineering standards; experience is turning disadvantage to advantage. Engines run more sweetly than they have done for many a year, *and* they are more powerful and economical than ever. The internal combustion engine is alive and well, yet there is no let-up in the search for other power sources, for better transmission systems, smoother bodies for better air flow, all-wheel drive, anti-lock braking: the ways of improving the motor car are endless. At each big motor show the public sees a new 'concept car' of some kind: and the 'concept car' usually turns out to be much nearer to reality than it seems.

One concept unlikely to change is that of personal transport, of the kind which gives man a freedom of movement that did not seem possible in 1885; and in 1985 the choice he is offered in terms of vehicles is wider than ever, if not in the way they can be used. Fortunately, not too much restriction of freedom has been needed so far, and to travel by road can still be a pleasure as well as a necessity.

It is the car makers themselves who are most subject to restraint and most balance sheets (like their products) are trim and neat, now that they are embarking on motoring's second exciting century.

LEFT **Mercedes-Benz 190, 1985.** 'Daimler' and 'Benz' are still combined in the maker's title: a reminder that motoring technology began in Germany. A tendency apparent now after a century of motoring is to make cars more efficient, more compact. Mercedes-Benzes were medium to large until the mid-1980s – then came the 190, which presented Stuttgart splendour on a smaller scale than usual. Cautiously received, it soon displayed worthy, traditional values.

CHRONOLOGY OF THE MOTOR CAR

These landmarks have been selected from among many, with a view to giving motoring some historical perspective.

1885: Carl Friedrich Benz produces first motor car with internal combustion engine; Gottlieb Daimler and Wilhelm Maybach apply the same basic principle to create the first motorcycle.

1891: Panhard and Levassor lead the world in series production.

1895: Emile Levassor (Panhard) wins first inter-city race, Paris–Bordeaux–Paris, at 24 km/h (15 mph); Dr Frederick Lanchester makes first practical all-British car.

1896: Henry Ford shows his first car. Britain's 'Red Flag Act' repealed.

1897: Daimler of Coventry becomes Britain's first series producer.

1898: Fernand Charron (Panhard) is first man to win a race crossing national boundaries – Paris to Amsterdam and back – at nearly 43 km/h (27 mph).

1899: Camille Jenatzy (Belgium) sets world land speed record of over 105 km/h (65 mph) with electric-powered car.

1900: Napier is Britain's first 'sports' car. First year of international racing (Gordon Bennett cup), won by France.

1901: Daimler of Bad Cannstatt introduces new 'Mercedes' design by Wilhelm Maybach, generally regarded now as the first modern car.

1902: S. F. Edge (Napier) wins Gordon Bennett race from Paris to Innsbruck, all other entrants having retired. (This was part of the Paris–Vienna road race, won by Marcel Renault.) Charles Jarrott (Panhard) becomes first Briton to win a major race outright – the 512 km (318-mile) Circuit des Ardennes.

1903: Irish Gordon Bennett race won by Jenatzy for Mercedes. British speed limit increased from 12 to 20 mph (19 to 32 km/h). Ford's first production car.

1904: The Rolls-Royce is born. France wins back Gordon Bennett trophy from Germany. Olds produces over 5000 'runabouts'.

1905: Léon Théry (Brasier) wins Gordon Bennett race for second year running; France plans to end series. First Shelsley Walsh hill climb won by Ernest Instone (Daimler); course still in use.

1906: Fred Marriott (Stanley steam car) exceeds two miles a minute, an unofficial world record. First Targa Florio won by Alessandro Cagno (Itala); first closed-circuit Grand Prix of the ACF won by Ferenc Szisz (Renault). First Austin cars.

1907: Japan makes its first production car, the American-engined Takuri. Count Borghese (Itala) wins Peking to Paris marathon. Brooklands speed track, Surrey, England, opened.

1908: First American Grand Prix, at Savannah, won by Louis Wagner (FIAT). New York to Paris (immortalized as the Great Race) won by an American car, the Thomas flyer. Ford Model T manufactured.

1909: Daimler (Great Britain) and Minerva (Belgium) adopt American Charles Knight's sleeve-valve engine design, soon to be followed by Panhard.

1911: First Monte Carlo Rally won by Henri Rougier (Turcat-Méry). First Indianapolis 500 won by Ray Harroun (Marmon).

1913: First person to exceed 160 km/h (100 mph) for an hour is Percy Lambert (Talbot) at Brooklands track. Georges Boillot (Peugeot) wins Grand Prix for second year running. First Morris cars.

1914: Christian Lautenschlager (Mercedes), the 1908 victor, wins last pre-war Grand Prix. Telegram reads: 'His Majesty the Kaiser is delighted. . . '. Over 200,000 Fords built this year.

1916: First tanks in action on the Somme; Paris taxis commandeered to move troops.

1918: Armistice.

1919: W. O. Bentley's first car; Hispano-Suiza introduces servo-assisted four-wheel brakes. World's first traffic lights (Detroit).

1920: Leyland introduces Britain's most expensive car, featuring torsion bars in rear suspension (only 18 cars made).

1921: Jimmy Murphy (in a Duesenberg with the first hydraulically operated four-wheel brakes) wins first post-war Grand Prix, at Le Mans; the first major American victory in Europe. Georges and Maurice Sizaire develop all-independent suspension for production.

1922: Tatra 11 is first volume production car to have central tube (or 'backbone') chassis; San Giusto rear-engined, all-independently sprung, 'backbone' car shown same year, but shortlived. Austin Seven launched; Ford makes over one million cars in the year. Lancia first with unit construction.

1923: First year of Le Mans 24-hour race (won by French Chenard-Walcker); Henry Segrave (Sunbeam) gives Britain its first-ever Grand Prix victory, at Tours. Mid-engined Rumpler-type Benz races in Italian GP at Monza (Minoia fourth, Hörner fifth).

1924: Dodge and Budd collaboration leads to first volume production of all-steel bodies; Milan–Varese *autostrada* opened.

1925: Closed cars outsell open ones in the USA for the first time; Harry Miller introduces front-wheel-drive racing car.

1926: Briton wins Monte Carlo Rally (Hon. Victor Bruce in AC); J. A. Grégoire introduces Tracta car with front-wheel drive, for series production soon after. First traffic signals and Keep Left signs in London's West End. Benz and Daimler (Mercedes) merge.

1927: Henry Segrave (Sunbeam) takes world speed record past 320 km/h (200 mph). First Mille Miglia held; winner Ferdinando Minoia (OM).

1928: Synchromesh gearbox introduced by Charles Kettering for 'clashless' Cadillac and LaSalle. Britain's first production car with front-wheel drive (Alvis).

1929: America's first front-wheel-drive production cars, the Cord and the Ruxton. Chevrolet becomes second make to achieve a million deliveries in a year. Wall Street crash and start of the Depression.

1930: The last great Vintage year, and the last great year for Bentley (fifth victory in Le Mans 24-hour race). Cadillac goes into production with a V16 engine – a 7.4-litre 185 bhp unit.

1931: The world's only other series-production 16-cylinder car is introduced – the 8.1-litre 200 bhp Marmon – but all production ceased in 1933. First four-cylinder mass-production car to sell in Britain for just £100 (Morris Minor side-valve tourer). Effect of Depression still strong, leading to collapses, and to mergers including Bentley with Rolls-Royce, Lanchester with Daimler, etc.

1932: Lanchester car wins first RAC Rally. The Ford V8 is introduced.

1933: Adolf Hitler becomes chancellor and begins to affect German motoring.

1934: American car production exceeds 2,000,000; British exceeds 250,000. Auto Union and Mercedes-Benz set out on six-year German state domination of GP racing. Citroën front-wheel-drive range introduced.

1935: Fiftieth anniversary of birth of the car. British victory at Le Mans, by Lagonda. Sir Malcolm Campbell's *Bluebird* exceeds 480 km/h (300 mph). SS Cars Ltd introduces its Jaguar range.

1936: M.G.'s T series is born. Mercedes-Benz markets diesel-engined car.

1937: Mercedes-Benz GP cars develop up to 646 bhp. Best pre-war year for world car production (United States nearly 4,000,000; Great Britain number two at just under 400,000; Japan still not listed).

1938: Richard Seaman of Britain wins the German GP in a Mercedes-Benz. Hitler lays foundation stone of Volkswagen works, but car is named KdF (*Kraft durch Freude* or 'Strength through Joy').

1939-45: World War 2 limits or halts world production, but motor car technology continues to be developed.

1946: Triumph is first British make to have steering-column gearchange.

1947: John Cobb (*Railton Mobil Special*) breaks his own World Land Speed record, exceeding 640 km/h (400 mph) in one direction.

1948: Modern tubeless tyres introduced by B. F. Goodrich Co.

1949: Pre-war car production records exceeded by the United States (5,000,000 plus), Britain (400,000 plus) and Canada now third with just under 200,000. Ferrari takes first of nine Le Mans victories. Chrysler introduces the key start.

1950: GP World Drivers' Championship introduced. First winner: Giuseppe Farina (Alfa Romeo). Stirling Moss has his first major race win (TT, Jaguar). Fuel rationing ends in Britain. Rover gas turbine car demonstrated.

1951: Juan Manuel Fangio takes first of five personal world GP titles.

1952: First disc-brake race victories (Stirling Moss, Jaguar); Nissan negotiates to make Austins under licence in Japan. British driver (Sydney Allard) wins Monte Carlo Rally in his own make of car.

1953: Helmut Polensky of Germany wins first European rally drivers' title from Ian Appleyard of Britain. Ferrari wins first World Sports Car Championship from Jaguar. Michelin launches radial-ply tyre.

1954: Standard Vanguard is first British diesel-engined production car. Jensen 541 is Britain's first production car to have glass-fibre body (a year after USA's Chevrolet Corvette). Mercedes-Benz 300SL 'gull-wing' coupé is first production car with fuel injection as standard.

1955: VW 'Beetle' is first European model to pass 1,000,000 production mark. America leads world annual car output (nearly 8,000,000), from Britain (900,000), with West Germany (800,000) about to take second place. Citroën introduces futuristic DS19. Stirling Moss (Mercedes-Benz) becomes first Briton to win Mille Miglia. Mercedes-Benz wins World Sports Car Championship.

1956: Monte Carlo Rally and Le Mans won by same make of car (Jaguar); fuel rationing reintroduced briefly following Suez crisis.

1957: Stirling Moss and Tony Brooks share in first World Championship GP victory for a British car (Vanwall, British GP, Aintree). Jaguar wins Le Mans for fifth time. Lotus Elite introduced with glass fibre as structural material.

1958: First British winner of World GP championship (Mike Hawthorn). Vanwall is first winner of new Manufacturers' title.

1959: Introduction of the Austin and Morris Mini. First driver and manufacturer to take World GP titles using rear-engined vehicle (Jack Brabham, Cooper-Coventry Climax). Aston Martin takes World Sports Car Championship.

1960: Rear engine and all-independent suspension are new features of Chevrolet Corvair compact car.

1961: American driver wins World GP championship for first time (Phil Hill, Ferrari).

1962: More than 2,000,000 Chevrolet cars made this year. Total Japanese car output still under 300,000. BRM's first and only World F1 title (Graham Hill).

1963: NSU starts production of Wankel rotary-engined car. First European Touring Car race championship won by Peter Nöcker (Jaguar); Rover-BRM gas turbine car completes Le Mans 24-hour race.

1964: Donald (son of Sir Malcolm) Campbell averages over 640 km/h (400 mph) to take the world's speed record for internal combustion wheel-driven vehicles (as opposed to jet, rocket etc.), with gas turbine *Bluebird*.

1965: Introduction of compulsory exhaust emission controls in California. Robert Summers uses four fuel-injected Chrysler V8 engines to take internal combustion wheel-driven world record to nearly 660 km/h (410 mph); then Breedlove beats 960 km/h (600 mph) in jet-powered *Spirit of America*.

1966: New Formula One for GP cars (3 litres unsupercharged, 1.5 litres supercharged) won by Jack Brabham: his third title, but the first for his own make of car. Ford takes first of four Le Mans victories.

1967: Jim Clark equals Juan Manuel Fangio's record number of World Championship GP victories. Last year of Panhard marque.

1968: From less than 1,000,000 in 1966, Japan surpasses 2,000,000 annual car production: now third to America and West Germany. BL formed. Ford UK wins first World Rally Championship.

1969: Top ten motor vehicle-makers this year (in millions): GM, USA, 5.3; Ford, USA, 2.7; VW, West Germany, 1.6; Chrysler, USA, 1.6; Toyota, Japan, 1.5; FIAT, Italy, 1.3; Nissan, Japan, 1.1; BL, UK, 1.0; Renault, France, 1.0; Opel, Germany, 0.8.

1970: Gary Gabelich (rocket-powered *Blue Flame*) exceeds 1010 km/h (620 mph) to retain World's Land Speed Record in the USA. First Porsche Le Mans win.

1971: Rolls-Royce group declared bankrupt, but successful motor division introduces new models and stays in business. Japan now second to America in car production.

1972: GM and Ford still first and second motor vehicle producers, but Toyota and Nissan now third and fourth. All-time record for British car production (1,921,311).

1973: Car output in America reaches all-time high (9,667,571 produced). Jackie Stewart wins third world crown, to become most successful GP driver ever, with 27 championship wins, beating previous title holders Jim Clark (25) and Juan Fangio (24). OPEC oil embargo.

1974: First big drop in world production for many years, and many countries introduce fuel rationing. Ryder investigation of British Leyland. Hat-trick of Le Mans wins for Henri Pescarolo (Matra).

1975: Ferrari wins first GP world crown for over a decade, through new star Niki Lauda of Austria. For most countries the slump continues, but West German production improves slightly, and Japanese car output exceeds pre-crisis records. BL fully nationalized. BMW drivers take first of nine successive European Touring Car Drivers' Championships.

1976: Japanese car production surpasses 5,000,000 for the first time. James Hunt (McLaren) is world GP champion.

1977: Michael Edwardes begins BL rescue plan. Niki Lauda recovers from his accident to be champion for Ferrari again.

1978: General Motors' associated companies around the world produce a record 9,297,395 motor vehicles. Lotus gains its seventh world GP 'makes' title, with help from ground effect, Mario Andretti, and Ronnie Peterson.

1979: Turbocharged Renault wins its first GP; Ford wins its third world rally title and its eighth successive RAC Rally. America's A. J. Foyt wins USAC Championship for seventh time. Richard Petty, also of America, takes NASCAR title for seventh time.

1980: Japan produces over 7,000,000 cars (nearly a quarter of the world's total for the year) and overtakes United States as world leader.

1981: Even Japanese output drops slightly as world new-car market contracts. Britain's Williams-Ford GP team takes second 'makes' title in succession.

1982: World car output continues to fall: Japan to just below 7,000,000, United States to little more than 5,000,000. Trends in sport shown by turbocharged Ferrari and four-wheel-drive Audi taking world GP and rally makers' championships respectively; record sixth Le Mans victory for Jacky Ickx of Belgium (with Britain's Derek Bell in Porsche).

1983: Ford withdraws from competition. Ford-Cosworth DFV wins 155th championship GP, but is beaten by turbocharged cars for both makes and drivers GP championships. Ford announces a new Cosworth-Ford family of competition engines for late 1980s. Lancia scores a record fifth win in world rally makes series. Finland's Hannu Mikkola (Audi) wins world rally drivers' crown. BMW's Dieter Quester wins a record fourth European touring car race title. Richard Noble (R-R-engined *Thrust II*) takes World Land Speed Record for Britain, beating 1970 figures.

1984: Twice-crowned world rally champion Walter Röhrl (Audi) wins Monte Carlo Rally, equalling Trévoux and Munari's record of four victories. Britain agrees plan for Nissan UK assembly plant; factory to be built at Sunderland; production scheduled for 1986. Decentralization of BL completed.

1985: Many new and advanced cars announced with optimism, as the centenary of the birth of the motor car is celebrated. Great centenary festival scheduled for Silverstone (25 to 27 May).

Figures in *italics* refer to captions to illustrations.

Aaltonen, Rauno 112, *112*, 113, 125
AC 48, 70, 142, 156
Adler 24, *44*, 73, 92
Albion 59
Alfa Romeo 24, 47, 71, *73*, 76, 84, 96, *96*, 110, 129, 134, 148, 151, 157
Allard 100, 137
Alpine 113, 131, *131*, 134, 144
Alvis *54*, 64, 70, 100, 112, 116, 156
Amédée Bollée (cars) 41
American Motors Corp. (AMC) 86, *87*, 120, 121, *142*, 148
Argyll 59
Armstrong Siddeley 59, 100, *100*
Arrol-Johnston (Arrol-Aster) 29, *48*, 59
Ascari, Alberto 96, *97*
Aston Martin 70, 71, 103–4, *104*, 110, 116, *116*, 126, *127*, 142, 157
Attwood, Richard *111*, *127*
Auburn 38, *38*, 82, 83
Audi 24, 73, 125, 134, 136, 144, 145, *145*, 151, 157
Austin 9, *26*, 32, *34*, 51, 54, *54*, 55, 60–1, 64–5, 67, 68, 69, 71, 76, 77, 83, 86, 91, 100, 103, 112, 113, 133, *137*, 138, 142, *142*, 157. *See also* Bantam; British Motor Corp.
Austin, Sir Herbert (Lord Austin) 29, 54, *54*, 55, 59, 61, 65
Austin-Healey 100, 112, 113, *113*, 124
Austin-Rover *137*, 138
Austro-Daimler 24, 44, *54*, 92
Autodelta 129
Auto Union 56, 70, *70*, *71*, 73, 76, 92, 118, 125, *127*, 156

Babs 48
Ballot 39, 47
Bantam; American Bantam Co. 65, 83
Barnato, Woolf 50, *50*
Bastien, Paul 38
'B. Bira' 70, *70*
Beardmore 59
Bell, Derek 137, *160*
Bennett, J.G. 21, 22
Bentley 32, 50, *50*, 51, 56, 58, 70, *70*, *102*, 103, *136*, 142, 156
Bentley, W.O. 29, 50, *50*, 58, 70, *104*, 156
Benz 8, 10, 12, *13*, 15, 16, 18, 20, 24, 42, 44, *44*, 47, 156. *See also* Daimler-Benz; Mercedes-Benz

Benz, Carl Friedrich 8, 10, 12, 15, *17*, 44, 156; Eugen 21
Berna 24
Biddle 38
Birkigt, Marc 24, *25*, 41, *41*
Biscuter 99
Bitter 148, *154*
Black, Sir John 60, 61, 62, 64, 100, *101*, 103
Blomqvist, Stig 128, *145*
Bluebird 48, 70
BMW *4*, 20, 54, *63*, 71, 72, 76, 92, *93*, 100, 108, 116, 124, *125*, 127, 143, 151, 155, 157. *See also* EMW
Böhringer, Eugen 112, 125
Boillot, Georges 27, 156
Bollée family 8; Amédée Sr *12*, 15; Amédée Jr 16; Léon 15, 29. *See also* Amédée Bollée (cars)
Bond 118
Borgward (cars) 73, 108, 128; Borgward, Carl 73, 127–8
Bouton, Georges *19*
Brabham 132, *132*, 144; Brabham-BMW 144; Brabham-Repco 132; Brabham, Jack 107, *107*, *110*, 132, *132*, 157
Brasier 22, 41, 156
Brennabor 73
Bristol 100, *102*, 116, 142
British Leyland (BL) 9, 108, 115, 116, 118, 136, 151, 157; British Leyland Motor Corp. (BLMC) 116, 138
British Motor Corp. (BMC) 100, 103, 108, 112, *112*, 113, *113*, 115, 118, 138
BRM 84, 107, 110, 132, 157
Broadley, Eric *111*, 121
Brooks, Tony 104, *104*, *107*, 157
Brown, Sir David 103, 104, 116
Brozincevic, Franz 24. *See also* FBW
BSA 17, 24, 56, 58, 59, *59*, 114, 115
bubble cars (Heinkel, Isetta, Messerschmitt) 92
Bucciali TAN 41
Budd bodies 54, 71, 79; Budd, Edward 68, 100
Buehrig bodywork 82–3, 86
Bugatti *4*, 39, *40*, 41, 42, 47, *47*, *48*, 70, 76–8, 77, 78, 99, 131, *151*
Bugatti, Ettore 23, *23*, 35, 39, 40–1, 50, 77, 96; Jean 40, 77
Buick (cars) *31*, 35, 145; Buick, David 34; Tojeiro-Buick *111*
Burney Streamline 59

Cadillac 34, 35, 36, *37*, 38,

81, *81*, 88, *88*, 98, 120, 145, 156
Campbell, Sir Malcolm 48, *49*, 69–70, 143, 156; Donald 143, 157
Carlsson, Erik 112, *113*
Castro *see* Hispano-Suiza
Cattaneo, Giustino 47
CGV 16
Chalmers 35
Chaparral 132, 143
Chapman, Colin 107, 118, 133
Charron, Fernand 16, 21, 24, 156
Chenard-Walcker 41, 156
Chevrolet *31*, 34, *34*, 35, 36, 51, 86, 88, *88*, 108, 118–20, 121, *121*, 145, *149*, 157
Chevrolet, Louis *31*, 34–5, 44
Chiron, Louis 47, *70*
Chiti, Carlo 110, 129
Christie *28*, 30
Chrysler 35, 36, 39, 78, 81, *81*, 82, 84, 86, *86*, *87*, 88, 89, 90, 92, 108, 115, *117*, 120, 136, 145, 150, 156, 157
Chrysler, W.P. 35
Cisitalia 92
Citroën 40, 42, *42*, 51, 56, 65, 78, *78*, 79, 82, *93*, 99, 103, 108, 112, 113, 129–31, *131*, 136, 150–1, *151*, 156, 157
Citroën, André 42, *42*, 79
Clark, Jim *6*, 108, *110*, *111*, 132, 133, 157
Clement, Frank 50, *50*
Clément-Bayard 136
Coatalen, Louis 29, 47
Cobb, John *49*, 70, 143, 156
Collins, Peter 104, *107*
Colombo, G. 96, *96*, 151
Connaught 104, 107
Cooper *6*, 84, 104, 107, 108, 110, 128, 132, 133; Cooper-Coventry Climax 104–7, *107*, 157
Cord (cars) *38*, 39, 73, 82–3, *83*, 156; Cord, E.L. 38, *38*, 39, 82
Cornelian 44
Crosley 86
CTA-Arsenal 131
Cugnot, Nicolas Joseph 8
Cunningham 89, 110

DAF 128, 149
Daihatsu 90, 121, 148
Daimler 12, *12*, 15, 20, 22, 42, 156
Daimler, Gottlieb 8, 10, 12, *12*, 15, 16, *17*, 18, 22, 24, *24*, 42, 125, 156; Paul 24, 42–4
Daimler-Benz 9, 12, 15, 44, 47, 73, 84, 92, 95–6, 108, 125, 127, 145, *154*, 155, 156. *See also* Mercedes-Benz

Daimler (Coventry) 10, 12, 15, 17, 18, 24–6, 50, 56, 58–9, *59*, 99, 101, 114, 115, *117*, 118, 139, 156
Darracq (cars) *19*, 21, 60, 129; Darracq, Alexandre 15, *19*
DAT 89, 90, 91; Datsun 90, *90*, 91, 124–5, *124*, 148; Datsun-Nissan 121–4
Davis 86
Decauville 15, 20, 23
de Dion-Bouton 10, 15, 18, 23, 34, 41
Delage 42, *43*, 47, 76, 99, 129
Delahaye (cars) 42, *43*, 76, 78, 99, 129; Delahaye, Emile 15
Delaunay-Belleville 23, 32, 41
de Lavaud 41
DeLorean *4*, *139*, 142
DePalma, Ralph 35
DeSoto 35, 36, 78, 81, *81*, 89
de Tomaso 129, 151
Detroit Automobile Co. 34, 37. *See also* Cadillac
Detroit Edison 37
Deutz 15, 41
DFP *29*, 50
Dick, Alick 103, 115
Dietrich, Baron de 40–1
Dion, Count Albert de 15, *19*
Dixi 54, 64, 71. *See also* BMW
DKW 73, 92, 113, 125
Doble steamer 81
Dodge 35, 81, 88, 145, 156
Don, Kaye *54*
Doorne, Hubert and Wim van 128
Dort, J.D. 34
Duesenberg (cars) 38–9, *38*, 82, 83, *83*, 156; Duesenberg brothers 38
Dunlop 16
Durant, Clifford 39; William *31*, 34, 35, 51
Duryea (cars) 29; Duryea brothers 20

Eagle 35
Eagle (American Motors Corp.) 148
Earl, Harley J. 36, 120
Eberan-Eberhorst, Robert *71*, 76
Edge, S.F. 16, 18, 21, *21*, 22, *23*, 24, 48, 51, 156
Edsel 89
Edwardes, Sir Michael 136, 139, 149, 157
Egan, John 142, 143
Eisenach 20, 54. *See also* BMW; Dixi; EMW; Wartburg
electric vehicles 20, 23, 29
Elford, Victor 126, *127*
EMW 92
ERA 70, *70*

Essex 36
Excelsior 50
Eyston, George *49*, 70

Faccioli, Aristide *14*
Facel Vega; Facellia 99
Falkenhausen, Alexander von 127
Fangio, Juan Manuel 95, 96, *96*, *97*, 104, 108, 157
Farman, Henri 21, 22; Maurice 41
FBW 24
Feeley, Frank 103–4, *104*
Fenaille, Pierre 41
Ferrari 76, 84, 96, *96*, *97*, 99, 104, 107, 110–12, *111*, 126, *128*, 129, 132, 133, 134, 139, 144, *145*, 151, *151*, 156, 157;
Ferrari, Enzo 35, 47, 96, 110, 151
Fessia, Franco 76, 77, 129
FF Developments 148
FIAT *12*, *14*, 18, 22, 23, 24, 27, *43*, 46, 47, *48*, 56, 61, *73*, 76, 77, 89, 129, 134, *139*, *145*, 149, 151, 156, 157
Fiedler, Fritz 71, 72, 100, *102*
Fisher, Lawrence P. 36
Flint 35
Ford (Australia) 134, 135
Ford (Gt Britain, Europe) 42, 51, 56, 68, *68*, 69, 70–1, *101*, 103, 108, *111*, 112, 113, 120, *121*, 127, *127*, 128, 132, 134, *136*, 138, *138*, 144, 157; Ford Cortina-Lotus 113, 133
Ford (USA) 9, 10, 30, 31, 32, 34, 35, 36, *37*, 38, 79, 81, 84, 86, *88*, 89, 91, 120, *121*, 145, 151, 156, 157
Ford, Henry 9, 10, 20, 30, 34, 36, 37, 38, 51, 89, 156; Henry, II 89; Edsel 38, 89
Franklin 80, 81
Fraschini, Oreste 24. *See also* Isotta-Fraschini
Frazer 86
Frazer Nash 70, 100, 116; Frazer Nash-BMW 71
Frazer Nash-Bristol *see* Bristol

GAZ 91
Ganz, Joseph 73
General Motors (GM) 9, 27, 29, *30*, *31*, 32, 34, *34*, 35, 36, 38, 42, 51–4, 60, 68, 70, 79, 81, 84, 86, 88, 89, 103, 108, 113, 118, 120, 127, 138, 145, *149*, 157
Giacosa, Dante 76, 77
Ginther, Richie 110, 115
Girardot, Léonce 21. *See also* CGV
Gobron-Brillié 23
Goertz, Albrecht *93*, 124

Golden Arrow 48
Gonzalez, José Froilan 96, *96*
Gordini 99, 110; Gordini, Amédée 131
Gorham 89
Graham 82, 83, *83*, 86
Grégoire, J.A. 41–2, 99, 131, 156
Gutbrod, Wilhelm 73

Hall, Jim 132
Hammel 20
Hanomag 44, *44*, 71, 91, 92
Hansa-Lloyd-Goliath 128
Harriman, Sir G. 115, 116
Harroun, Ray 38, 156
Hassan, Walter 70, 115
Hawthorn, Mike 104, *106*, *107*, 132, 157
Healey, Donald 70, 100, 116. *See also* Austin-Healey
Henry, Ernest 24, 39
Hermes-Simplex 40
Heynes, Bill 62, 115
Hill, Graham 110, 115, 132, *132*, 133
Hillman 60, *63*, 64, 91, 103, 113, 136
Hindusthan 91
Hino 121
Hispano-Suiza 24, *25*, 32, 41, *41*, 50, 78, 99, 156
Holden 89
Honda 9, 90, 110, 121, 132, 136, 139, 148
Hopkirk, Paddy *112*, 113
Horch (cars) 42, 71, 73, 125; Horch, August 12, 24. *See also* Audi
Hotchkiss 41, 54, 76, *78*, 99, 129; Hotchkiss-Grégoire 131
HRG 70
Hudson 36, 84, 86, *87*. *See also* American Motors Corp.
Hulme, Dennis 132, *132*
Humber *26*, 60, 62, 103, 112
Hunt, James 134, 157
Hupmobile 82, 83, *83*
HWM 104, 107
Hyundai 136

Iacocca, Lee 120, *120*, 145
Ickx, Jacky 132, 157
Imperial 88
Innocenti 151
Invicta 70
Ishikawajima 89, 90, 91
Iso 129
Isotta-Fraschini 24, 47, *48*, 96, 99
Issigonis, Alec *101*, 103, 112, 113, 138
Isuzu 121, 148
Itala 24, 156
Ital Design 148, *151*

Jaguar *26*, 54, 60, *62*, 84, 99–100, 101, 103, 104, *104*, *106*, 110, *111*,

114–15, *115*, 118, 125, 136, *137*, 139, 142–3, 156, 157
Jano, Vittorio 47,' *73*, 76, 96, *97*, 151
Jaray, Paul 71
Jarrott, Charles 21, 22, 29, 51, 156
Jeep 56, 83, 86
Jeffery, Thomas B. 35
Jellinek, Emil 22, 42
Jenatzy, Camille 21, *21*, 22, 156
Jensen (cars) 62, 116, *117*, 142, 157; Jensen brothers 62, 116; Jensen-Healey 116
Jitsuyo 89, 90
Johnson, Claude 29, 50, 51
Jowett 103

Kaiser 86, Kaiser-Frazer 83, 86
KdF-Wagen *see* Volkswagen
Keech, Ray 48
Kettering, Charles F. 35, 36, 51, 156
Kimber, Cecil 100
King, Spencer 115
Kissel 38

La Cuadra 24
Lago, Antonio 78, 129
Lagonda *50*, 58, 69, 70, 103, 104, *104*, 116, *116*, 142, 156
Lamborghini 129, *129*, 151, *151*
Lampredi, Aurelio 96, 151
Lanchester 16, 17, *17*, *48*, 50, 56, 58, 59, *59*, 101, 156
Lanchester brothers 18, 26; Frank 17, 18; Dr Frederick 16, 17, *17*, 18, 50, 156; George 16, 17, *17*, 18, 50
Lancia *4*, 23–4, 44–7, *48*, 56, 76, 77, *81*, 84, 96, *97*, *99*, 110, 129, 134, 144, *144*, 145, *145*, 151, 156
Lancia, Gianni *97*; Vincenzo *12*, 23, 44, *48*, 76, 77
Land-Rover *see* Rover
Langen, Eugen 15
Lanza 18
LaSalle 35–6, *37*, 156
Laurin-Klement 24
Lea-Francis *54*, 100–1
Ledwinka, Hans (Jan) 18, 24, 44, 73, 118, 149, *149*
Leland, H.M. 34, 35, 38; Wilfred 38
Lenoir, Jean-Joseph Étienne 8, 12
Levassor, Emile 9, 10, 12, 15, 16, 156
Levegh, Pierre 95
Leyland 48, *48*, 115, 156. *See also* British Leyland
Ligier 144
Lila 89

Lincoln 38, 81, *81*, 89
Lion-Peugeot 23
Locomobile 20-1, 29, 35, 39
'Locomotives on Highways Act' 18
Loewy, Raymond 82, 86, 87, 120, 124
Lohner, Jacob 18, 24, 92; Lohner-Porsche 18
Lola; Lola-Ford *111*
Lord, Sir Leonard 100, 103, 112, 115
Lorraine-Dietrich 23, 24, 41, *41*
Lotus 84, 107, *107*, 108, 110, *110*, *111*, *115*, 116, 118, 124, 132, 133, 142, 144, 157; Lotus-Ford *132*
Lunn, Roy *121*
Lutzmann 18-20, 42. *See also* Opel
Lyons, Sir William 54, 60–1, 62, *62*, 100, *104*, 114, 115

Makinen, Timo *112*, 113
March 144
Marmon 38, 81, 156
Maserati 70, 84, 96, *97*, 110, 112, 129, 131, *131*, 151, *151*
Mason, George 86
Mathis (cars) 41; Mathis, Emile 40, 41
Matra 132, 144
Maudslay, John 62; Reginald 60, 62
Maxwell 35
Maybach 44, 71, 73
Maybach, Karl 44; Wilhelm 12, 15, 22, 24, 44, 156
Mays, Raymond 70, *70*
Mazda 90, 121, 124, *124*, 143, 148
McLaren 132, 144, 157
Mercedes 15, 22, *24*, 27, 42, 44, 156
Mercedes-Benz 9, 12, 44, *44*, *47*, *48*, 56, 70, *70*, 71, *71*, 73–6, 84, 92–5, *94*, 96, 97, 104, 110, 112, 113, 118, 125–6, 128, 142, *154*, 155, 156, 157
Mercer 38
Mercury 89, 91, 120
M.G. 54, *61*, 65, 68, 70, 100, 103, 113, *115*, *137*, 138, 156
Michelin 78, 79, 157; Michelin, André 16, *20*, 22
Mikkola, Hannu 138, 145, *145*, 157
Miller (cars) *35*, 38, 39; Miller, Harry *38*, 39, 41, 156
Minerva 24, 156
Mitsubishi 89, 121, 145
Moore-Brabazon, J.T.C. (Lord Brabazon) 24
Morgan *60*, 118, 139, *139*

Morris *24*, 54, 56, *60*, 64, *64*, 65, 68, *68*, 69, 79, 91, 100, *101*, 103, 112, 113, 139, 156, 157. *See also* British Motor Corp.
Morris, William (Lord Nuffield) *24*, *42*, 54, 65–8, 79, 100, 112
Mors 22, 23, 42, 79
Moskvich 91
Moss, Pat 112, *113*, 145; Stirling *94*, 95, 104, *104*, 107, 110, 112, 116, 132, 157
Mouton, Michèle 145, *145*
Mundy, Harry 116–18
Murphy, James 38, 47, 156

NAG-Voran 73
Nami 91
Napier (cars) 18, 21, 22, *23*, 24, *24*, *25*, 29, 48, 50, *51*, 58, 156; Napier, Montague 18, 48
Nash 35, 84, 86, 87, 100. *See also* American Motors Corp.
Nesselsdorf 18, *18*, 21, 24, 44, *44*. *See also* Tatra
Neubauer, Alfred 92, 95
Nibel, Hans 73, 92
Nissan 90, 91, 124, *124*, 148, 151, 157. *See also* Datsun
Noble, Richard *49*, 143
Nöcker, Peter 114, 157
North-Lucas 44
NSU 73, 76, 92, 125, *125*, 157
Nuffield, Lord *see* Morris, William
Nuffield Group 56, 65, 101, 103, *103*, 113
Nuvolari, Tazio *61*, *70*, *71*, 76

Oakland *see* Pontiac
Ogle (designs) *117*, 118; Ogle, David *117*, 118, 124, 142
Olds, R.E. 9, 29, *30*, 156
Oldsmobile 22, 30, 34, *34*, 35, 88, 120, *120*, 145
Opel 42, 68, 70, 78, 81, 91, 127, 134, 138, *139*, 145, 148, 151–5, *154*
Opel, Adam 20; Fritz 42
Otto, Nikolaus August 8, 15

Packard (cars) 35, *40*, *80*, 81, 84, 86, *90*; Packard, J.W. and W.D. 35
Panhard *14*, 16–18, 21, 22, 23, 78, 79, 99, 101, 108, 131, 156, 157
Panhard, René 9, 10, 15, 16
Panhard et Levassor, Système *13*
Panther 139
Pathfinder *34*
Peerless 22
Pegaso 99, 129

Peugeot *14*, 16, 18, 23, *23*, 24, *27*, 39, 41, 42, 79, 81, 99, 108, 131, 136, 150, 151, 156, 157. *See also* Lion-Peugeot
Peugeot, Armand 10, 15; Robert 23
Pierce-Arrow 35, 38, 81
Piquet, Nelson 144
Playboy 86
Plymouth 35, 38, 86, 145
Pobieda 91
Pomeroy, Laurence, Sr 26, 27, 51, 59; Jr 27
Pontiac 34, 36, 120, *121*, 145–8, *149*
Porsche 26, *86*, 92, 110, 112, 113, 124, 126, *127*, 129, 134, *154*, 155, 157, *160*
Porsche, Dr Ferdinand 18, 24, 44, 73, 76, 92, 112, 118; Dr Ferdinand, Jr 92; Ferdinand 'Butzi' 126
Praga 24
Price, Barrie 101
Prince 91, 121
Princeton 35
Prost, Alain *142*, 144

Quester, Dieter 143, 157
Qvale, Kjell 116

Railton-Mobil 70
Rambler 35, 86, 121
Range-Rover *see* Rover
Rasmussen, J.S. 73, 92
'Red Flag Act' 16, 18
Reliant *117*, 118, 142
Renault 9, 15, *18*, 23, *23*, 24, 42, 78, 79, 91, 99, 118, 131, 134, *142*, 148, 149, 156, 157
Renault, Louis 15, 99; Marcel 21, 22, 156
Reo 29
Ricart, Wilfredo 129
Riley 64, 68, 70, 100, 101, 103, *103*, 118, 139
Rindt, Jochen 132
Roamer 38
Rochas, Alphonse Beau de 8
Roesch, Georges 24, 59, 60
Roger, Emile 12, 15
Roger-Benz 16
Röhr 73
Röhrl, Walter *144*, 145, *145*
Rolls, Hon. Charles Stewart 24, 26, 29, 50, 51
Rolls-Royce 24, 29, 32, *41*, 50, 51, *51*, 56, 58, 59, *59*, 70, 103, 108, 116, *118*, *136*, 142, 156, 157
Rolt, Tony 70, 116
Romeo, Nicola 24. *See also* Alfa Romeo
Rootes brothers 60, 64, 115; William, Sr 60
Rootes Group 56, 60, 65, 68, 100, 103, 113, 115,

120, 129, 136
Rosemeyer, B. *70*, 73, 76
Rover 26, *63*, 64, *90*, 103, 115, *137*, 139–42; Land-Rover 115; Range-Rover 139
Royce 26; Royce, Frederick Henry 15, 26–9, 35, 50, 51, *59*
Rumpler 44, *44*, *127*; Rumpler, Edmund 18, 24, 44, *44*, 71, 73, 118
Ruxton 39, 156
Ryder, Sir Don 136, 139, 157

Saab 90, 92, 112, 113, *113*, 128, 149
Sacha-Gordine 131
Salmson 129
Salvadori, Roy 104
San Giusto 44, 156
Sarazin, Edouard 12, 16
Saurer 24; Saurer, A. 24
Scheckter, Jody 144
Seaman, Richard 47, 70, 76, 156
Segrave, Sir Henry *42*, 47, 48, *49*, 69, 156
Selden, G.B. 20, 30
Serpollet, Léon 15, 23
Shelby, Carroll 104
Siddeley, John 55, 59
Sidgreaves, Arthur 50
Simca 76, 99, 136, 150; Simca-Gordini 131
Simms, Frederick Richard 16, 18
Singer 26, 60, 69, 70, 103
Sizaire, G. and M. 156
Sizaire-Naudin 23
Skoda 149
Sloan, Alfred P. 35, 36, 38, 51, 54
Spijker (Spyker) 24, *24*
SS 54, 60, 61, 62, *62*, 156; SS Jaguar 62, *63*, 65, 70, 71, 100. *See also* Jaguar
Standard 60, 61, 62, 65, 101, 103, 115, 157
Standard (Germany) 73
Standard-Triumph group 100, 103, 115, 128
Stanley Steamers 16, 21, 29, 156; Stanley, F. 20
steam vehicles 8, 10, *12*, 15, 16, 18, *19*, 20–1, 23, 29, 30, 81
Stewart, Jackie 6, 7, 108, 110, 115, 131, 132, 157
Steyr 73, 92
Stoewer 71, 73
Stokes, Donald (Lord Stokes) 115, 117, 136
Stuck, Hans 70, 73
Studebaker 35, 38, 81, 84, 86, *87*, 91, 118, 120–1; Studebaker, Clem and Henry 35, 87
Stutz 38; Stutz, Harry 38
Subaru 121, 148, *149*
Sunbeam 26, *29*, 32, 42, 47, 48, 60, 120, 136, 156; Sunbeam-Talbot 42,

60, 103, 136
Šustala, Ignác 18, *18*
Suzuki 121, 148
Swallow 54, 60, 61, 62, 100
Szisz, Ferenc 23, 156

Takuri 89, 156
Talbot (France) 78, 129, 150; Talbot-Lago 110, 121
Talbot (Gt Britain) 24, 42, 59–60, 103, 136, 138, 156; Talbot Sunbeam-Lotus 136
Tatra 18, 32, 44, *73*, 73, 149, *149*, 156
Théry, Léon 22, 156
Thomas, John Parry 48–50, *48*, *49*
Thomas, Sir Miles 101, 112
Thrust II 49, 143
Thunderbolt-R-R 70
Tjaarda, John *81*, 89
Toivonen, H. 136; P. 126
Toyota 81, 90, 91, 121, 124, *124*, 157
Tracta 41, 156
Triumph 9, 64, *68*, 70, 99, 100, 103, 115, 134, 139, 156
Tucker 86; Tucker, Preston T. 86
TVR Tasmin 139
Tyrrell (car) 7, *144*; Tyrrell, Ken 132

Uhlenhaut, Rudolf 92, 125

Vandervell, Tony 104
Vanwall 84, *104*, 107, 110, 157
Vatanen, Ari *136*, 138
Vauxhall 26, 27, 51–4, *51*, 65, 68, 103, 113, 138, 139, *139*, 145, 148
Voisin (cars) *42*, 78, 99; Voisin, Gabriel *42*, 99
Volkswagen 36, *44*, 73, 76, 84, 92, 108, 112, 116, 118, 125, 148, 151, *154*, 156, 157
Volvo 71, 81, *90*, 91–2, 112, 113, 118, 128, 131, 149–50

Walmsley, W. 54, 61, 62
Wanderer 73, 125
Warszawa 91
Wartburg 20
Wilks, Maurice 64; Spencer *63*, 64
Wills Sainte Claire 38
Williams 144, 157
Willys 83, 86
Winton 22, 35
Wisdom, Ann 112, *113*; Tom 70, 112
Wolseley 29, 54, 55, 59, 61, 62, 65, 68, 89, 100, 103
Wyer, J. 116, *121*, 126, *127*
Wyss, Joseph 24. *See also* Berna

Zündapp 73, 92

Great names, great racing: long-tail Porsche 917 on the long, long road of Le Mans (Derek Bell and Jo Siffert, 1971).

Acknowledgements

The publishers wish to thank the following individuals and organizations for their kind permission to reproduce the photographs in this book:

Autocar Magazine 51 below right; Automotive History Collection, Detroit Public Library 31 below; BBC Hulton Picture Library 59 below, 112 below; Neill Bruce Photographic 25 above, 30, 100 above, 102 below, 116, 117 above; Jean Paul Caron (DPPI) 6 far right, 13 above right, 23 right, 92 above, 111 below, 124 above, 126, 131, 132, 133 inset above, 133 below, 136, 145; Chevrolet, USA 34 centre, 148; Citroën Cars Ltd 79 below; Classic and Sportscar/Mel Drew 90 above right; Hugh Conway Collection 78 above; Richard Cooke 90-1; Colin Curwood 149 below; Daimler-Benz AG 155; Ian Dawson (Octopus Books) 1 above, 61 above, 62-3, 64-5, 77 above, 84-5, 105, 106 above, 114 below, 118-9, 127, 129, 137 above and below, 154 above; FIAT, Italy 14 below, 43 below, 73 below; Ford Motor Company Ltd 138 left; Henry Ford Museum, The Edison Institute, Dearborn, Michigan, USA 37 below, 38; Geoffrey Goddard 6 right, 7 left, 14 above, 21, 22 left and right, 23 left, 47 below, 48 below right, 49 above, 50, 55 below, 59 above, 61 below, 62 below, 70 above centre and below, 71 left and right, 73 above, 96 left, 97 below, 106 below, 110, 111 above, 133 above; Illustrated London News 25 below right; Chris Linton (Octopus Books) 28 above, 51 above, 56-7, 114 above; Monitor Group/Lotus Cars 115; Morgan Motor Co/C. G. Smedley & Associates Ltd 138 right; Andrew Morland 43 above, 63 below, 76 above, 98 above; Don Morley 6 far left, 142-3; Peter Myers 49 below; The National Motor Museum, Beaulieu 13 above left, 16 left, 28 below; Oldsmobile, USA 34 above; Ogle Design Ltd 117 below; Cyril Posthumus 20 right, 24 right, 32-3, 34 below, 35, 40 below, 42 above, 44 left and right, 51 below left, 54 left, 60 right, 68 above right, 76 below, 78 below, 92 below, 94 above, 96 above right, 100 below, 104 below; Renault, France 143 inset; Peter Roberts 12 below, 15, 18 left and right, 19 below, 20 left, 24 left, 25 below left, 27 below, 46 below left, 60 left, 77 below, 81 below left, 94 below, 96 below right, 107 right; Rolls-Royce Motors Ltd 134-5; Rainer Schlegelmilch (Octopus Books) 2-3, 8, 9, 12 above, 13 below, 45, 46-7, 72 above, 93 above, 94-5, 125 below; Halwart Schrader 86; Shell, UK 54 right; Nigel Snowdon 108-9, 160; Subaru (UK) Ltd 149 above right; Roger Swan 124 below; Colin Taylor 112 above, 144; VAG (UK) Ltd 125 above, 154 below; Vauxhall Motors/Broadway Arts 139; Andrew Whyte 6 left, 7 below right, 10-11, 72 below, 90 above and below left, 107 below left, 113 above and below, 149 above left; Nicky Wright 31 above, 36, 39 below, 41, 80 below, 81 above and below right, 82-3, 83 above and below, 87 below, 88 above and below, 89, 101 above and below, 120 above and below right, 128 above, 150 above; Nicky Wright (Octopus Books) 39 above, 80 above, 93 below, 98-9, 120 left; Franco Zagari 19 above, 29, 37 above, 40 above, 42 below, 46 below right, 48 above, 97 above, 128 below, 150 below, 151.

Special photography by:

Ian Dawson 1 below, 4-5, 17 above and below, 26 below, 26-7, 48 below left, 52 inset, 52-3, 55 above, 58, 66-7, 69, 74-5, 79 above, 102 above, 103, 104 above, 107 above left, 121, 122-3, 130, 140-1, 146-7, 152-3, 154 centre.

In addition the publishers would like to thank the owners and custodians of those cars photographed specially for the book (see captions), in particular the Nigel Dawes Collection and the Patrick Collection and its curator John Ward.